Ethics
and
Public
Administration

Bureaucracies, Public Administration, and Public Policy

Kenneth J. Meier
Series Editor

Bureaucracies, Public Administration,
and Public Policy

Ethics
and
Public
Administration

With a Foreword by John A. Rohr

H. GEORGE FREDERICKSON
Editor

M.E. Sharpe
Armonk, New York
London, England

Library of Congress Cataloging-in-Publication Data

Ethics and public administration / H. George Frederickson, editor.
p. cm. — (Bureaucracies, public administration, and public policy)
ISBN 1–56324–096–3 (cloth). — ISBN 1–56324–097–1 (pbk.)
1. Public administration—Moral and ethical aspects.
2. Public administration—United States.
3. Political ethics—United States.
4. Conflict of interests—United States.
5. Political corruption—United States.
I. Frederickson, H. George.
II. series.
JF1525.E8E854 1993
172′.2—dc20
92030046
CIP

Printed in the United States of America

The paper used in this publication meets the minimum requirements of
American National Standard for Information Sciences—
Permanence of Paper for Printed Library Materials,
ANSI Z39.48–1984.

∞

BM (c)   10   9   8   7   6   5   4   3   2   1
BM (p)   10   9   8   7   6   5   4   3   2

Contents

About the Contributors

GREGORY G. BRUNK is associate professor of political science at the University of Oklahoma. He has recently published papers on ethics and professional behavior in the *International Studies Quarterly, Western Political Quarterly, Administration and Society, Journal of Peace Research*, and the *Journal of Political and Military Sociology*. Along with Howard Tamashiro and Donald Secrest, he is finishing a book manuscript on American elite attitudes toward warfare issues.

J. PATRICK DOBEL is associate professor at the Graduate School of Public Affairs at the University of Washington. He has served as the Chair of the King County, Washington, Board of Ethics for six years and has written *Compromise and Political Action: Political Morality in Liberal and Democratic Life* (1990) as well as numerous articles on public ethics. He is presently working on a book on political prudence.

LINDA FOSS is manager of Maternal-Child Services at Yuma Regional Medical Center, Yuma, Arizona. She received her Ph.D. from the Graduate School of Public Affairs, University of Colorado at Denver and maintains an active interest in the practical application and teaching of medical ethics.

H. GEORGE FREDERICKSON is Edwin O. Stene Distinguished Professor of Public Administration at the University of Kansas. He received the 1991–92 Dwight Waldo Award of the American Society for Public Administration and the 1990–91 Distinguished Research Award of the National Association of Schools of Public Affairs and Administration and the American Society for Public Administration. He is a fellow of the National Academy of Public Administration and the editor-in-chief of the *Journal of Public Administration Research and Theory*.

THOMAS M. HOLBROOK is an assistant professor of political science at the University of Wisconsin-Milwaukee. He has published articles on state politics and electoral behavior in several journals, including the *American Journal of Political Science, Western Political Quarterly, Journal of Politics*, and *American Politics Quarterly*. His current research projects include a study of the determinants of state economic development, a study of state legislative elections, and a study of the effects of campaign events on presidential elections.

HENRY D. KASS is currently professor of public administration and director of professional development in the Public Administration Program at Lewis and Clark College. His fields are management, organization theory, human resource management, and administrative ethics. He has taught at American University and Eastern Washington University. Dr. Kass is co-editor and contributor to *Images and Identities in Public Administration* (1990), an editor and contributor to a special issue of the *International Journal of Public Administration* on ethics in public administration, and co-author of *Welcoming Change* (1979). He has also written a number of articles on management and administrative ethics.

CAROL W. LEWIS is a professor of political science at the University of Connecticut and teaches administrative ethics in the graduate program in public administration. She is author of *The Ethics Challenge in Public Service: A Problem-Solving Guide* (1991).

PAUL C. LIGHT is a professor of planning and public affairs at the Humphrey Institute of Public Affairs, University of Minnesota. He was senior adviser to the National Commission on the Public Service (Volcker Commission), and has written widely on American government, including *The President's Agenda: Domestic Policy Choice from Kennedy to Reagan* and *Forging Legislation*. His current work, *Monitoring Government: Inspectors General and the Search for Accountability*, will be published in 1993 by the Brookings Institution.

KATHRYN L. MALEC is an assistant professor in the School of Public and Environmental Affairs, Indiana University Northwest. She is currently teaching courses on organization theory, ethics, and human resource management. She has co-authored a number of articles in *Corruption and Reform* and is the author of several conference papers concerning public corruption and citizen response. She is currently exploring, using the discipline of applied ethics, responses by public administrators to public corruption.

KENNETH J. MEIER is professor of political science at the University of Wisconsin-Milwaukee. He previously served as the Chair of the Oklahoma Ethics and Merit Commission, which had jurisdiction over all civil service ethics violations. His current research projects include the politics of drugs, and minority access to equal educational opportunities.

DONALD C. MENZEL is professor of public administration and political science in the Department of Government and International Affairs at the University of South Florida. Recent and forthcoming publications in the area of government ethics include "Ethics Attitudes and Behavior in Local Government: An Empirical Analysis," *State and Local Government Review* (1992); "Ethics Stress in the Local Government Workplace," *Public Personnel Management* (forthcoming); and "Ethics Complaints and Local Government: The Case of Florida," *Journal of Public Administration Research and Theory*, 1:4 (October 1991). He is currently conducting research on the ethical environment of local government managers in Florida and Texas.

DOUGLAS F. MORGAN is professor of public administration and director of the master's program in public administration at Lewis and Clark College in Portland, Oregon. His articles on administrative ethics have appeared in various journals and books, including *Administration and Society, Problemi di Administrazione pubblica, Administrative Discretion and Public Policy Implementation,* and *Images and Identities in Public Administration.*

E. SAM OVERMAN is associate professor at the Graduate School of Public Affairs, University of Colorado at Denver. He has published books on *Public Management* (1983) and *Methodology and Epistemology for Social Science* (1988). He currently studies the effects of information on managerial control, and the politics of information in state health policy making. This research includes the ethics of information use.

JAMES L. PERRY is professor in the school of Public and Environmental Affairs, Indiana University, Bloomington. He is the co-author or editor of four books, including the *Handbook of Public Administration* (1989), and many articles appearing in journals such as *Administrative Science Quarterly, American Political Science Review,* and *Public Administration Review.* He is a recipient of the Yoder-Heneman Award for innovative personnel research and the Charles H. Levine Memorial Award for Excellence in Public Administration. His current research focuses on whistleblowing, comparative civil service systems, and public service motivation.

JOHN A. ROHR is professor of public administration at Virginia Polytechnic Institute and State University. He is the author of *Ethics for Bureaucrats: An Essay on Law and Values* (1989).

DONALD E. SECREST, Professor Emeritus of Political Science, University of Oklahoma, specializes in international relations theory, American foreign policy, and normative issues in international relations. He is the author and co-author of several articles concerning the moral issues of war. He is currently working on a book manuscript based upon empirical studies of the normative views toward war of American elites.

NORMAN A. SPRINTHALL is a professor and former head of the counselor education graduate department at North Carolina State University. Awards and honors include Phi Beta Kappa, fellow status in the American Psychological Association, and membership in the Academy of Outstanding Teachers. He is author of numerous articles and has co-authored two textbooks, *Educational Psychology: A Development Approach* (5th ed.), and *Adolescent Psychology: A Developmental View* (2nd ed.) His research in administrative ethics has been in collaboration with Debra Stewart and includes chapters in *Ethical Frontiers in Public Management* (J.S. Bowman, ed., 1991), and in *Handbook on Administrative Ethics* (T.L. Cooper, ed., 1992). He and Professor Stewart created the *Stewart Sprinthall Management Survey* as an assessment technique for the issues involved in this area of research.

ANDREW STARK is assistant professor of policy, Faculty of Management, University of Toronto. His work in the area of government ethics is forthcoming in the *American Political Science Review*, *Public Administration Review*, and the *Canadian Journal of Political Science*. He is currently completing a book on public-sector conflict of interest, and was a 1991–92 fellow in the Harvard University Program in Ethics and the Professions.

DEBRA W. STEWART is a professor of political science and public administration at North Carolina State University. Professor Stewart is the author or co-author of three books and numerous articles. Her scholarly works have addressed administrative theory, equal employment opportunity policy, and women and politics. Her current research focuses on ethics and managerial decision making in public administration.

HOWARD TAMASHIRO is an assistant professor of political science at Allegheny College. Besides works on policy ethics, he has published articles on computational modeling.

Foreword

This volume is an empirical examination of questions of government ethics. The topics speak for themselves: ethics codes, ethics commissions, ethics agencies, inspectors general, whistleblowers, and an impressive range of attitudinal studies.

It is not surprising that serious attention is being given to empirical questions of government ethics. It is surprising that it is *academics* who are giving that attention. For nearly two decades, academics in the ethics field, while sitting in the "shadow of the organization," have indulged their passion for "social equity" by calling for "moral reasoning" about civil servants' "sense of vocation," always mindful, of course, of the rigorous demands of "active citizenship" and "civility," and of "democratic responsibility" on the one hand and "regime values" on the other.

It is practitioners who have been most concerned with conflict of interest, financial disclosure, and the other mundane ethical questions that most academics have ignored in writing and research.

If academics have ignored ethical questions that are of considerable interest to practitioners, it is time our research agenda is expanded to include these interests. As government ethics scholars, we need only *expand* our agenda and not *abandon* it. We need not apologize for the body of administrative ethics literature we have compiled over the past two decades. But we must not end up simply talking to ourselves. I am not telling stories out of school when I say that there has always been considerable tension between the practitioners and the academics in public administration. Yet this bifurcated focus, for all its discomfiture, has been part—and an important part—of public administration's success and vitality.

For a fuller discussion of the points touched upon in this foreword, see the author's article, "On Achieving Ethical Behavior in Government," *The Public Manager*, 21 (Spring 1992):47–51.

Why is it that the academic literature on administrative ethics has paid relatively little attention to questions of conflict of interest and financial disclosure? Without pulling any punches, let me answer my own question with brutal candor. We find such questions technical, narrow, negative, and dull. This is why we ignore them. We are teachers. We make our living by discussing ideas that at least hold our students' attention and at times even raise their vision. This is what makes our work interesting and rewarding. If we get bogged down in the intricacies of a conflict-of-interest statute, we end up directing the energies of our students to the less-than-ennobling task of figuring out how to stay out of the slammer! To use more high-toned language, we know that the study of ethics deals with doing good and avoiding evil. Being positive thinkers, we choose to emphasize the opportunities to do good rather than the difficulties of avoiding evil. Hence, the emphasis on moral reasoning, vocation, civility, and so forth.

We have chosen well, but the unfortunate result is that we have paid too little attention to the negative questions that are of tremendous importance in the careers of practitioners in our field. The solution to this problem is not to abandon the high road of positive, interesting, and elevating ideas, but rather to look for such ideas in the ares of conflict of interest and financial disclosure.

For example, conflict-of-interest regulations frequently prohibit appearances of impropriety, a point mentioned explicitly in President Bush's Executive Order of 17 October 1990. The appearance stand is troublesome, however, because, unlike overt behavior, it does not easily yield to the definitional exigencies of law and administrative regulation. The argument for regulating appearances seizes the high ground by asserting that they weaken public confidence in the integrity of governmental institutions and thereby threaten the foundations of a free society.

This is a fine old argument, tracing its pedigree back to the *Federalist Papers*, wherein Publius argued that sound administration was the best way to win the affection of Americans for the government that would be created by their new constitution. Despite its venerable heritage, however, what do we know about its accuracy? It seems plausible enough, but, as a matter of fact, is there an empirically verifiable connection between popular perceptions of impropriety and diminished beliefs in the integrity of governmental institutions? If so, are these improprieties related to conflict of interest and, again if so, to which types of conflict of interest? That is, are they more strongly correlated with officials' owning stock in an industry they regulate, or with government employees' accepting jobs in corporations they once dealt with officially, or with procurement officers accepting gifts from government contractors, and so on?

My instincts tell me that there is a connection between popular perceptions of such conduct and diminished confidence in government, but I would be much more comfortable if my instincts were confirmed by solid empirical findings. Further, I would like to know if the diminished confidence is detected even when the value of the stock is small or the gift inconsequential. I know of no convincing, rigorous studies in these important matters. Without such data, we continue to impose legal disabilities upon government officers and employees without really knowing if they are apt means for achieving the stated goals.

The area of postemployment restrictions is particularly troublesome because many employees see these obligations as punitive measures that unfairly prohibit them from participating fully in a capitalist society. A careful examination of advisory letters issued by the Office of Government Ethics (OGE), however, clearly suggests that the purpose of postemployment restrictions is not to keep former government employees from benefiting financially from what they learned in government service but to protect the integrity of governmental decision-making processes from improper influence by such persons. This entire field of postemployment restrictions bristles with questions demanding empirical investigation. For example, can the anecdotes about the morale problems created by postemployment restrictions be supported by empirical data? If so, are federal employees aware that the purpose of the restrictions is prophylactic rather than punitive? If they were aware of this distinction, would this awareness diminish the severity of the morale problem?

In mentioning questions of appearances of impropriety and postemployment restrictions, I have suggested in a nonempirical way that civil servants resent certain aspects of these burdens that are placed upon them. But these are not the only burdens they bear. In other matters related to conflict of interest, they must be careful about what sorts of severance bonuses they can accept from companies they leave in order to work for the government, and what sort of help they can give to others who may be having problems with government agencies. Their family life is invaded to the extent that certain restrictions are placed upon the jobs and property their spouses and minor children may hold.

In addition to these financial burdens, they are held to the strict standards of the Hatch Act in their political activities. Depending on the nature of their employment, their freedom of speech can be severely restricted in matters pertaining to national security, trade secrets, and medical records. Again, depending on the particular job they hold, they can be held to certain grooming and dress standards and can even be put in uniform. Finally, they must all take an oath to uphold the Constitution of the United States. To be sure, this last obligation is one that few would find burdensome, but in our country we tend to look askance at the idea that the government can tell what one must say or believe, even if one does believe it.

To put all this in perspective, consider OGE's response to the complaint of many civil servants that people in the business world are not burdened with the kind of rules that descend even to such picky matters as accepting lunches from persons doing business with the government. OGE's position is that different standards apply in the public sector because of the duty of public employees to instill public confidence in the institutions of government.

This response is absolutely correct. Government service is different. Correct as this response is, however, one might ask if it proves too much. Just *how different* is government service? From the long list of burdens just rehearsed, we might conclude that government service is *very* different. All these restrictions tend to make government employees a group apart from the rest of us and subject, like military personnel, to a special discipline and perhaps even to a special way of life.

If this is the case or if this is in any way becoming the case, it signals a dramatic change in the nature of the American civil service. Although Jacksonian spoils began to be corrected over a century ago, the Jacksonian idea of civil servants who are close to the people and indeed of the people themselves was left undisturbed. The merit exams that were established at that time eschewed the British model that emphasized the classical learning of the gentleman, thereby giving a distinctively Oxbridge flavor to the British civil service, whose higher reaches once excluded all but a favored few. Unlike the French, we have never had an elite civil service academy whose rigors constitute a rite of passage for those who ambition distinguished careers in the civil service.

Our relaxed recruiting patterns allow lateral entries at relatively high levels of the career civil service and at the very highest levels for political appointees. If our civil servants, both political and career, lack the elegance of the British and the brilliance of the French, that is all right with Americans. It seems more compatible with our democratic and egalitarian ways.

But if the restrictions we now impose upon our civil servants tend to remove them from the people and make them a group apart from the rest of us, will we not eventually have to think about them differently? Indeed, will they not have to think about themselves differently as a special corps separate from the rest of Americans because they govern the rest of us? Can we impose strict obligations upon them and at the same time withhold from them the prestige that their European counterparts enjoy? I find these questions unsettling, not least because I support most of the restrictions that are imposed upon our civil servants. But in supporting these burdens we place on civil servants, I wonder how we can do so in good conscience without conferring a very special status upon them as well. And yet we know that this is not our way.

Perhaps an empirical study would be in order on the self-perception of civil servants in light of the special burdens placed upon them and on the perception of the public at large as well. Is there any support for going further in the direction of separating them from the rest of us not only in imposing burdens but also in conferring benefits, such as heightened guarantees against reductions in force, restrictions against lateral entries, and so forth?

Just recently, I had the opportunity to spend nine months in France, where I could not help but be impressed by the rich, normative notion of *l'État* in public affairs. In France, high-ranking civil servants are imbued with a profound "sense of the state" that helps to explain much of the best and, alas, the worst in French public administration. The French rely much more upon this internalized "sense of the state" to help check corruption than upon detailed rules and regulations. It is the "sense of the state" that gives French civil servants a certain psychological distance from the citizenry at large and enables them to see themselves as a group apart from the rest. In our country we do not have this strong sense of the state. Much of our present effort to prevent corruption may have the unintended effect of gradually making American civil servants a group apart from the rest of us, despite our weak notion of the state. If they are to become a group apart from the rest of us only because of burdens and restrictions placed upon them—that is, with no compensating privileges—they will become increasingly demoralized and disgruntled. Public service will present an attractive career only for those who can do nothing else—dispirited men and women willing to endure humiliations in order to retain their jobs. If this outcome is to be avoided, then the burdens of public service must be counterbalanced by compensating privileges—as is the case for those in military service with their special exchanges, commissaries, hospitals, chapels, clubs, libraries, recreation centers, and retirement provisions. Such a system of extraordinary benefits and burdens involves a logic of separatism—the civil service will become increasingly separated from society at large, as the military is today. The logic of such a system would also counsel expanding civil service protections to increasingly higher positions in government—far beyond the modest recommendations put forward not long ago by the Volcker Commission. If we are to achieve integrity in government by treating public servants as different from the rest of us, then there is no reason to exempt those in the most important positions from the logic of this plan.

I do not really believe all this is going to happen. If it did, it might have devastating effects on American democracy as we know it today. I merely point to an unsettling logic of reform that we seem to have set in motion by relying on burdens imposed on public servants as the primary means to assure ethical behavior.

I am quite ambivalent about this. For the most part, I look favorably upon conflict-of-interest prohibitions, financial disclosure requirements, Hatch Act restrictions, and the other burdens we place on civil servants; and yet I am uneasy about where all this might be leading us. And this is why it is so important that we have solid empirical data to illuminate just what it is we are accomplishing through these various policies of achieving ethical behavior by imposing burdens.

We should recall the wise words of the ancient lawgiver Solon: "Attempt no more good than the nation can bear."

John A. Rohr
Virginia Polytechnic Institute
and State University

Ethics
and
Public
Administration

Introduction

H. George Frederickson

The Ethics Movement

It was in the city and state governments of America, as well as in the national government, that corruption provided much of the impetus for the development of modern public administration. By the early years of the twenty-first century the structures and policies of American governments were being changed for the purpose of reducing corruption. These changes were of two types: first, to reduce procedurally the potential for corruption by the use of management concepts such as awarding contracts to the lowest bidder, pre- and post-auditing, council–manager government, and the prohibition of conflicts of interest; and second, to bring into government service "better types" through merit civil service systems for administrators and through concepts such as nonpartisan and at-large elections for politicians. The government reform movement, while not driven by what would today be described as a concern for ethics, was certainly driven by a concern for corruption.

The contemporary government ethics movement appears to have essentially the same purpose as the reform movement of a century ago—to reduce government corruption. The present ethics movement has, however, considerably different emphases. Structures and programs such as whistleblowing; ethics hot lines; ethics boards and commissions; ethics education programs for elected, politically appointed, and administrative officials; agency ethics officers; financial or other conflict-of-interest disclosure systems; and professional codes of ethics typify the modern approach to guarding against or reducing public corruption. While the ethics movement may lack the fervor of the reform movement, it is nevertheless a self-conscious, visible, and growing assemblage of government offices and officials with ethics titles and responsibilities. In modern public life not only are issues of ethics pervasive, the implements of ethics enforcement are ubiquitous.

Much of the normative and philosophical leadership of the governmental reform movement was in the universities, and so it is today with the ethics movement. Virtually every major university has an institute or center for ethics or human values. There is, however, a difference between the role of universities in the reform movement and their role in the ethics movement. Academic programs, particularly public administration programs, were influential in the governmental reform movement, and most leading universities had such programs. They were almost all located in political science departments. The perspective was historical, legal, philosophical, and deductive. The development of political science as an empirically based social science, the emergence of public administration as interdisciplinary applied social science, and the more recent advent of policy studies all postdate the governmental reform movement. As a consequence, the contemporary study of ethics in universities, while still primarily philosophical and deductive, is significantly informed by social and policy science research.

By the application of research findings to the primary theories of government ethics it should be possible, at least in a preliminary way, to indicate whether these theories work. Which theories, when applied, are most effective? Are they uniquely effective in particular settings but not in others? Which theories of ethics, while compelling, seem incapable of application? When is governmental ethics purchased at too high a price in administrative effectiveness or political responsiveness? These and similar questions can be met, even if as a beginning, by the results of research and analysis.

This is not to suggest that moral truths or human values are empirically testable. They are not. Human behavior as an expression of values can, however, be judged to be honest or dishonest as long as the concept of honesty is defined. Democratic government, including the Constitution and the laws, can be seen as a collective expression of agreed-upon values, or as the definitions of values. Other forms of pregovernmental or extragovernmental social agreement are accepted as collective values. Individual and group behavior, judged against social convention, the laws, and the Constitution, can be said to conform and therefore to be ethical, or not to conform and therefore be unethical. Given the tools of modern social science it is possible to assess ethical behavior in this way. In addition, governments institute policies, programs, and organizations that are designed to improve the prospects for individual and group ethics. The social sciences should help determine the extent to which these policies, programs, and organizations are ethics enhancing.

There is a second important difference between the governmental reform and the ethics movements. At the time of the governmental reform movement in the early 1900s, the people knew what they did not like—government corruption. Many of the correctives adopted were administrative and managerial. By the mid-1930s government began to grow dramatically. By the 1950s it was routine to refer to the "administrative state" (Waldo) and to think of the civil service as "the fourth branch of government." By the 1980s, bureaucracy, especially as a symbol of big government, was the issue. Bureaucrat bashing and fighting "waste, fraud, and abuse" were the political weapons of choice. Government corruption was becoming an issue again, but this time it was made to be an issue in and of the bureaucracy, effectively bringing together public concerns for big government and high taxes on the one hand, and concerns about corruption on the other. During the government reform movement, corruption was generally understood to mean political corruption. In the present ethics reform movement, corruption is most often associated with bureaucracy. Is there evidence to suggest that contemporary governmental ethics issues are primarily manifestations of big government or bureaucracy? Or is the bureaucratic machine, however inefficient, still more ethical than prereform politics? Are contemporary governmental ethics problems essentially political rather than administrative or bureaucratic in nature? This volume attempts to address these questions.

Does the Ethics Movement Have Staying Power?

Whether the current ethics movement is going to endure is, of course, arguable. It is suggested here that the 1990s is the beginning of an era of ethics. In looking back on the sweep of time, we categorize the past in terms of eras or epochs. Affixed to each epoch is the symbol or metaphor that was most influential in public affairs in that particular period. In American domestic affairs, for example, the 1960s was the era of concern for poverty and social injustice. By the 1970s the dominant concern and the controlling policy metaphor was law and order. The 1980s will be known as the era of privatization, government cutback, or degovernmentalization. The policy emphasis in each epoch is a response to the accumulation of either unsolved social problems or unresolved social issues. Certainly the political rhetoric of the 1960s tapped our shared concern for fairness and justice and our sensitivity to the failure of African Americans to achieve social, economic, and political equality.

It is popular to put the cycles of time in binary or dichotomous categories. In 1984 the political scientists Herbert McClosky and John Zoller, using public opinion survey research, found a continuing struggle between capitalist values (the sanctity of private property, the maximization of profit, the cult of the free market, the survival of the fittest) and democratic values (equality, freedom, social responsibility, and the general welfare as an end to be promoted when necessary by public action regulating property and restricting profit). While neither side wishes to abolish the other, those most firmly attached to democratic values exhibit least support for capitalism, and those most firmly attached to capitalist values exhibit least support for democracy. The historian Arthur M. Schlesinger, Jr., took the contrast in values further in 1986, defending the hypothesis that there is "a continuing shift in national involvement between public purpose and private interest." Using the concept of generations, Schlesinger described an America especially influenced by capitalist values in one epoch and by democratic values in the next. While history informs America's understanding of the past and its perspectives on the present and future, it is the instant tension between the values of private interest and public purpose and the contemporary context of policy and implementation choices that challenges the nation's democratic experiment.

Considerable evidence shows that the present generation or epoch is dominated by the values of private interest. But there is also evidence that there is a major shift away from private interests.

What will be the dominant issue in domestic public affairs in the 1990s? Homelessness is certainly an important problem. AIDS is a contender. Abortion continues to be a divisive issue. The economy is slow to recover. And there are others. But the issue that does and will continue to dominate public policy in the 1990s is ethics, particularly ethics as a metaphor for an increasing concern for democratic values and public purposes.

There has always been governmental corruption, so why is ethics so important now, and why will it dominate policy in the 1990s?

First, the level of government corruption has increased dramatically. Lee Alexander, the longtime mayor of Syracuse, New York is in prison for taking bribes. After it was revealed that Tom Bradley, the five-term mayor of Los Angeles, had received funds from firms doing business with the city, the Los Angeles City Council adopted the strictest ethics laws in the country. Governor Ray Blanton of Tennessee went to prison for selling pardons and paroles. During the Reagan administration over 100 federal officials were either indicted or convicted. At the state level, postelection investigations of possible breeches of campaign financing laws are now almost routine. In the Ill Winds defense contracting scandal over thirty officials have pled guilty or have been convicted of accepting of bribes and kickbacks. Both Abscam at the national level and state-level "scams" have resulted in the conviction of prominent federal and state legislators. The check overdraft scandal in the House of Representatives in 1992 resulted in a significant turning out of incumbents. While these are the more notable breeches of government ethics, there are hundreds of less well publicized scandals at all levels of government. Taken together, they are both the substance and the symbols of a pervasive and enduring public issue.

Second, unlike other policy issues, the people do not equivocate about government corruption. It is wrong and they are against it.

Third, government corruption is a policy issue with a strong "carrying capacity." A policy issue's carrying capacity is determined in part by its drama. Without drama the media and the public lose interest. The saturation of the public arena with repeated cases of corruption dramatizes the issue. Repeated bombardment of the public with messages of new symbols or events about corruption redramatizes the issue of corruption.

Fourth, in politics both the bad side (being exposed as less than ethical) and the good side (being able to expose others or to occupy the ethical high ground) of ethics are understood. The political use of the powerful symbols of ethics is now commonplace.

Fifth, matters of government ethics are being increasingly institutionalized. Cities, counties, and states are passing new ethics laws many of which establish review boards, inspectors general, ethics officers, and the like. In the national government every department now has both an inspector general and a designated ethics officer, and all of this in addition to the Office of Government Ethics, the General Accounting office, and other ethics-related offices. This institutionalizes ethics and provides a continuing means by which matters of government corruption are kept in the public eye.

Sixth, ethics cut across the policy fields. Medical ethics are significant in health policy, especially in abortion, life prolongation, insurance, and service distribution matters. Business ethics are critical in the world of commerce, particularly in light of the junk bonds issue and the collapse of the savings and loans. The Social Security system coupled with corporate use of pension systems for capitalization raises serious issues of intergenerational ethics. Environmental ethics are also essentially intergenerational. Housing, transportation, education, public safety, national defense, and foreign affairs all have compelling ethical concerns. Ethics, these days, seem to be everywhere.

In the very real competition among social problems for enduring public attention, government ethics has the advantage of relative public certitude as to what is right and wrong, the media's interest in continuing dramatic exposés, the political use of the powerful symbols of ethics, and the governmental institutionalization of ethics. The ethics movement is here to stay.

Research on Government Ethics

If the contemporary concern for ethics in government is going to endure, will it be informed by social science research or will the study of ethics remain primarily philosophical and normative? On the basis of evidence can we determine, at least in a tentative way, which features or "implements" of the ethics movement have salutary effects on the ethical conduct of government officials? This volume answers "yes."

We began with John Rohr's eloquent defense of why government officials should tend their ethical fences by an increased concern for substantive issues of public disclosure and conflict of interest. And, he argues persuasively that these same issues are equally important to scholars of ethics.

Following this introduction, Part One assumes that contemporary government ethics are at least partially derivative of the problem of public corruption. In Chapter 1, Kathryn Malec reviews a large volume of research on the attitudes of citizens toward public corruption. This is a rich and varied body of research and analysis that informs the question of whether and how citizens view public corruption. Malec capably shows that citizens have a fairly sophisticated ability to distinguish between those forms of corruption that should be taken seriously and are unacceptable and those forms of corruption that are regarded as petty. In our time, of course, the definition of what constitutes public corruption is in the midst of a sea change.

Malec's work is followed with an analysis of political corruption in the American states by Thomas Holbrook and Kenneth Meier. Their treatment of the importance of history and culture as salient indicators of corruption is compelling. They capably take up the long-standing argument that corruption can be dealt with by changing governmental structure. They demonstrate links between politics, race, and the use of ethics for political advantage.

Part One concludes with Andrew Stark's contrasting perspectives on the concept of conflict of interest in the United States and Canada. He argues that government structure does make a difference both in how conflict of interest is defined and in the ethical behavior of public officials.

As indicated earlier, in the contemporary ethics movement the emphasis is on controls, oversight, whistleblowing, and the like. Part Two of this volume examines several aspects of the control perspective on government ethics. It begins with James Perry's analysis of the research and literature on whistleblowing in American government. He puts whistleblowing research into the triad of exit, voice, and loyalty developed by Hershman. Obviously, whistleblowers engage in voice. Perry analyzes the effects of this approach to organizational performance.

In Chapter 5, Paul Light examines the role of inspectors general in the federal government. He reviews the conduct of the HUD inspector general in the context of the HUD scandal. He evaluates the limited effectiveness of the inspector general model in dealing with "high-level wrongdoing." Sam Overman and Linda Foss, in Chapter 6, address the question of professionalism and its effects on ethics in public organizations. In their "separatist thesis" they contend that professionals have "higher" standards of ethical behavior than the general population.

In Chapter 7, Carol Lewis looks at the capacity of ethics codes and the agencies that manage ethics codes to affect the behavior of governmental officials. She not only asks whether ethics codes and ethics agencies make a difference, she assesses the possible negative side-effects of elaborate and detailed codes of ethics and the vigorous enforcement of such codes. Patrick Dobel then considers the politics of the adoption of ethics codes in Chapter 8. This is an examination of the difference between the ethics of politics and the politics of ethics. His findings with respect to the political uses of ethics are both informative and disturbing.

In Part Three we turn away from viewing ethics and control to seeing ethics as a matter of administration or policy. This begins in Chapter 9 with Douglas Morgan and Henry Kass's conception of the "the ethical crisis of role reversal" in a world of policy gridlock. Public administrators are often put in the position of having to take up the slack so as to make government work. This is, of course, a fundamental question of legitimacy. Do public administrators have the moral obligation to act if their political policy file leaders fail to act?

In Chapter 10, Donald Menzel examines the question of the effects of the ethics movement on both organization values and performance. Are improved ethics and high governmental performance compatible? As governments become more procedural and bureaucratic are they less effective? Is a strong ethical climate compatible with a strong productivity commitment? Debra Stewart and Norman Sprinthall then examine the effects of demography and professional and organizational factors on public administrators' moral reasoning. How do variables such as gender, race, education, age, region, and organization purpose affect patterns of moral reasoning among public administrators? In other words, is everything situational or are there some generalizations that can be made regarding patterns of moral reasoning?

Part Three concludes with an examination of policy ethics based on the work of Howard Tamashiro, Donald Secrest, and Gregory Brunk. Here they examine the contrasting attitudes of members of Congress and military officers toward war. This is an especially compelling analysis in view of the decision of the United States to pursue the Gulf War. Do elected officials see the morality of war in a different way than military professionals? Their findings are a splendid prediction of the contrasting views of President Bush, Secretary Chaney, and General Powell with regard to when and how to enter the Gulf War.

In the closing part of *Ethics and Public Administration*, I summarize and synthesize the research presented in this collection and develop some research assertions. This is an attempt not only to summarize what we know about government ethics but to assert some hypotheses in the hope that scholars will test them.

Ethics, Philosophy, and Empirical Research

Much of the professional discourse on ethics in public administration and in government generally is normative and philosophical. Does field-based or empirical research on ethics impoverish an interesting and otherwise lively process of moral reasoning? Is such research beside the moral point (Jos 1993)?

Philosophy, norms, and theory are the guides for both the structure and the actions of government. If research on ethics does not inform larger issues of philosophy or theory, then that research is beside the point. But if field-based research on ethics in the management of government affairs tests the validity of theoretical or philosophical claims, then it can significantly inform the practices of government.

How, for example, corruption is defined is filled with moral and philosophical issues. In this volume corruption has been defined as essentially a legal matter and tied to breaking the law. Corruption is also described here as grounded in public opinion as to what constitutes acceptable behavior. And, corruption is also described here as deviating from Kantian principles of ethical behavior. But, in research there is always some compromise between the definition of a problem, the "quality" of the data, and the philosophical issues to be tested. As Jos (1993) reminds us:

> Choosing to rely on either the law or public opinion to define corrupt activities will . . . fall short of encompassing the full range of acts that corrupt government and politics. As a result, both the legalistic and public opinion perspectives have purchased empirical utility at the expense of normative relevance.

Without empirical research, however, philosophy and moral discourse are absent experience beyond descriptions of ethics based on single cases in unique settings. We search here for knowledge based on both single cases and on generalizations based on multiple observations. Understanding ethics in the management of government affairs requires a grounding in philosophical issues and a knowledge of the effectiveness, practicality, or utility of particular practices established to enhance honest government.

References

Etzioni, Amitai. 1988. *The Moral Dimension: Toward a New Economics*. New York: The Free Press.

Hilgartner, Stephen, and Bosk, Charles L. 1988. "The Rise and Fall of Social Problems: A Public Arenas Model," *American Journal of Sociology*, vol. 94, no. 1 (July): 53–78.

Jos, Philip. 1993. "Empirical Corruption Research: Beside the (Moral) Point?" *Journal of Public Administration Research and Theory*, vol. 3, 2.

Lasch, Christopher. 1978. *The Culture of Narcissism: American Life in an Age of Diminishing Expectations*. New York: Norton.

McClosky, Herbert. 1984. *The American Ethos: Public Attitudes Toward Capitalism and Democracy*. Cambridge, MA: Harvard University Press, pp. 162, 291–92.

Schlesinger, Arthur M., Jr. 1986. *The Cycles of American History*. Boston: Houghton Mifflin, p. 27.

Smith, T. Alexander. 1988. *Time and Public Policy*. Knoxville, TN: The University of Tennessee Press.

Part One

The Problem—Understanding Public Corruption

1

Public Attitudes toward Corruption: Twenty-five Years of Research

Kathryn L. Malec

Several definitions of political corruption have been proposed, and generally can be classified according to three criteria: definitions based on legality, definitions based on the public interest, and definitions based on public opinion. . . .The definition of political corruption based on *legalistic* criteria assumes that political behavior is corrupt when it violates some formal standard or rule of behavior set down by a political system for its public officials. . . . Definitions of political corruption based on notions of the *public or common interest* significantly broaden the range of behavior one might investigate. . . . The researcher has the responsibility of determining what the public or common interest is before assessing whether a particular act is corrupt. A third approach to the definitional problem suggests that a political act is corrupt when the weight of *public opinion* determines it so. (Peters and Welch 1978a; 974–75, emphasis added)

Varieties of Corruption Definitions

Over the past twenty-five years, official corruption has frequently been a topic of public concern. Scandals such as Watergate, Abscam, the Iran–Contra Affair, and their state and local counterparts have lead to prosecutions and the ouster of elected officials, and legislatures have often responded by creating or strengthening official misconduct and campaign finance statutes. At the same time, specialists in political science and public administration have sought to increase understanding of corruption as a form of political behavior and as a management problem. As a result of this increased attention, there is now an extensive body of research literature documenting the many forms corruption has taken (see, for example, Malec and Gardiner 1987) and analyzing the philosophical issues involved in labeling behaviors as ethical or unethical.

As John G. Peters and Susan Welch indicated, corruption scholars have defined their subject matter in different ways. Joseph S. Nye (1967, 419) defines official corruption as "behavior which deviates from the formal duties of a public role because of private-regarding (personal, close family, private clique) pecuniary or status gains; or violates rules against the exercise of certain types of private-regarding influence". Examples of behavior violating "formal duties" include bribery (use of compensation to pervert the judgment of a person in a position of trust); nepotism (bestowal of patronage positions by reason of ascriptive relationships rather than merit); misappropriation (illegal allocation of public resources for private uses); and willful failure to enforce laws or invoke sanctions that are appropriate to a situation. This definition assumes that behavior is corrupt only when it violates a formal standard or rule, which can happen only if legislators have labeled it corrupt.

Other scholars have built their definitions around the *effects* of corruption. Rogow and Lasswell (1963, 132–33) argue that

> a corrupt act violates responsibility toward at least one system of public or civic order and is in fact incompatible with (destructive of) any such system. A system of public or civic order exalts common interest over special interest; violations of the common interest for special advantage are corrupt.

That is to say, corruption exists if the public trust or good is betrayed whether or not a violation of legislated standards transpires.

Public Attitude-Centered Corruption Research

This chapter will review and synthesize research that has used elite and mass interview techniques to explore public attitudes about official corruption. Barry Rundquist and Susan Hanson (1976, 2–3) provide a clear focus for this analysis: "Political corruption [involves] behavior by an individual or group (party, administration) which violates citizens' conceptions of acceptable official behavior within their political community."

Arnold Heidenheimer (1970) notes that corruption can be "black," "white," or "gray." "Black" corruption involves actions that are judged by both the public and public officials as particularly abhorrent and therefore requiring punishment. "White" corruption might be political acts deemed corrupt by both the public and officials, but not severe enough to warrant sanction. "Gray" corruption involves those actions found to be corrupt by either one of the groups, but not both. The importance of such variations in attitudes is clear: "What may be corrupt to one citizen, scholar, or public official is just politics to another, or discretion to a third" (Peters and Welch 1978a, 74). If a society defines certain behaviors as

Table 1.1

Citizens' Estimates of the Extent of Bribery and Other Illegal Activity in City Government

						Response					
		Great Deal		Some		A Little		Almost None		Other	
	N	N	%	N	%	N	%	N	%	N	%
Albuquerque	471	51	11	176	37	94	20	66	14	84	18
Atlanta	469	116	25	202	43	73	16	20	4	58	12
Baltimore	500	172	35	155	30	108	22	14	3	51	10
Boston	507	172	34	182	36	62	12	21	4	70	14
Denver	357	27	8	145	40	73	20	38	11	74	21
Kansas City, KS	193	31	16	47	24	34	18	20	10	61	32
Kansas City, MO	383	64	17	153	40	53	14	33	9	80	20
Milwaukee	443	31	7	157	35	96	22	83	19	76	17
Nashville	426	91	22	158	37	89	21	24	6	64	14
San Diego	517	47	9	197	38	105	21	79	15	89	17
Total	4,266	802	19	1,572	37	787	18	398	9	707	17

Source: David Caputo, *Urban America: The Policy Alternatives* (1976, 65). Data were collected as part of the Urban Observatory Program funded by the Department of Housing and Urban Development. The question asked was "In some cities, officials are said to take bribes and make money in other ways that are illegal. In other cities, such things almost never happen. How much of that sort of thing do you think goes on in [this city]?"

corrupt and then supports the legal system in enforcing that definition, then, and only then, will the legal system be able to enforce ethical standards effectively and over a long period of time. However, if a society defines certain behaviors as not corrupt but the legal system defines them as corrupt, the legal system will be unable to enforce legal standards of ethical behavior.

A major problem in corruption research has been the lack of reliable data to indicate the prevalence of corruption. Media reports and indictments may only indicate whether or how frequently journalists or prosecutors have gone *looking* for corruption, rather than how often it occurs (Malec and Gardiner 1987). However, a comparative study of ten major cities undertaken in 1970 by the National League of Cities attempted to measure prevalence by asking several questions that focus on public perceptions of the extent of political corruption (Caputo 1976, 63–66). When citizens were asked about the honesty of local public officials, their responses were, for the most part, relatively favorable. Although there was some variation among cities as shown in Table 1.1, about one-fifth of the respondents from all ten cities thought that local government officials were less honest than most other people; two-thirds thought that government officials were about the same as most other people. When asked how many public officials "take bribes and make money in other ways that are illegal," 56 percent responded "a great deal" or "some."

Hierarchies of Seriousness

Analogous to Heidenheimer's scale of black, gray, and white corruption, a series of survey research projects have sought to construct hierarchies suggesting the factors that make some behaviors more or less "corrupt" in the eyes of the public. It is apparent from the research by Beard and Horn (1975), Gardiner (1970), Gibbons (1989), Howe and Kaufman (1979), Johnston (1983), Joseph (1988), Lane (1962), Peters and Welch (1978b), and Smigel and Ross (1970) that people judge the severity of corruption by who is involved and what is done. Over and over, the research found that respondents judged elected officials more severely than they judged appointed officials; judges more severely than police officers; bribery and extortion more harshly than conflict of interest, campaign contributions, and patronage; and harmful behavior more harshly than petty behavior.[1]

As Lane (1962) discovered, a majority of the fifteen working- and lower-middle-class men of an Eastern seaboard city whom he interviewed believed that politics and corruption go hand-in-hand. It was not surprising to those interviewed that politicians would cheat a little when it came to campaign contributions, conflict of interest, and special favors. Beard and Horn's (1975) study of fifty congressmen of the Ninetieth Congress found that a number of congressmen believed that "it is none of our business" to interfere with someone's personal choices. If a fellow congressman accepted an honorarium for a speech, it was his business and no one else's. If a politician had a secretary who could not type, it was his business and no one else's. And if a politician hired his wife to be his office manager, it was his business and no one else's. Smigel and Ross (1970, 7) determined in their study of crimes against bureaucracy that for many, "theft appears to be easier to excuse when the victim has larger assets than the criminal, as exemplified by the Robin Hood myth." Therefore, size and the accompanying characteristics of impersonality, bureaucratic power, and red tape were the main reasons given for stealing from large organizations such as corporations and government.

Gardiner (1970) expanded the study of public attitudes toward corruption by surveying attitudes of non-elites in a small Eastern city ("Wincanton" or Reading, Pennsylvania) with a long history of political corruption and influence by organized crime. He asked whether widespread local corruption could be attributed to the preferences and attitudes of city residents by examining the question of public acceptance of official misconduct, especially in relation to nonenforcement of laws against gambling. While interviewing 180 randomly selected residents, Gardiner found that upper-status residents, who were better informed about politics and corruption, were less tolerant of official corruption. Those who gambled and those who had spent most of their lives in the city were most tolerant of gambling. However, in respect to acceptance of corruption, those who had spent most of their lives in Wincanton were less tolerant of corruption than those who had lived elsewhere. In addition, the study found relatively lower levels of tolerance of corruption among younger respondents and among those with more education.

In their analysis of responses by state senators to a series of items concerning ten hypothetical actions by public officials, John G. Peters and Susan Welch found that situations judged most corrupt by legislators were those that involved clearly illegal activity and/or direct personal financial gain by the public official: the driveway of the mayor's home being paved by the city crew; a public official using public funds for personal travel; a state assembly member, while chairperson of the Public Roads Committee, authorizing the purchase of land he had recently acquired; a legislator accepting a large campaign contribution in return for voting "the right way" on a legislative bill (Peters 1977; Peters and Welch 1978a, 1978b, 1980; Welch and Peters 1977, 1980).

In the Peters and Welch survey, minor forms of influence peddling were least likely to be regarded as corrupt: a public official using his influence to get a friend or relative admitted to law school, or a congressman using seniority to obtain a weapons contract for a firm in his district. A variety of conflict-of-interest situations produced the lowest consensus among the respondents: a judge hearing a case concerning a corporation in which he has $50,000 worth of stock; a presidential candidate who promises an ambassadorship in exchange for campaign contributions; a secretary of defense who owns $50,000 in stock in a company with which the Defense Department has a million dollar contract; a congressman who holds about $50,000 worth of stock in Standard Oil of New Jersey and is working to maintain the oil depletion allowance.[2]

In a survey of contemporary planners, Howe and Kaufman (1979) discovered that certain variables were associated with planners' responses to various types of corruption. These variables included the role models technician, political actor, or a combination of the two; political ideology measured from radical to conservative; agency's definition of the public interest versus the individual professional's definition; and value commitment. "Technicians" were the most conservative overall in their view of what is ethical, while "politicians" were more interested in influencing policy and were most willing to use a range of openly political tactics to do it. "Combinations" who were more active, independent, and skilled actors, in most cases, fell in between. The data indicated that "ethical standards in planning are relative. It is certainly true that some kinds of behavior, such as distorting information, are considered unacceptable by the vast majority of all planners. . . . And for many political tactics, planners disagree much more about acceptability, depending on such things as their role orientations, political views, value commitment, or sympathies toward the substantive issues at stake" (Howe and Kaufman 1979, 45).

In a 1983 study of the Pittsburgh metropolitan area, Michael Johnston analyzed the reactions of 241 citizens to perceived corruption; he also analyzed their judgments of the "corruptness" of a set of hypothetical examples of behavior. Over 95 percent of respondents, when asked how concerned they were about corruption, believed that it was an "extremely serious" or "somewhat serious" problem in the United States; when asked how they felt about corruption, approximately 95 percent responded that it tended to make them "very angry" or "somewhat angry" (Johnston 1986).

When they were presented with the set of hypothetical examples of behavior, Johnston's respondents supported the hypothesis that formally defined corrupt actions would be judged more corrupt than those of more doubtful status. A treasurer who embezzles $10,000, a definite illegality, was found to be more corrupt than a restaurant owner who provides free lunch to policemen.

Respondents judged more harshly those who took more than they did those who took less. A public official's embezzlement of $10,000 was regarded as significantly more corrupt than an embezzlement of $500. Also, direct styles of taking were judged more corrupt than indirect styles. A policeman who asks for $20 from a speeding driver so that he can "forget" a ticket was judged to be more corrupt than a policeman who asks/accepts a free lunch from a restaurant on his beat.

Actions of public officials were judged more harshly than those of private citizens. A public official who falsely claimed a management degree was judged more corrupt than a homeowner who conceals remodeling from the tax assessor. The judgment of what is corrupt and what is not depends upon mitigating circumstances. An official's taking a cut of a contract was seen as slightly less corrupt if he gave the money to his political party instead of keeping it for himself, and as much less corrupt if he used the money to pay his sick child's hospital bill. The same held true for a person who "bounced" a check if she/he did so in order to buy clothes for her/his children. If there was a "compassionate" reason for the behavior, respondents tended to forgive more readily.

Finally, Johnston found that judgment of rule-breaking behavior varied with the nature of both the perpetrator and the victim. When a prominent person takes from a large organization, judgments are relatively harsh. When a prominent person or organization takes from ordinary citizens, judgments are also relatively harsh. But when ordinary citizens take from a large organization, judgments are more lenient. A homeowner who offers trash collectors $20 to take away trash they are not supposed to pick up, or a homeowner who conceals from the tax assessor the fact that he has remodeled his basement is less corrupt, if corrupt at all, than a county treasurer who embezzles $500 or a supermarket in a poor neighborhood that raises the prices of basic food items on the days when welfare checks come out. In the first two cases, it is the "little guy" taking from the large system and in the last, it is the prominent person or large organization taking from the "little guy." The latter is seen as much worse than the former, and the former is the "little guy" getting back at large organizations.

Johnston compared social class—low, lower-middle, middle, upper-middle, and upper—with perceptions of corruption. He found no consistent relationship between class and the severity of judgment. However, he did find that various kinds of wrongdoing matter more to some classes than to others. Cases of official theft are much more the concern of middle- to upper-status respondents than of lower-status groups. Johnston also found a strong tendency for lower-middle and middle-status respondents to resent cases of favoritism, and for upper-middle and upper-status respondents to be tolerant of them. Class variation was not significant in "personal taking" situations. In cases of official theft, it may be that middle- and upper-status individuals are more aware of what constitutes wrongdoing in public settings, and are more familiar with the public misconduct that does come to light. Favoritism for upper-middle- and upper-status individuals may be seen as the reward for merit and expertise; for lower-middle and middle-status individuals favoritism may be regarded as illegitimate favors and advantages.

Johnston's study of Pittsburgh residents was replicated in 1984 and 1987 in Great Britain. His hypothetical examples were used by Social and Community Planning Research in the British Social Attitudes Surveys as a measure of public attitudes toward corruption. Johnston later conducted follow-up interviews with fifty-five of the 1984 respondents. He discovered that in many situations, British citizens reacted to corruption the same way as Americans. Both groups condemned elites/public officials who misuse their office: for example, the policeman who asks for a bribe or the public official who embezzles. However, Americans tended to condemn just as severely private citizens who take, while British were more lenient: "The citizen who tries to purchase preferential treatment is just as wrong for many Americans as the official who puts his or her discretion up for sale" (Johnston 1989, 428).

The British were also more lenient about public officials who take in small amounts. When the stakes were smaller, or the connections between giving and receiving less direct, respondents were more tolerant. Americans, on the other hand, judged public officials more harshly. To Americans, it does not matter how much public officials take; it is just as wrong.

Dolan, McKeown, and Carlson (1988), using Q-methodology[3] and Johnston's set of hypothetical examples of behavior (plus twenty-four more), replicated Johnston's study with twenty-five persons representing a mix of occupations and sensitivities to corruption. Their findings support those of Johnston. Considered most corrupt were those situations where a public official misappropriates public resources and engages in clear conflicts of interest: a judge with $50,000 worth of stock in a corporation who hears a case concerning that firm; a legislator who accepts a large contribution in return for voting the way a contributor wants him to on a certain bill. Allowable behaviors were more indicative of private life: a homeowner conceals from tax assessors the fact that he has remodeled his basement; a state employee makes personal long-distance calls from his office phone;

a company's purchasing agent accepts personal gifts from the supply company that seeks to do business with his company.

Respondents believed that using the system is acceptable as long as one works within and works according to its informal rules, which legitimate a certain degree of elite use of power not available to non-elites. It is permissible for a public official to use his influence to get a friend admitted to law school or a city council member to obtain a city job for his son; it is not permissible for a person to write a bad check, knowing there is not enough money in the bank to cover it, in order to buy clothing for his children. Influence peddling is acceptable unless it negates the law or a personal code of right. Respondents felt that the behavior of a homeowner who pays $20 for extra trash removal, or a person who maintains his voter registration in a town he no longer lives in, or a city councilman who uses his political influence to get tickets to a sold-out concert is most corrupt. However, when "politics as usual" is involved, people in high positions may take advantage of their good fortune. Therefore, it is permissible for the driveway of the mayor's home to be paved by the city crew, or a presidential candidate to promise an ambassadorship to someone in exchange for campaign contributions.

Respondents judged those acts that include large amounts of money or influence as more corrupt than those acts that do not. An embezzlement of $10,000 is more corrupt than an embezzlement of $500. They also judged as more corrupt misrepresentations, especially for personal gain. A supermarket in a poor neighborhood that raises the price of basic food items on the day welfare checks are issued is more corrupt than a public official who uses public funds for personal travel.

It is apparent that the respondents react most strongly to behavior that relates primarily to local or state affairs. Corrupt acts are defined in terms of theft, such as embezzlement and stealing. Permissible behaviors stress limited forms with which to exercise influence. In the terms of Heidenheimer, corruption is defined by black, white, and gray areas. Embezzlement and stealing are definitely black areas. Influence peddling to a limited extent is white. In between are actions that tend to be gray.

Lawrence Joseph (1988), also using hypothetical examples, conducted in-depth interviews with fifty-eight community and civic leaders in Chicago. Included in the sample were leaders of the business community, public interest groups, neighborhood and community development organizations, civil rights groups, and political advocacy groups. The overall rankings of types of cases are generally compatible with the findings of Peters and Welch and of Johnston. Chicago elites judged situations that involved bribery and extortion as most corrupt, while "petty" bribery, along with conflicts of interest, were judged less harshly. Cases that involved campaign contributions and political patronage were least likely to be considered corrupt. A police officer who takes money from drug pushers or a city inspector who demands money in exchange for overlooking building code violations is more corrupt than a city employee who accepts

Table 1.2

Correlates of Corruption Attitudes

Respondent Characteristic	Stricter	More Lenient
Socioeconomic Status	Higher	Lower (Carlin, 1966; Gardiner, 1970; Joseph, 1988; Gibbons, 1989; Johnston, 1986)[5]
Age	Younger	Older (Gardiner, 1970)
	Older	Younger (Gibbons, 1989)[6]
Residency	Long-time	Short-time (Gardiner, 1970)
	Rural	Urban (Atkinson & Mancuso, 1985)
Institutional setting	High courts	Lower courts (Carlin, 1966)
Ethical concerns	High ethical concerns	Low ethical concerns (Carlin, 1966; Howe & Kaufman, 1979)
Political culture	Moralistic	Individualistic/Traditionalistic (Peters & Welch, 1978a, 1978b; Welch & Peters, 1980; Nice, 1983; Johnston, 1983)
Region of country	Quebec	Atlantic, Ontario, Prairie, British Columbia (Gibbons, 1989)[7]
Alienation	More alienated	Less alienated (Gibbons, 1989)
Ideology	Liberal	Conservative (Peters & Welch, 1978b; Howe & Kaufman, 1979; Gibbons, 1989; Atkinson & Mancuso, 1985)[8]
Gender	Female	Male (Peters & Welch, 1978b)
Political experience	Previous	None (Peters & Welch, 1978b)
Role model	Technician	Political actor (Howe & Kaufman, 1979)

money to expedite the issuance of a liquor license or an alderman who uses his position to influence a zoning change for a business in which he has a financial interest. Examples of situations judged least corrupt were a mayor who awards a city contract to one of his major campaign contributors or an alderman who uses his influence to obtain a city job for a party precinct captain.

Joseph's study also suggested that some public officials (judges) were held to higher standards than others (police officers). Other things being equal, elected officials were thought to have a greater responsibility to uphold the public trust than were appointed officials. Actions perceived to have more harmful consequences were likely to be judged more corrupt.

These studies have identified a number of correlates of attitudes toward corruption. Recognizing that the studies used differing survey instruments, Table 1.2 presents the respondent characteristics associated with stricter and more lenient views. (For purposes of this presentation, "stricter" respondents label more forms of behavior as corrupt, and "more lenient" respondents so classify fewer forms of behavior.)[4]

Implications and Conclusions: Integrity as a Policy Preference

> In the past 20 years, South Carolinians have moved by the thousands from the farms to the suburbs. Republicans now give the once monolithic Democratic party a serious contest. And from the marshy coast to the Piedmont plateau, the place has been infiltrated by outsiders, notably vacationers, retirees, and powerful corporations that have bought hometown banks and newspapers and brought a new standard for doing business. These changes have upset the old social order, and with it the old rules. "All of a sudden we don't play by local rules any more, we play by national rules. . . . What used to be agreements among gentlepersons now amounts to crime." [Schmich 1991]

The literature we have reviewed clearly shows that "corruption" means different things to different people, and many respondents do not see as "very corrupt" some acts that are forbidden by official misconduct statutes, let alone other improper activities. Even among respondents who *in the abstract* prefer honest government, some will find other values more important if they are forced to make a choice. In some cases, for example, a public policy preference is more significant; in other cases, loyalty to friends or colleagues may mean that little will be done to counteract improper practices.

Gardiner's (1970) study clearly showed that the residents of Reading, Pennsylvania, did not tolerate corruption per se. However, he concluded that public attitudes did facilitate the growth of corruption in law-enforcement agencies. Residents saw little wrong with gambling and believed that many forms of petty gambling were locally popular and, therefore, seldom criticized those who indulged in them. They in turn questioned the wisdom of the state's antigambling laws and supported the legalization of most forms of gambling. When residents were confronted with the choice between strictly upholding the antigambling laws and "looking the other way," the residents preferred that elected and appointed public officials look the other way.

Beard and Horn's (1975) survey of the Ninetieth Congress examined congressmen's perceptions of the behavior of their colleagues and knowledge of congressional behavior as regards conflict of interest, campaign financing, and peer-group pressure on ethical behavior. They discovered that the majority of respondents regarded behavior in the House as not especially bad or as no worse than that found elsewhere in American society. Outside financial interests were seen as legitimate and often necessary to supplement congressional income. The assisting of private parties dealing with the government was viewed as a necessary part of the representative function. Finally, congressmen believed that they should not oversee their colleagues' behavior unless it reflected adversely on the House as a whole.

> It is like your relations with your wife. Your relationship with your constituency is your business. Adam Clayton Powell's sin was that he embarrassed the House. No member really cares if X cleaned up on the sugar bill. But you do care if Congress as such gets a bad name. [Beard and Horn 1975, 67]

Williams's (1985) similar study on conflict of interest involving members of Parliament in Great Britain[9] found that a majority of M.P.'s believed that corruption arises only where personal financial interest overcomes or distorts a member's duty as an M.P. Like the U.S. Congress, Parliament is reluctant to intervene in the area of personal interests of members. Members of Parliament, like congressmen, believed that they should not interfere with their colleagues' behavior unless it reflected adversely on the party or Parliament as a whole. Trust is fixed on the honor and integrity of the individual and the mutual trust of the collectivity. The privacy of the individual is respected and he or she is entrusted with the discretion to judge what interests should be disclosed (Williams 1985, 136).

Rundquist and colleagues in two separate studies (Rundquist, Strom, and Peters 1977; Rundquist and Hansen 1975, 1976) examined how awareness of elected representatives' corruption affects the behavior of voters.[10] In both studies, it was found that citizens seem to prefer other things more intensely than they prefer honest government. "When they are made to choose between a corrupt official who is 'right' on those other things [preferences], and a clean official who is 'wrong' on them, they tend to support the corrupt official" (Rundquist and Hansen 1976, 10). And the more the voters agreed with a candidate's policy, preferences, and party, the more they discounted a credible message that the candidate was corrupt (Rundquist, Strom, and Peters 1977).[11]

In a study of government employees in India, Sengupta (1982) measured the effect of the organization, the family, and the neighborhood on attitudes toward corruption. He concluded that a corrupt environment in the office is largely responsible for the formation of favorable attitudes toward corruption; that a corrupt environment in the family can influence attitudes toward corruption; and that a corrupt environment in the neighborhood has very little effect on attitudes toward corruption. "This shows that an employee learns the habit of corruption mainly from his fellow employees. . . . The corrupt environment in the family and the corrupt environment among the neighbours and relatives hardly contributed toward it" (Sengupta 1982, 8). Sengupta concludes his analysis by stating that:

the effect of organisational environment ruling over that of family and neighbourhood may be appreciated better by considering two persons both coming from similar types or same families and similar neighbourhood, but one joining police or excise department and the other joining teaching profession. It is natural and very logical to conclude that the first employee will get involved in corruption due to organisational environment of the department, whereas the latter will be less involved in corruption. [Ibid.]

Joseph's (1988, 72–73) interviews with Chicago elites found that "most organizational leaders did not perceive that political corruption had a significant direct impact on the organization, on its work, on its membership, or on its broader constituency." Very few respondents had any first-hand experience with corruption and most reported few, if any, specific complaints about corruption from their members. On the other hand, many community and civic leaders believe that corruption does have some sort of indirect impact on their organization. Some leaders maintain that corruption breeds incompetence and inefficiency in government, while others draw a distinction between problems of corruption and quality of public services. Business leaders believe that corruption in government discredits the overall impression of Chicago, thus discouraging businesses from locating or expanding in the city. Leaders of African American and Hispanic organizations believe that corruption as favoritism subverts fairness and impartiality in government, especially in relation to hiring, contracting, and the delivery of services. Some community leaders believe that corruption creates cynicism and apathy among citizens, thus "making it more difficult for community and civic organizations to get people involved in trying to address public issues and affect public policy" (Joseph 1988, 74).

Varying policy preferences might be relevant in an explanation of why one community is tolerant of corrupt behavior and another is not. "Citizens seem to prefer other things more intensely than they do honest government" (Rundquist and Hanson 1976, 10). And citizens might have other needs more pressing than the need for honest government. According to Maslow's (1954) study of needs, unless the needs for security and acceptance are satisfied, a person is unable to move forward in his psychological development. If citizens are more concerned about shelter and food, they will accept any official who will provide those needs, whether she/he is corrupt or not.

Our review of research on public attitudes toward corruption provides a mixed message for those who wish to increase integrity in government: some citizens are very sensitive to the issue and others are not.

As Joseph (1988, 74) concludes,

in order to mobilize Chicago's community and civic organizations (and their constituencies) on the issue of political corruption, appeals to their sense of ethics or their sense of civic virtue will not be sufficient. They will have to be convinced that the problem of corruption has a significant effect on those issues that directly concern them. They will have to be shown that proposed reforms will somehow make the work of their organizations easier, will benefit their constituencies in a relatively specific way, or will improve the quality of government as it affects them.

In some areas, public support for standards of official integrity might be so widespread that corruption is unlikely to be a major problem. In some areas, demands for illegal goods and services might overwhelm *any* attempt to reduce corruption. Everywhere else, however, the preferences of citizens—the "issues that directly concern them"—establish more important issues that dominate public discussion.

Notes

1. These findings support Peters and Welch's definition of official corruption. Characteristics that seem to determine whether behavior is to be judged corrupt or not are the political nature of the public official's role, the status of the donor and recipient of the political favor, and the nature of the favor (1978a, 976–77). An act will be considered more corrupt, according to Peters and Welch, if the official involved is acting in a public rather than in a personal capacity and holds a judicial or other nonpolitical post. It will also be judged more corrupt if either the contributor or the recipient of the favor is a nonconstituent or is a public official. Any favor intended to benefit only one individual or corporation is likely to be considered more corrupt than a favor benefiting many. Finally, any payment that is large, unrelated to campaign expenses, consists of cash, and is immediately accepted will be seen as more corrupt than a payment that has the opposite characteristics.

2. Atkinson and Mancuso (1985) in their study of Canadian members of Parliament came to conclusions similar to those of Peters and Welch.

3. Q-methodology is a technique for contextual rank-ordering of stimuli based on a method of social research that assumes the centrality of self-reference (Dolan et al. 1988; 9).

4. Strictly speaking, this assumes that the component items in a questionnaire form a single ordinal scale. It is likely, however, that respondents may see in the items a variety of issues going beyond a consistent degree-of-corruptness dimension. Without the original data, it is impossible to judge whether this is true.

5. Johnston found that cases of official theft were much more the concern of middle- to upper-status respondents than of lower-status groups, while for cases of favoritism, lower-status groups were more concerned than middle-to upper-status groups. Joseph supported these findings in his study.

6. Gardiner found that tolerance of corruption increased with age. Gibbons found that older students were more critical of irregularities in campaign finance and in bureaucratic conflict of interest.

7. Depending on the type of corruption, regions within Canada had different responses to corrupt behavior. Respondents from Quebec were less critical of nepotism than the other four regions. However, they were more critical of campaign finance irregularities than the other four regions. The Atlantic provinces were more critical of patronage.

8. Gibbons found that in Canada the influence of federal party preference was felt on patronage, campaign finance, and some conflict of interest. Atkinson and Mancuso found that party affiliation was a significant factor in their models. New Democrats were consid-

erably less tolerant than either the Liberals or the Conservatives of acts of corruption associated with either constituency service or conflict of interest.

9. Williams randomly interviewed as part of her Ph.D. research a number of members of Parliament and House of Commons staff from 1978 to 1980, using a structured interview schedule that consisted of thirty-seven questions.

10. Knowledge of a candidate's illegal activities is rarely comprehended by voters for several reasons. The first is that the candidate usually seeks to conceal that he is involved in illegal activities. Second, both candidates have similar motivation to accuse each other of being corrupt. Third, only when the corruption message comes from a source outside the electoral setting is it likely to be given credibility.

11. This was particularly true with those voters who had intense feelings about the Vietnam War.

References

Atkinson, Michael M., and Mancuso, Maureen. 1985. "Do We Need a Code of Conduct for Politicians? The Search for an Elite Political Culture of Corruption in Canada." *Canadian Journal of Political Science* 18 (September): 459–80.

Beard, Edmund, and Horn, Stephen. 1975. *Congressional Ethics: The View from the House.* Washington DC: Brookings Institution.

Caputo, David A. 1976. *Urban America: The Policy Alternatives.* San Francisco: W.H. Freeman.

Carlin, Jerome E. 1966. *Lawyers' Ethics: A Survey of the New York City Bar.* New York: Russell Sage.

Dobel, J. Patrick. 1978. "The Corruption of a State." *American Political Science Review* 72 (September): 958–73.

Dolan, Kathleen; McKeown, Bruce; and Carlson, James M. 1988. "Popular Conceptions of Political Corruption: Implications for the Empirical Study of Political Ethics." *Corruption and Reform* 3 (1): 3–24.

Gardiner, John A. 1970. *The Politics of Corruption: Organized Crime in an American City.* New York: Russell Sage.

Gibbons, Kenneth M. 1989. "Variations in Attitudes toward Corruption in Canada." In *Political Corruption: A Handbook*, edited by Arnold J. Heidenheimer, Michael Johnston, and Victor T. LeVine, 763–80. New Brunswick, NJ: Transaction.

Heidenheimer, Arnold J. 1970. "The Context of Analysis." In *Political Corruption: Readings in Comparative Analysis*, edited by Arnold J. Heidenheimer, 3–28. New York: Holt, Rinehart and Winston.

Howe, Elizabeth, and Kaufman, Jerome. 1979. "The Ethics of Contemporary American Planners." In *Ethics in Planning*, edited by Martin Wachs. New Brunswick, NJ: Center for Urban Policy Research.

Johnston, Michael. 1982. *Political Corruption and Public Policy in America.* Monterey, CA: Brooks/Cole.

_____. 1983. "Corruption and Political Culture in America: An Empirical Perspective." *Publius* 13 (Winter): 19–39.

_____. 1986. "Right and Wrong in American Politics: Popular Conceptions of Corruption." *Polity* 18 (Spring): 367–91.

_____. 1988. "The Price of Honesty." In *British Social Attitudes: The Fifth Report*, edited by Roger Jowell, Sharon Witherspoon, and Lindsay Brook. London: Gower.

_____. 1989. "Corruption and Political Culture in Britain and the United States." *Innovation* 2 (4): 417–36.

Johnston, Michael, and Wood, Douglas. 1985. "Right and Wrong in Public and Private

Life." Chapter 5 in *British Social Attitudes: The 1985 Report*, edited by Roger Jowell and Sharon Witherspoon. London: Gower.

Joseph, Lawrence B. 1988. *Attitudes of Community and Civic Leaders toward Political Corruption: A Report to the Chicago Ethics Project*. Chicago: Chicago MetroEthics Coalition.

Lane, Robert E. 1962. *Political Ideology: Why the American Common Man Believes What He Does*. New York: Free Press.

Malec, Kathryn L., and Gardiner, John A. 1987. "Measurement Issues in the Study of Official Corruption: A Chicago Example." *Corruption and Reform* 3 (3): 267–78.

Maslow, Abraham. 1954. *Motivation and Personality*. New York: Harper.

Nice, David C. 1983. "Political Corruption in the American States." *American Politics Quarterly* 11 (October): 507–17.

Nye, J.S. 1967. "Corruption and Political Development: A Cost–Benefit Analysis." *American Political Science Review* 61 (June): 417–27.

Peters, John G. 1977. "Politics and Corruption: The View from the State Legislature." Unpublished manuscript.

Peters, John G., and Welch, Susan. 1978a. "Political Corruption in America: A Search for Definitions and a Theory." *American Political Science Review* 72 (September): 974–84.

_____. 1978b. "Politics, Corruption, and Political Culture: A View from the State Legislature." *American Politics Quarterly* 6 (July): 345–56.

_____. 1980. "The Effects of Charges of Corruption on Voting Behavior in Congressional Elections." *American Political Science Review* 74 (September): 697–708.

Rogow, Arnold A., and Lasswell, Harold D. 1963. *Power, Corruption and Rectitude*. Englewood Cliffs, NJ: Prentice-Hall.

Rundquist, Barry S., and Hansen, Susan B. 1975. "Political Corruption and Voting Behavior: The Case of Watergate." Unpublished manuscript.

_____. 1976. "On Controlling Official Corruption: Elections vs. Laws." Unpublished manuscript.

Rundquist, Barry S.; Strom, Gerald S.; and Peters, John G. 1977. "Corrupt Politicians and Their Electoral Support: Some Experimental Observations." *American Political Science Review* 71: 954–63.

Schmich, Mary T. 1991. "Scandals Mark a Passing Era in S. Carolina." *Chicago Tribune*, April 4.

Sengupta, P.B. 1982. "Impact of Corrupt Environment on the Formation of Favourable Attitudes towards Corruption." *Social Defence* 18 (July): 5–9.

Smigel, Erwin O., and Ross, H. Laurence. 1970. *Crimes against Bureaucracy*. New York: Van Nostrand.

Welch, Susan, and Peters, John G. 1977. "Attitudes of U.S. State Legislators Toward Political Corruption: Some Preliminary Findings." *Legislative Studies Quarterly* 2 (November): 445–63.

_____. 1980. "State Political Culture and the Attitudes of State Senators Toward Social Economic Welfare, and Corruption Issues." *Publius* 10 (Spring): 59–67.

Williams, Sandra. 1985. *Conflict of Interest: The Ethical Dilemma in Politics*. London: Gower.

2

Politics, Bureaucracy, and Political Corruption: A Comparative State Analysis

Thomas M. Holbrook and Kenneth J. Meier

Ethics in government is an issue that has drawn the attention of both academics and the general public. Certainly, in the American case, interest in government ethics has been heightened by such notorious scandals as Watergate, Koreagate, Iran–Contra, the HUD scandal, ABSCAM, and presidential chief of staff John Sununu's travels. Although systematic empirical research on political corruption is not extensive (Peters and Welch 1978a, 1987b, 1980; Johnston 1983; Nice 1983), elaborate theories and attempts to integrate case literature abound (Johnston 1983; Rose-Ackerman 1978; Nye 1967; Nas, Price, and Weber 1986; Heidenheimer 1970; Heidenheimer, Johnston, and LeVine 1990; Wilson 1966). This chapter seeks to contribute to the literature by combining various explanations of political corruption with an empirical examination of corruption in the American states. First, we discuss the distinction between corruption and unethical behavior. Second, we define corruption so that comparable measures are possible. Third, we examine four general explanations of political corruption—historical/cultural, political, structural, and bureaucratic; this will be followed by the presentation of a combined model. Fourth, we address the question of political opportunism: Can actions against corruption be linked to racial and partisan politics? Finally, we discuss the possibility of other administrative sources of corruption.

This chapter is a somewhat modified version of the authors' article "I Seen My Opportunities and I Took 'Em," *The Journal of Politics*, Volume 54, Number 1, February, 1992.

Corruption versus Ethics

Students of public administration have devoted substantial effort to the examination of administrative ethics. Unethical behavior in general is considered more than just illegal behavior (our definition of corruption). Appleby (1952), for example, included as unethical the unwillingness to assume responsibility, the inability to deal with people, the failure to use institutional resources effectively, and the failure to anticipate bureaucratic problems, among others. None of these behaviors in the abstract would be considered illegal, but Appleby and his followers (Bailey 1966; Jos 1990) would consider them unethical.

Corruption or illegal behavior is probably only a small subset of the behaviors that might be considered unethical. Rohr's (1989) approach to ethics, for example, defines appropriate behavior in terms of regime values that include equity, fairness, equal opportunity, property, and similar terms. Collectively, regime values cover a far broader scope than illegal activities.

Students of administrative ethics, including Rohr, also hold that administrative ethics are situational; what is ethical is determined in part by the context in which the action takes place (Denhardt 1988). Illegal bureaucratic behavior, at least within a single political jurisdiction, generally remains illegal regardless of the context.

Even the ability to define a given behavior as ethical is subject to challenge. Terry (1990) and Burke (1986) argue for a neutral competence approach to administrative ethics where administrators would refer decisions with ethical components to political officials. Only if administrators have been delegated the responsibility for making ethical determinations should they do so. Wamsley et al. (1987), on the other hand, reject the notion that ethical behavior can exist unless administrators have discretion; they feel that bureaucrats should not yield this discretion to politicians. Similarly, Appleby (1952) stresses the moral ambiguity of action; few black-and-white moral issues arise, shades of gray predominate. Definitions of morality, therefore, are always open to challenge.

Some students of ethics avoid the issue of defining ethical behavior by advocating a process approach to ethics (Denhardt 1988). In a process approach, organizations or individuals establish a process that ensures ethical and moral considerations are brought to the attention of decision makers and are incorporated in the decision calculus. The outcome of such a process can be judged as ethical only by understanding the organizational structure, political demands, and other contextual factors that condition the decision (Cooper 1987).

Ethical behavior might even include some actions that are illegal—what is known as the dirty hands problem (Burke 1986). Although Rohr (1989) contends that administrators should never violate the law, one can see situations in which implementation of unjust laws might call for an administrator who violates the law. To allow an action to be ethical simply because it has the endorsement of legislation would be to abrogate the moral responsibility of a public servant (Wamsley et al. 1987; Denhardt 1988).

While we feel that questions of ethics are inherently more interesting than questions of illegality, questions of ethics have characteristics that make them difficult to study empirically. First, there is no consensus on which acts are ethical and which acts are unethical. One person might perceive the acts of Oliver North, for example, as ethical support for the office of the president. At the same time others could logically condemn his actions. Second, if ethics are contextual, then what is ethical will vary from situation to situation and from organization to organization. Ethical behavior in Wisconsin might well differ from ethical behavior in Louisiana. Third, if ethical decisions are rarely clear cut, then any attempt at an operational definition is sure to be inadequate.

Because questions of ethics face major theoretical and empirical barriers, we have focused our study on illegal behavior. We do not contend that by examining illegal behavior we are able to deal with the nuances of ethical behavior. We cannot. Rather we offer our research as an examination of a more limited but not less important topic, illegal behavior by public employees. Corruption, like ethics, has ramifications for effective governance. Corruption is quite clearly a violation of the contract between citizens and public officials. It is likely also to alienate citizens from their government and breed cynicism among the populace. For those reasons alone it merits study.

Defining Political Corruption

In his comparative analysis of political corruption, Heidenheimer (1970) groups definitions of political corruption into three categories. First, public office definitions specify corruption as deviation from legal and public duty norms for the purpose of private gain. Second, market system definitions characterize corruption as part of the rational utility maximizing behavior of public officials. Third, public interest definitions view corruption as the betrayal of some broad "public interest." Peters and Welch (1978a, 976) argue that no matter what definition of corruption is used, individual actions still vary in degree of corruption. They use a survey approach to define relative corruption as a function of the type of public official, the relationship of the beneficiary to the public official, the type of favor performed, and the nature of the payoff. Johnston (1986a) distinguishes among four different types of corruption and suggests that the number of participants and the severity of consequences vary among the four categories. Johnston (1986b) has also analyzed the ways in which the public defines corruption. Based on a Pittsburgh area survey, he found that respondents viewed "personal taking," "official theft," "misrepresentation," and "favoritism" as distinct forms of corruption, and that differences in concern about corruption had some social class correlates.

In its broadest terms such as Heidenheimer's public interest definition, corruption becomes similar to unethical behavior. Using the narrowest definition— the public office definition—corruption is restricted to illegal behavior. While a

Table 2.1

Judicial Resources and Corruption Convictions

Independent Variables	Slope	Beta	t-score
U.S. Attorneys per 100,000 Population	−0.1022	−0.05	0.25
Federal Judges per 100,000 Population	0.8091	0.15	0.80
Percentage of Cases Backlogged	0.0018	0.09	0.56
R^2 = 0.02			
Adjusted R^2 = 0.00			
F = 0.34			

narrow definition of corruption excludes a great many interesting political phenomena, it has the aforementioned empirical advantages over broader definitions.

This study uses a narrow definition of corruption—illegal activities for private gain—recognizing the exclusion of politically interesting actions that such a definition entails. Our specific measure of corruption is the number of public officials in each state who have been convicted for violating laws against public corruption per one hundred elected officials in that state. To eliminate the random yearly variations that occur because a single investigation might produce several convictions, the measure is based on the total number of convictions from 1977 to 1987. Data were gathered by the United States Department of Justice's (1988) Public Officials Integrity Section. Nearly six thousand public officials were convicted of corruption charges during this time period. The average state had 1.69 convictions per one hundred elected officials; the standard deviation was 1.71. Because the data are positively skewed, a log transformation of this variable was used in all analysis.

We are reasonably confident that this convictions measure is a good surrogate for the level of corruption in a state for four reasons. First, a similar measure of corruption used by both Nice (1983) and Johnston (1983) produced theoretically informed results.[1] Second, Peters and Welch (1987b, 351) compared a similar measure of corruption with elite survey data on perceived levels of corruption in the states. They found a positive correlation. Third, the measure has reasonable face validity, with such states as Oklahoma, New York, and Maryland ranking high on corruption and states such as North Dakota, Oregon, and Wisconsin ranking low. Fourth, the measure is unrelated to federal prosecution or court resources in the state. If convictions were simply the result of slack prosecution resources rather than levels of corruption, we would expect that convictions would be positively related to the number of federal prosecutors and the number of judges and negatively related to court backlogs.[2] Table 2.1 shows that each of these factors is only weakly related to the corruption convictions measure. To make sure our findings are unaffected by court-related resources, each explana-

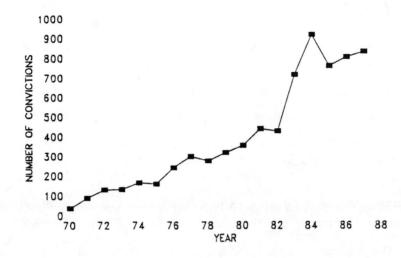

Figure 2.1. **Convictions of Corrupt Public Officials**

tion below will include controls for these three variables if any of these variables are statistically significant.

Although this chapter focuses on the pattern of corruption across states, it is interesting to examine the pattern of corruption over time, which shows an interesting development. Figure 2.1 presents the change in corruption convictions from 1970 to 1987. One is struck by the increase in convictions of corrupt public officials, ranging from a low of thirty-two in 1970 to a high of 936 in 1984. Though the increase in convictions is fairly constant from 1970 to 1982, there was a sharp increase between 1982 and 1983, an increase that was maintained through 1987.

Although the increase in convictions for corruption cannot be denied, this does not necessarily mean that something is wrong with the system. Elder Witt (1989, 33) poses the interesting question, "Are we electing rascals to office in record numbers, or are we simply finding and punishing actions that used to be routinely ignored?" According to Witt, at least part of this increase in convictions does not reflect an increase in corruption. Instead, a proliferation of ethics legislation since Watergate and changes in investigation technology (audio- and videotaping) have boosted indictments and convictions. Even considering these influences, however, some of the increase in convictions probably reflects "the higher monetary stakes involved in state and local government decisions" (Witt 1989, 35). This, of course, illustrates the utility of the states as units of analysis during this time period. Another interesting possibility is that the Justice Department is dedicating more resources to the prosecution of corrupt public officials than it did in the past. Unfortunately, the information required to test this hypothesis—personnel and budgetary data for the Public Integrity division—is not readily available.

Explanations of Political Corruption

Public officials act in a corrupt manner for a very simple reason: they perceive that the potential benefits of corruption exceed the potential costs (Rose-Ackerman 1978). Perceived benefits and costs, in turn, are a function of values associated with various outcomes and the probability that each outcome will be obtained. As Klitgaard (1988, 70) expresses it, if the benefits of corruption minus the probability of being caught times the penalties for being caught are greater than the benefits of not being corrupt, then an individual will rationally choose to be corrupt. While such statements border on tautology, they suggest that explanations of corruption can be clustered in groups that affect either perceived benefits or perceived costs (penalties times probability of apprehension) of corruption.[3] Within this general benefit/cost approach, we will consider four explanations of corruption—historical/cultural, political, structural, and bureaucratic.[4]

Historical/Cultural Explanations of Corruption

Historical/cultural explanations of political corruption proliferate in American politics. The corruption of urban political machines as they facilitated the rise of immigrant groups to power in the United States is well documented (Greenstein 1964). Urban environments, in particular, loosen the social controls of family and religion and at the same time concentrate government programs and resources. In short, urbanism fosters conditions conducive to corruption. In these environments, political machines were established to benefit individuals who supported the machine; and corruption was used to compensate machine operators for their efforts. At times cultural explanations of corruption border on pop psychology: "There is a particular political ethos or style which attaches a relatively low value to probity and impersonal efficiency and relatively high value to favors, personal loyalty, and private gain" (Wilson 1966, 30). This "cultural-flaw" argument gained support among middle-class reformers who sought to eliminate corruption and/or lower-class, immigrant influences from government (Magleby 1984, 24).

The historical/cultural explanation of political corruption, therefore, holds that corruption is the result of the weaknesses of individuals or a pattern of politics that has routinely accepted corruption. In other words, corruption exists because individuals perceive that there are benefits to corruption and that the costs are relatively low compared to the benefits. As succinctly put by Tammany Hall's George Washington Plunkitt, "I seen my opportunities and I took 'em" (Riordan 1963, 3).

Four indicators of historical/cultural explanations of political corruption will be used: urbanism, middle-class preferences, immigration, and other criminal activities. Although most American cities have been subjected to substantial structural change to eliminate corruption (see below), major cities have historically been the province of political machines. Cities still provide weaker social controls and greater opportunities for corruption. Accordingly, we expect that traditionally corrupt governments will continue to be corrupt (Johnston 1986c, 23). Recent indictments (1990–91) in Chicago and New York, for example, suggest some corruption continues in our major cities. Our measure will be the percentage of state population living in urban areas.[5]

The middle-class preferences opposing corruption can be tapped by the education levels of the population, in this case by the percentage of the population with college degrees. While immigration and corruption have often been linked (Werner 1983, 148; Nye 1967, 417; Wilson 1966, 30), in the United States these arguments clearly are not intended to apply to all immigrants. Within the context of political corruption, the word "immigrants" means to many the Irish or Italian immigrants who first challenged Yankee hegemony in the major cities. Our immigration measure will be the percentage of the population who identify their ancestral group as Irish or Italian.[6] Since immigrants have few economic resources to lose, they might perceive that the costs of corruption are fairly low. Finally, Nice (1983, 509) argues that political corruption is merely the extension of private behavior in the public realm, and that crime rates might be a good surrogate for tolerance of corruption.[7] High crime rates should indicate the inability of the political system to establish penalties severe enough or certain enough to deter crime (and thus corruption). The historical/cultural explanation of corruption, therefore, suggests positive correlations between political corruption and urbanism, Irish/Italian ancestry, and crime rates; it suggests a negative correlation with education.[8]

Table 2.2 reports the standardized and unstandardized regression coefficients for the historical and cultural variables. Urbanization and education have the anticipated impact on the rate of corruption convictions: An increase in urbanization yields an increase in convictions while an increase in the number of college graduates is associated with a decline in convictions. The crime rate is not statistically significant although the coefficient is in the expected direction. The Irish/Italian variable is highly significant but in the *wrong* direction. States with concentrations of people of Irish or Italian ancestry have less political corruption. Since the immigrants hypothesis is strongly rejected by these results, this variable will no longer be used for analysis. With these variables, the number of judges per capita becomes a significant influence (unlike Table 2.1). In terms of relative importance, urbanization has a somewhat greater impact on corruption than does education although the difference in magnitude is modest. Finally, the overall fit of the model indicates that historical and cultural factors affect convictions for political corruption, but much of the variation remains unexplained.

Table 2.2

Historical and Cultural Impacts on Political Corruption

Independent Variables	Slope	Beta	t-score
Percent Urban	0.0175	0.71	4.69*
Percent College Graduates	−0.0645	−0.35	2.82*
Crime Rate	0.0081	0.15	0.96
Irish and Italian Immigrants	−1.7259	−0.38	3.42*
Control Variables			
Attorneys per Capita	−19.1101	−0.09	0.61
Judges per Capita	154.7827	0.29	2.09*
Backlogs	−0.0022	−0.10	0.83

$R^2 = 0.53$
Adjusted $R^2 = 0.46$
$F = 6.89$
*$p < 0.05$

Political Explanations of Corruption

Perhaps the most political explanation of corruption is presented by political economist Susan Rose-Ackerman (1978). Using formal modeling, Rose-Ackerman rejects the common economic prescription of decentralization and economic competition as a remedy for the evils of government. Politics, in her view, can be used to combat corruption if political actions increase the cost of corruption by increasing the probability that a corrupt individual will be punished. Focusing on elected officials, she states, "politicians may sell their votes on particular issues if they are either very confident of reelection or practically certain to be defeated" (Rose-Ackerman 1978, 213). Competitive elections, however, are not a sufficient condition for reducing corruption; an intelligent electorate is also required. She concludes: "Combining an informed and concerned electorate with a political process that regularly produces closely contested elections leads to a world in which corruption is limited by competition" (Rose-Ackerman 1978, 213).

The linkage between corruption and electoral defeat has received a fair amount of empirical research. Peters and Welch (1980) found that charges of corruption reduced a candidate's vote totals by 6 to 11 percent in congressional elections. Other studies have also found an electoral impact to charges of corruption (Rundquist, Strom, and Peters 1977; Ragsdale and Cook 1987; Krasno and Green 1988).

The most obvious indicator of competitive elections is party competition (Bibby et al. 1990), operationalized for this study as the competitiveness of state-level elections from 1974 to 1986. The relative turnout in House elections from 1974 to 1980 is used to tap the informed electorate dimension.[9] Johnston (1983) found that turnout was negatively related to corruption but found no relationship between party competition and corruption. In addition to turnout, the college graduates measure in the historical/cultural section might also indicate an involved, politically informed electorate (Campbell, et al. 1960; Verba and Nie 1972; Nie, Verba, and Petrocik 1976).

If contested elections contribute to less corruption, then another aspect of politics that should be considered is how isolated public officials are from the electorate. One measure of electoral isolation is the appointive power of the governor. The broader the governor's appointive power, the fewer the high-ranking officials that need be concerned about the electoral consequences of corruption.[10] Finally, political ideology could be linked to the toleration of corruption. One argument might be that conservative electorates would be more tolerant of politicians who view politics as a means to maximize personal utility, thereby leading the politicians to believe that the chances of punishment for corrupt practices is fairly low. Alternatively, conservatives generally are supporters of law enforcement and are less likely to appreciate tax money wasted because of corruption. The Wright, Erikson, and McIver (1985) measure of political ideology is used in this analysis.[11] The political explanation of corruption, therefore, predicts that corruption is negatively related to voter turnout and party competition, positively related to governor's appointment power, and either positively or negatively related to conservative electorates.

The analysis of political influences on corruption is presented in Table 2.3. Political participation (voter turnout) is negatively related to political corruption, which confirms Rose-Ackerman's theory that potential exposure to electoral retribution acts as a deterrent to potentially corrupt public officials. This theory is not, however, fully supported by the coefficient for party competition; that coefficient is in the expected direction but not statistically significant. Colinearity is one possible explanation for the lack of significance; party competition is highly correlated with voter turnout ($r = 0.65$). The coefficient for appointive power is not statistically significant either, although it too is in the anticipated direction. The political conservatism relationship supports the hypothesis that conservatives are less tolerant of corruption than nonconservatives are, but the relationship is not statistically significant. Unlike party competition, appointive power and political conservatism are not highly correlated with the other independent variables, so colinearity is not an explanation for the null findings. To summarize, there is strong support for the party competition hypothesis and weak support for the turnout, appointive power, and political conservatism hypotheses.

Structural Explanations of Corruption

Within American politics, the primary perceived deterrent to corruption has been the advocacy of structural reforms. Variation in governmental structures is perceived to be an influence on corruption. Wilson (1966, 35) argues that American

Table 2.3

Political Forces and Political Corruption

Independent Variables	Slope	Beta	t-score
Voter Turnout	−0.0283	−0.48	3.26*
Party Competition	−1.1674	−0.21	1.43
Appointive Power	0.0092	0.171	0.33
Political Conservatism	−0.5034	−0.08	0.61

$R^2 = 0.42$
Adjusted $R^2 = 0.37$
$F = 8.21$
$*p < 0.05$

political systems, because they are fragmented, allow individuals to exploit politics for their own gain.[12] Fragmented political systems make public officials less visible and thus reduce the perceived probability that corrupt actions will be discovered (Klitgaard 1988, 58). Walsh (1978) and Henriques (1986) argue that the fragmentation of political authority resulting from the proliferation of single-purpose special districts (water districts, public corporations) is a stimulus to corruption. Such districts are obscured from public view yet control substantial public funds; thus they provide good opportunities for corruption (Henriques 1986).

The political reform movements of the early twentieth century explicitly stressed structural reforms with city managers, nonpartisan elections, at-large elections, and so forth. Populist reforms at the state level such as direct election of senators, initiative, referendum, and recall also provide structural changes for voter actions. In their study of corruption, Berg, Hahn, and Schmidhauser (1976, 23) suggest that direct democracy methods such as these can do a great deal to limit corruption by increasing political action.[13] In contemporary government, campaign contributions are perceived as a source of corruption; advocacy groups such as Common Cause support laws that require more complete campaign finance reporting. All in all, an elaborate series of structural reforms have been considered and adopted. As Harold Seidman and Robert Gilmour (1986, 4) contend, an enduring myth of American politics is that we can solve deep-seated problems of government by structural change. The purpose of these structural reforms quite clearly is to make government more visible and thus increase the costs to a corrupt official by increasing the probability of apprehension.

Structural reforms designed to increase the risks to corrupt public officials can be grouped into four sets. First, a series of reforms seeks to centralize political authority and thus make actions more visible and increase the probability that those engaged in corrupt activities will be caught.[14] We use two measures of centralization: first, a state centralization measure, which is simply the percent-

Table 2.4

Political Reform and Political Corruption

Independent Variables	Slope	Beta	t-score
Computer Audit Capability	0.0109	0.10	0.61
Campaign Report Filing	0.0509	0.11	0.65
State Centralization	0.4031	0.07	0.42
Percent Special Districts	0.0084	0.29	1.86#
Initiative Requirements	0.0025	0.21	0.78
Referendum Requirements	0.0010	0.09	0.32
Recall Requirements	0.0014	0.09	0.55

$R^2 = 0.16$
Adjusted $R^2 = 0.02$
$F = 1.15$
$*p < 0.05$
$\#p < 0.10$

age of state and local employees who are employed by state government, and second, the number of special districts as a percent of all government units. Special districts, as noted above, are perceived as especially amenable to corruption.

Second, a greater use of audits to enable legislatures to deter corruption is advocated by many (Wilson 1966, 31; Walsh 1978; Rose-Ackerman 1978, 216; Fuchs 1986, 113; Klitgaard 1988, 53). An increase in auditing capacity should convince public officials that corrupt action will be more likely to be discovered and thus deter corruption (Gardiner and Lyman 1990, 833). Our measure of the audit capacity of the state legislature is the computer facilities available to the legislature.[15] Third, the requirements for campaign contributions reporting are used as a measure of efforts to control the corrupting influences of campaign contributions by increasing their visibility.[16] Finally, as a measure of the populist direct democracy reforms, we use the proportion of the electorate that must sign petitions to activate procedures for recall, referendum, and initiative.[17] Structural explanations of corruption, in short, predict that political corruption will be negatively related to centralization, computers, and campaign finance reporting, and positively related to special districts and restrictions on the initiative, the referendum, and the recall.[18]

Table 2.4 presents the evidence for structural effects on political corruption. With the single exception of special districts, none of the structural factors have an impact on convictions for corruption. Many of these coefficients are also in the wrong direction. While there is some colinearity among the direct democracy measures, this does not explain their lack of significance because they all perform as poorly when entered separately. Perhaps the most devastating finding is that as a group the structural variables do not significantly explain any variation in corruption ($F = 1.15$, $p = 0.35$). Clearly, except for special districts, the structural factors measured here do not play a significant role in deterring political corruption.

The relationship of special districts to political corruption is especially intriguing because of the rapid increase in the number of such units. While the total number of governmental units declined almost 30 percent between 1952 and 1982, the number of special districts increased almost 600 percent during the same period. From 1977 to 1985, roughly the period of this analysis, employment in special districts increased almost 30 percent (Stanley and Niemi 1988, 263–64). If this relationship continues to hold (see below), it means that we can expect corruption to increase.

Bureaucratic Explanations of Corruption

According to Wilson (1966, 31) "men steal when there is a lot of money lying around loose and no one is watching." In other words, all public servants are susceptible to corruption, and corruption is increased by the opportunity for it (an increase in perceived benefits). As the size of government increases, the potential rewards of corruption should also increase (Johnston 1986c, 27). Parallels to this reasoning are often found in the comparative politics literature: corruption exists because public service offers a way to become rich that is not available to private citizens (Nye 1967, 418; Nas et al. 1986, 109; Huntington 1968). One explanation offered for the increase in state and local corruption is that the states are spending more money because the "new federalism" requires more state action (Witt 1989). This logic suggests that corruption should increase as the size of government increases and more opportunities for corruption are presented.

The size of the bureaucracy may be related to corruption for reasons other than increased opportunities. Corruption can be used to overcome bureaucratic inertia and make bureaucracies respond to demands for change (Nas et al. 1986, 109; Werner 1983, 148; Klitgaard 1988, 37). Bureaucracy is viewed by many as an obstacle to change, and corruption is perceived as positive since it can be used to motivate the bureaucracy to act in support of some public good.

Another bureaucratic hypothesis is related to what can be called the income inequality argument or the poverty argument (Huntington 1968, 66; Nye 1967, 418). Because government service provides opportunities for corruption, governments need to reduce temptations for corruption on the part of government employees. Positive incentives can be used rather than reliance on negative incentives like penalties and audits. Civil servants can be better paid. This should attract better qualified persons and also lessen the temptation toward corrupt activities. Higher pay could also be associated with a more professional bureaucracy, which Heidenheimer (1990, 579) believes is more difficult to bribe.

Each of these hypotheses concerning bureaucracy and political corruption recognizes that an increase in the perceived benefits of corruption will produce greater corruption. Another possibility is that bureaucracies also might act in such a manner as to increase the temptations of corruption. Police enforcement associated with organized crime is perceived as a potentially corrupt area of public administration. Greater enforcement in such areas as gambling, drugs, and prostitution will likely increase the need for police "protection" and thus generate more bribe attempts (Johnston 1986c, 25). Nas et al. (1986, 109) suggest that arrests for crimes such as gambling and prostitution may be an indicator of the "lack of congruence between the legal system and social demand," and thus may be considered a determinant of corruption, since both consumers and producers of the illegal activities may bribe public officials to overlook violations of high demand crimes.

Four indicators will be used in the analysis of bureaucratic explanations of political corruption. First, the number of government employees per 1,000 population is a direct measure of size and bureaucracy. Second, the mean salary of public employees should indicate the relative temptation of inducements to corruption. Third, the ratio of budgets to employees should indicate, in Wilson's terms, the relative amount of money lying around.[19] Finally, the arrest rate for gambling is used as an indicator of police enforcement against high demand crimes.[20] Bureaucratic theories of corruption predict a positive relationship between corruption and total government employment, budgets per employee, and gambling arrests, and a negative relationship with mean salary.

According to the results in Table 2.5, the bureaucratic arguments concerning corruption have some validity; the size of the public sector and gambling arrests are both related to levels of public corruption. While both relationships are significant, the coefficient for gambling is especially strong. Corruption, however, is not responsive to the salary levels of government employees or expenditures per employee. For salaries, an explanation exists. Most corrupt activities involve a fair amount of money rather than just the modest amount needed to supplement incomes. When compared with the large potential gains available for corrupt action, differences in salaries may be too small to alter incentives to be corrupt. The overall fit of the bureaucratic model is impressive for a partial explanation.

Determinants of Corruption

The analysis presented thus far has been enlightening. Four categories of explanation have been offered; each has found some degree of empirical support. Among the historical and cultural variables, urbanization and education are important influences on corruption. Among the political explanations, voter turnout and, to a lesser degree, party competition stand out as relevant influences. Of the structural and reform measures, only special districts exhibit a relationship, while the size of the public sector and gambling arrests are important bureaucratic explanations of corruption.

Table 2.5

Opportunities and Political Corruption

Independent Variables	Slope	Beta	t-score
Total Government Employment	0.0012	0.25	2.33*
Budget per Employee	0.0001	0.13	0.76
Mean Government Salary	−0.0000	−0.00	0.00
Gambling Arrests	0.5487	0.69	6.92*

$R^2 = 0.57$
Adjusted $R^2 = 0.53$
$F = 14.90$
*$p < 0.05$
#$p < 0.10$

A combined model of political corruption is presented in Table 2.6. This model includes two variables from each of the four partial explanations. The variables included were either statistically significant in the initial analysis or, in the case of party competition and access to computers, are considered because of theoretical significance. The results of the combined analysis generally support all four explanations. First, we note that urbanization and level of education are important historical/cultural determinants of corruption. Second, party competition emerges as a significant influence from the political environment while voter turnout loses the level of significance found in the earlier analysis. Third, among the structural and reform variables, access to computers has a small negative impact on corruption. An increase in audit capacity is associated with less corruption. Special districts, which were marginally significant in the earlier analysis, lose significance when other controls are introduced. Finally, both bureaucratic variables are significant, reaffirming again that the size of the public sector and the number of gambling arrests influence the level of corruption.

In terms of relative importance, the historical/cultural factors (especially urbanism) carry the most weight, followed by bureaucratic factors, then political influences and, finally, structural and reform variables. The explanatory power of the combined model is impressive; the four different explanations together account for 78 percent of the variation in convictions for corruption across states.

Partisan and Racial Targeting

One final consideration has to do not with the influence of the state environment on corruption but with the motivations of those who prosecute corrupt public officials. Given that our analysis is based on federal prosecutions, some variation in convictions might be related to differences in aggressiveness of federal prosecutors. Corruption prosecutions are only about 1.5 percent of the federal case

Table 2.6

Determinants of Political Corruption

Independent Variables	Slope	Beta	t-score
Percent Urban	0.0138	0.56	4.45*
Percent College Graduates	−0.0521	−0.28	2.19*
Voter Turnout	−0.0027	−0.05	0.37
Party Competition	−1.5499	−0.28	2.78*
Access to Computers	−0.0182	−0.16	1.84#
Special Districts	0.0007	0.02	0.26
Government Employment	0.0023	0.45	4.14*
Gambling Arrests	0.2325	0.29	2.45*

$R^2 = 0.78$
Adjusted $R^2 = 0.73$
$F = 17.91$
$^*p < 0.05$
$^\#p < 0.10$

load so that changes in prosecution priorities can be accomplished without reallocating substantial resources. We need to consider why the Department of Justice might pursue corruption more vigorously in some states than in others. Prosecution of corrupt public officials has the potential to build or destroy political careers (Heidenheimer 1990, 576). Accordingly, politics might motivate some prosecutions. Heidenheimer (1990, 583–84) suggests as much when he notes that prosecutions of Democrats appeared to increase during the Nixon–Ford and Reagan administrations (Ruff 1990, 635). The recent, highly publicized trial of Marion Barry generated charges that black public officials were targeted for prosecution. The first targeting hypothesis we examine is based on partisan control in the state and the party of the president. Specifically, we expect that a presidential administration will be more energetic in its pursuit of corrupt officials in states where the opposition party controls government than in states controlled by the president's party.[21] Presidents in other situations have not been shy about using the powers of government to aid their friends and harm their enemies. In effect, we argue that the Justice Department is but one of the many tools of government available for partisan advantage.

In order to measure partisan targeting, we broke the analysis into two different periods: 1977–80 for the Carter administration and 1981–87 for the Reagan administration. We then created an independent variable that measured control by the opposition party in each state during each of the two administrations.[22] This variable was included with all significant variables from the combined model in Table 2.6.

The results of the partisan targeting analysis are presented in Table 2.7. Positive coefficients for the partisanship variable will indicate targeting under presi-

Table 2.7

Partisanship and Political Corruption

	Standardized Regression Coefficients for Convictions under President	
Independent Variables	Carter	Reagan
Percent Urban	0.59*	0.50*
Percent College Graduates	−0.48*	−0.25#
Party Competition	−0.33*	−0.22*
Access to Computers	−0.12	−0.23*
Government Employment	0.46*	0.51*
Gambling Arrests	−0.06	0.25*
Partisan Targeting	0.06	0.21*
R^2	0.43	0.74
Adjusted R^2	0.33	0.69
F	4.50	16.69

*$p < 0.05$
#$p < 0.10$

dents Carter and Reagan. There is little indication of partisan targeting during the Carter administration; the coefficient is not significant ($t = 0.34$, $p = 0.74$) even though it is in the expected direction. During the Reagan administration, however, the coefficient for partisan targeting is significant and in the anticipated direction, which indicates that prosecution of corrupt officials was more intense in Democratic states than in Republican states during the Reagan years. While such a relationship does not conclusively demonstrate that partisanship determines Justice Department actions, it is consistent with the notion of partisan targeting.

To examine whether or not racial targeting might exist, we added a single variable to the equations in Table 2.7, the percentage of elected officials who are black.[23] Positive coefficients would indicate that states with more black elected officials would have a higher rate of corruption convictions. The results of this analysis are presented in Table 2.8. During both the Carter and the Reagan administrations, the coefficient for black elected officials is positive and strongly significant. Again, while these relationships do not conclusively demonstrate that the Justice Department targets black public officials for prosecution, they are consistent with that notion.

Administrative Sources of Corruption

Beyond the variables discussed above, one might reasonably expect that a number of other characteristics of administration affect the level of corruption in a

Table 2.8

Targeting Black Public Officials?

Independent Variables	Carter	Reagan
Percent Urban	0.70*	0.49*
Percent College Graduates	−0.44*	−0.18
Party Competition	0.15	−0.13
Computers	−0.24*	0.24*
Number of Government Employees	0.46*	0.47*
Gambling Arrests	−0.30*	0.21#
Partisan Targeting	−0.10	0.18*
Black Public Officials	0.66*	0.23*
R^2	0.61	0.76
Adjusted R^2	0.54	0.72
F	8.06	16.59

Note: Dependent Variable = Log of Prosecutions per 100 Public Officials
$*p < 0.05$
$\#p < 0.10$

state. In a separate analysis (Holbrook and Meier 1991), several categories of administrative variables were added to the model developed in this chapter. Adding these variables to the analysis serves two purposes. First, we can more carefully scrutinize administrative sources of corruption. Second, as the other variables are added we can assess the strength and consistency of the core model developed in this chapter.[24] To the degree that the model survives unscathed by the addition of other variables, our confidence in the model should be heightened.

The first group of administrative variables we added were intended to capture the quality of state administration. These variables summarized the degree to which state employees were familiar with rules and procedures and the technological capability of state administration. The second group of variables we tested measured the ethical environment of state politics. These variables measured the stringency of state ethics laws as well as how open to public scrutiny state government is. The third group of administrative variables focused on the state personnel system. In particular, we were interested in the type of people employed in state government and the incentive structure of state government. Finally, we examined additional structural explanations, similar to those explored earlier in this chapter.

The results of the analysis of administrative influences was at once dismaying and encouraging. The results were dismaying in that, with the exception of nonwhite public employment, none of the administrative variables were statistically significant in the anticipated direction. They were encouraging in that the model of corruption developed here remained essentially intact. When the administrative variables were added to the analysis, the significance and size of the coefficients presented in Table 2.6 changed very little.

One issue that needs to be discussed before dismissing the impact of administrative variables is the manner in which the data are aggregated. The dependent variable is based on the total number of corruption convictions in the state. Both elected and administrative officials from state and local levels are included in the dependent variable. This may create a problem when certain explanations are tested. Why should elected officials respond to administrative structure or resources? Alternatively, why should administrative officials respond to election-related influences such as party competition and voter turnout? The point here is that although we believe that the data we are using are the best currently available, these data do bring certain problems to the analysis that might make direct tests of administrative hypotheses difficult.

Ideally, the data on corruption would include information on the nature of the office of the offender as well as personal characteristics of the offender. Separate data for career public servants would be especially valuable. With such data there are a number of interesting hypotheses that could be pursued. We could more accurately assess the validity of the racial and partisan targeting arguments. We could also conduct separate analyses of state and local public officials. Administrative hypotheses could be tested with administrative data. It might even be possible to analyze better the increase in corruption over time with more disaggregated data. These comments are not intended to undermine the preceding analysis but are extended as a caveat and to illustrate that a number of other interesting hypotheses could be addressed with more disaggregated data.

Conclusion

This study examined four general explanations of political corruption as measured by convictions of corrupt public officials. First, historical/cultural factors, especially the traditional corruption of urban areas and the informed nature of the electorate, affect the relative level of political corruption. Second, corruption is reduced by a political system that has closely contested elections and high voter turnout. Third, despite a wealth of arguments that link government structure to corruption, we were unable to find any structural correlates of corruption except for the capacity to conduct computer-based audits. Fourth, corruption is strongly related to bureaucratic factors; both the size of the bureaucracy and potential bribery (gambling arrests) are positively correlated with corruption. Finally, the prosecution of corrupt public officials was found to be associated with Democratic elected officials during the Reagan administration and black elected officials during both the Reagan and Carter administrations.

If we assume that corruption is a bad thing and government should act to limit it, this analysis offers encouragement in some areas while it also suggests that a degree of pessimism may be appropriate. A major attraction of structural explanations of political corruption is that government structures can be altered and changed by policy makers. Unfortunately for this optimistic view of political corruption, our analysis shows that many structural aspects of government are generally unrelated to political corruption. Among structural factors, only increase of the auditing capability of government appears to decrease corruption. Cultural/historical factors are by their very nature difficult to change. While we can conceive of a state slowly changing its level of education over time, changes in urbanization are not likely to be driven directly by government policies.

Turnout and competition are two areas where we have seen change in recent years; turnout has declined, and party competition at the state level has increased. What is interesting about voter turnout is that it is, to a degree, susceptible to manipulation. Although state governments have lost some control over barriers to voting, they still maintain direct control over a number of voter registration requirements that are strongly related to voter turnout. Wolfinger and Rosenstone (1980) estimate that a relaxation of state-level registration requirements could increase voter turnout by about 9 percent. What is especially interesting about this finding is that barriers to registration are most effective in dissuading the uneducated from voting. The effects of liberalizing registration laws could be particularly impressive by increasing turnout in areas with lower levels of education, which are also areas with higher levels of corruption (see Table 2.2). Voter registration laws may be one example of a structural factor that influences the level of corruption, albeit indirectly, through affecting turnout.

Perhaps the most manipulable variables are the bureaucratic ones. Size constraints on bureaucracy are difficult to maintain given the inertia of growing programs, but self-generated temptations are relatively easy to control. Policies that legalize gambling or policies of less stringent enforcement can be formulated and implemented with some degree of success. These policies could reduce the demand for special treatment in enforcement and thus eliminate the incentives for bribery. Governments, as a result, should be able to control some of the incentives for political corruption.

The benefit/cost framework allowed us to integrate a variety of theories and generate a rich explanation of political corruption. Political corruption is highest where the benefits are greatest and the probability of discovery is lowest, and it is lowest where benefits are lower and the odds of prosecution are higher. To be sure, our measures of factors that facilitate the potential costs and benefits of corruption do not constitute an exhaustive or a perfect list, but they are all theoretically plausible correlates of corruption, and collectively they provide a strong explanation.

Notes

1. Both Nice and Johnston had access to only a few years' data from the Department of Justice. None of their data were for the 1980s. Because the data fluctuate a great deal from

year to year, the more years available to study, the more confidence the researcher has concerning measurement reliability. Nice adjusted his measure for total state population; Johnston used only the raw number of convictions.

2. The per capita number of attorneys employed by the Office of U.S. Attorneys in the state was taken from the U.S. Department of Justice (1984, 2–3). Data on per capita federal judges and percent of backlogs were calculated from data contained in Administrative Conference of the United States Courts (1984, 459–61, 237–40).

3. By using a benefit/cost framework to discuss various explanations of corruption, we do not argue that individuals actually calculate these benefits and costs; nor do we argue that individuals might not engage in corruption activities for irrational reasons. Rather we find the benefit/cost approach useful in the integration of various explanations of corruption since each of the explanations can be linked to changes in costs or benefits.

4. These explanations overlap somewhat so that variables in one analysis might also be relevant to explanation in another analysis. In addition, some of the explanations are more amenable to empirical verification than are others.

5. Most cultural explanations of corruption rely on case studies so that the rich detail of culture can be examined. Quantitative studies such as this one must of necessity rely on explanations that are measurable across jurisdiction. As a result, our indicators are not as closely tied to the underlying concept as we would like. The measures for education and urbanism are taken from the 1980 U.S. Census.

6. We find this argument highly ethnocentric and we are skeptical that Irish or Italian immigrants are any more corrupt than other groups. Nevertheless, due to their role in urban political history these groups are frequently pointed to as sources of corruption. Data were taken from the 1980 Census. The measure included all individuals who claimed either Irish or Italian ancestry. A measure for percent foreign born was tried in this analysis, but it was unrelated to corruption convictions. A measure of percent Catholic was also tried as a surrogate for non-Anglo immigration, but it was negatively related with corruption. Both foreign-born percentages and Catholic percentages at the present time reflect large Hispanic populations rather than residents of other countries.

7. Nice implies that general perceptions of the acceptability of corruption will increase illegal acts in both the public and private sector. The crime measure is an average of the overall crime rate for the state for 1986 and 1987 and is taken from the Federal Bureau of Investigation, *Uniform Crime Reports*.

8. We do not use Elazar's (1972) political culture measure for two reasons. First, culture as a variable is often described in terms of participation, political corruption, and a wide variety of other factors. As a result, it is unclear if political culture is conceptually distinct from political corruption. Second, our reading of Elazar suggests that individualist cultures should have the most political corruption. Johnston (1983), however, presents evidence that moralistic cultures are most corrupt. Any hypothesis concerning culture and corruption, as a result, lacks precision. In our data set neither individualistic nor moralistic culture was significantly related to political corruption.

9. Turnout is taken from Bibby, Cotter, Gibson, and Huckshorn (1983, 62). Party competition is based on a folded measure of Democratic party strength (Bibby et al. 1983, 66; Bibby et al. 1990).

10. This measure of appointive power is taken from Beyle's (1983) work on gubernatorial power. The measure of appointive power reveals the degree to which the governor has sole control over the staffing of forty-six different functions or offices in the state. The scores range from 76 (New York) to 29 (South Carolina).

11. The Wright, Erikson, and McIver (1985) measure excludes Alaska and Hawaii due to lack of data. In order to include Alaska and Hawaii in this analysis, public opinion conservatism for these states was estimated, using the roll-call liberalism of the states'

congressional delegation (Holbrook-Provow and Poe 1987).

12. This argument makes little sense to us. Madison in *Federalist 10* suggests that fragmentation is the way to make sure that the private interests of individuals are used to check the ambitions of other individuals. Centralization appears only to increase the potential benefits of corruption by aggregating political units. In addition, it is not clear that the structural reforms actually increase centralization. The infusion of expertise (for example, the use of city managers) suggests that experts be placed in charge of all operations of policy. This should imply a decentralization and the proliferation of special districts rather than a centralization of control.

13. We disagree. The mechanisms of direct democracy, especially the initiative, produce a great many elections, often with low stimulus and low turnout. Many initiatives circumvent the existing political institutions and thus weaken their control over government. The initiative is also amenable to use by well-financed special interest groups who can succeed in low turnout initiative elections. In general, direct democracy reforms have been a disappointment (Hofstadter 1955).

14. Initially such measures will catch more individuals and thus be positively correlated with corruption convictions. Over time, however, they should become a deterrent and be correlated with fewer convictions. Since our dependent variable is measured over an eleven-year period, this chapter will treat structural changes as deterrents. Data are from the *Book of the States* (1986–87 edition).

15. *The Book of the States* (1986–87 edition) lists nineteen legislative functions that are performed by computers in some states. Our measure is the number of these functions for which the individual states use computers. The measure is not adjusted to population since we feel total computer volume increases audit capacity. This measure could also be interpreted as a measure of legislative professionalism.

16. This measure is defined as the number of groups or types of individuals that are required to file campaign finance statements. This data is taken from *Book of the States* (1986–87 edition), Table 5.4, 185–89.

17. To maintain consistent coding, states without these measures are coded as 100 so that this is a measure of restrictiveness of direct democracy measures. Neither this measure nor dummy variables measuring just the existence of initiative, referendum, and recall were able to explain political corruption.

18. Two reform measures were not usable. First, no data exist on the number of nonpartisan elections in the states; so antiparty reforms could not be used. Second, merit system coverage is a possible variable, however, the currently available measure has serious flaws. Several states have more merit employees than total employees according to this measure. Because we were unwilling to place any faith in this measure, we did not use it in the analysis.

19. The number of government employees is for 1984 and is taken from the *Book of the States* (1986–87 edition), page 275; the budget figures are from the same source (page 309); the salary figure is for all public employees for October 1984 (page 278). These individuals are generally not elected officials. We also tried the salaries of the governor and members of the legislature, but these were unrelated to corruption convictions.

20. Data are taken from the FBI *Uniform Crime Reports* for 1986 and 1987. This measure is highly skewed, so a log transformation was made. Gambling works better empirically than do arrests for drugs or prostitution. Drug arrests are correlated with corruption but less strongly than gambling arrests. Prostitution arrests are unrelated to corruption.

21. Ideally, we could do this analysis based on the party affiliation of the indicted official. The Justice Department does not provide this information; nor is such information contained in the summaries of those cases that the Justice Department publishes.

22. For the Carter years, states were given a score of 1 for each year the state was governed by a Republican governor and 1 for each year Republicans had a majority in both houses of the state legislature. For the Reagan years, states were given one point for each year a Democrat was governor and each year the Democrats controlled both houses of the legislature. If the legislature was under divided party control, one-half point was awarded. The maximum score was 8 for the Carter years and 16 for the Reagan years.

23. These data were provided by the Joint Center for Political Studies in their *National Roster of Black Elected Officials*. Data for 1980 were used for the Carter equation; data for 1987 were used for the Reagan equation.

24. The tables reporting the results of the analysis of administrative influences are not reproduced here. The authors would be happy to make these tables available upon request.

References

Administrative Conference of the U.S. Courts. 1984. *Annual Report*. Washington, DC: Author.

Appleby, Paul H. 1952. *Morality and Administration in Democratic Government*. Baton Rouge: Louisiana State University Press.

Bailey, Stephen K. 1966. "Ethics in the Public Service." In *Public Administration*, edited by Robert Golembiewski, Frank Gibson, and Geoffrey Y. Cornog, 22–32. Chicago: Rand McNally.

Berg, Larry L.; Hahn, Harlan; and Schmidhauser, John R. 1976. *Corruption in the American Political System*. Morristown, NJ: General Learning Press.

Beyle, Thad. 1983. "Governors." In *Politics in the American States*, 4th ed., edited by Virginia Gray, Herbert Jacobs, and Kenneth Vines, 180–221, 444–45. Boston: Little, Brown.

Bibby, John; Cotter, Cornelius; Gibson, James; and Huckshorn, Robert. 1983. "Parties in State Politics." In *Politics in the American States*. 4th ed., edited by Virginia Gray, Herbert Jacobs, and Kenneth Vines, 59–96. Boston: Little, Brown.

———. 1990. "Parties in State Politics." In *Politics in the American States*. 5th ed., edited by Virginia Gray, Herbert Jacobs, and Kenneth Vines. Boston: Little, Brown.

Burke, John P. 1986. *Bureaucratic Responsibility*. Baltimore, MD: Johns Hopkins University Press.

Campbell, Angus; Converse, Philip; Miller, Warren; and Stokes, Donald. 1960. *The American Voter*. Chicago: University of Chicago Press.

Cooper, Terry L. 1987. "Hierarchy, Virtue, and the Practice of Public Administration: A Perspective for Normative Ethics." *Public Administration Review* 47 (July/August): 320–28.

Denhardt, Kathryn G. 1988. *The Ethics of Public Service*. Westport, CT: Greenwood.

Elazar, Daniel J. 1972. *American Federalism: A View from the States*. New York: Thomas Y. Crowell.

Fuchs, Harry. W. 1986. "Auditing as a Political Instrument." In *Fraud, Waste and Abuse in Government*, edited by Jerome B. McKinney and Michael Johnston, 110–17. Philadelphia: ISHI Publications.

Gardiner, John A., and Lyman, Theodore R. 1990. "The Logic of Corruption Control." In *Political Corruption: A Handbook*, edited by Arnold J. Heidenheimer, Michael Johnston, and Victor T. LeVine, 573–86. New Brunswick, NJ: Transaction Books.

Greenstein, Fred I. 1964. "The Changing Pattern of Urban Party Politics." *Annals of the American Academy of Political and Social Science* 353: 1–13.

Heidenheimer, Arnold J. 1970. *Political Corruption: Readings in Comparative Analysis*. New York: Holt, Reinhart and Winston.

————. 1990. "Problems of Comparing American Political Corruption." In *Political Corruption: A Handbook*, edited by Arnold J. Heidenheimer, Michael Johnston and Victor T. LeVine, 573–86. New Brunswick, NJ: Transaction Books.

Heidenheimer, Arnold J.; Johnston, Michael; and LeVine, Victor T. 1990. *Political Corruption: A Handbook*. New Brunswick, NJ: Transaction Books.

Henriques, Diana B. 1986. *The Machinery of Greed*. Lexington, MA: Lexington Books.

Hofstadter, Richard. 1955. *The Age of Reform: From Bryan to F.D.R.* New York: Alfred Knopf.

Holbrook, Thomas, and Meier, Kenneth. 1991. "Bureaucracy and Political Corruption: Patterns in the American States." A paper presented at Conference on the Study of Government Ethics, Park City, UT, June 12–15, 1991.

Holbrook-Provow, Thomas M., and Poe, Steven C. 1987. "Measuring State Political Ideology." *American Politics Quarterly* 15 (July): 399–416.

Huntington, Samuel. 1968. *Political Order in Changing Societies*. New Haven, CT: Yale University Press.

Johnston, Michael. 1982. *Political Corruption and Public Policy in America*. Monterey, CA: Brooks/Cole.

————. 1983. "Corruption and Political Culture in America: An Empirical Perspective." *Publius* 13 (Winter): 19–39.

————. 1986a. "The Political Consequences of Corruption: A Reassessment." *Comparative Politics* 18 (July): 459–77.

————. 1986b. "Right and Wrong in American Politics: Popular Conceptions of Corruption." *Polity* 18 (Spring): 367–91.

————. 1986c. "Systematic Origins of Fraud, Waste, and Abuse." In *Fraud, Waste and Abuse in Government*, edited by Jerome B. McInney and Michael Johnston, 15–29. Philadelphia: ISHI Publications.

Jos, Philip H. 1990. "Administrative Responsibility Revisited: Moral Consensus and Moral Autonomy." *Administration and Society* 22 (August): 228–49.

Klitgaard, Robert. 1988. *Controlling Corruption*. Berkeley: University of California Press.

Krasno, Jonathan S., and Green, Donald Philip. 1988. "Preempting Quality Challengers in House Elections." *Journal of Politics* 50 (November): 920–36.

Lippmann, Walter. 1990. "A Theory about Corruption." In *Political Corruption: A Handbook*, edited by Arnold J. Heidenheimer, Michael Johnston and Victor T. LeVine, 567–72. New Brunswick, NJ: Transaction Books.

Magleby, David B. 1984. *Direct Legislation: Voting on Ballot Propositions in the United States*. Baltimore, MD: Johns Hopkins University Press.

Nas, Tevfik F.; Price, Albert C.; and Weber, Charles T. 1986. "A Policy-Oriented Theory of Corruption." *American Political Science Review* 80 (March): 107–19.

Nice, David C. 1983. "Political Corruption in the American States." *American Politics Quarterly* 11 (October): 507–17.

Nie, Norman H.; Verba, Sidney; and Petrocik, John. 1976. *The Changing American Voter*. Cambridge, MA: Harvard University Press.

Nye, J.S. 1967. "Corruption and Political Development: A Cost–Benefit Analysis." *American Political Science Review* 61 (June): 417–27.

Peters, John G., and Welch, Susan. 1978a. "Political Corruption in America." *American Political Science Review* 72 (September): 974–84.

————. 1978b. "Politics, Corruption, and Political Culture: A View from the State Legislature." *American Politics Quarterly* 6 (July): 345–56.

————. 1980. "The Effects of Charges of Corruption on Voting Behavior in Congressional Elections." *American Political Science Review* 74 (September): 697–708.

Ragsdale, Lyn, and Cook, Timothy E. 1987. "Representatives' Actions and Challengers' Reactions: Limits to Candidate Connections in the House." *American Journal of Political Science* 31 (February): 45–81.

Riordon, William L. 1963. *Plunkitt of Tammany Hall*. New York: Alfred Knopf.

Rohr, John. 1989. *Ethics for Bureaucrats*. New York: Marcel Dekker.

Rose-Ackerman, Susan. 1978. *Corruption: A Study in Political Economy*. New York: Academic Press.

Ruff, Charles F.C. 1990. "Federal Prosecution of Local Corruption." In *Political Corruption: A Handbook*, edited by Arnold J. Heidenheimer, Michael Johnston, and Victor T. LeVine, 627–38. New Brunswick, NJ: Transaction Books.

Rundquist, Barry W.; Strom, Gerald S.; and Peters, John G. 1977. "Corrupt Politicians and Their Electoral Support: Some Experimental Observations." *American Political Science Review* 71 (September): 954–63.

Seidman, Harold, and Gilmour, Robert. 1986. *Politics, Position, and Power*. 4th ed. New York: Oxford University Press.

Stanley, Harold W., and Niemi, Richard G. 1988. *Vital Statistics on American Politics*. Washington, DC: Congressional Quarterly Press.

Terry, Larry D. 1990. "Leadership in the Administrative State: The Concept of Administrative Conservatorship." *Administration and Society* 21 (February): 395–413.

U.S. Department of Justice. 1984. *Attorney Employment Fact Book*. Washington, DC: Author.

———. 1988. *Report to Congress on the Activities and Operations of the Public Integrity Section for 1987*. Washington, DC: Author.

Verba, Sidney, and Nie, Norman H. 1972. *Participation in America*. New York: Harper and Row.

Walsh, Annmarie. 1978. *The Public's Business*. Cambridge, MA: MIT Press.

Wamsley, Gary L.; Goodsell, Charles T.; Rohr, John A.; Stivers, Camilla M.; White, Orion F.; and Wolf, James F. 1987. "The Public Administration and the Governance Process: Refocusing the American Dialogue." In *A Centennial History of the American Administrative State*, edited by Ralph Clark Chandler. New York: Free Press.

Werner, Simcha B. 1983. "New Directions in the Study of Administrative Corruption." *Public Administration Review* 43 (March/April): 146–54.

Wilson, James Q. 1966. "Corruption: The Shame of the States." *The Public Interest* 1 (Winter): 28–38.

Witt, Elder. 1989. "Is Government Full of Crooks, or Are We Just Better at Finding Them?" *Governing* (September): 33–38.

Wolfinger, Raymond E., and Rosenstone, Steven J. 1980. *Who Votes?* New Haven, CT: Yale University Press.

Wright, Gerald; Erikson, Robert; and McIver, John. 1985. "Measuring State Partisanship and Ideology with Survey Data." *Journal of Politics* 47 (August): 469–89.

3

Public-Sector Conflict of Interest at the Federal Level in Canada and the U.S.: Differences in Understanding and Approach

Andrew Stark

Over the course of the past twenty years, and at the federal level, Canadian and American responses to public-sector conflict of interest have shared a rough chronology. In 1973, the Trudeau government tabled the *Green Paper on Members of Parliament and Conflict of Interest*, and in so doing became the first in Canadian history to propose a legislated approach to certain problems of public-sector conflict at the federal level. The *Green Paper*'s statutory proposals were eventually embodied in two bills, C-62 and C-6, which died on the order paper in 1978. In the United States, 1973 was the penultimate year of Watergate, an ordeal that set off an intense five-year debate in Congress over government ethics and culminated in the Ethics in Government Act of 1978. Both Parliament and Congress further considered the problem of conflict of interest throughout the early and mid-eighties, and then in 1988—responding to a rash of conflict of interest code violations by cabinet ministers—Canada's Mulroney government introduced Bill C-114, an "Act to Provide for Greater Certainty in the Reconciliation of the Personal Interests and Duties of Office of Members of the

---

A shorter version of this chapter appeared in the *Public Administration Review*, Volume 55, Number 5, September/October 1992, pp. 427-37. It appears here with the permission of the American Society for Public Administration.

Senate and House of Commons." C-114 died on the order paper in the fall of 1988 but was reintroduced, with minor modifications, as Bill C-46 in November 1989 (the bill was reintroduced a third time as Bill C-43 in November, 1991, and a parliamentary committee reported on it in June, 1992). Meanwhile—also in November 1989, and in response to a rash of conflict-of-interest transgressions by administration and congressional office-holders—the U.S. Congress passed the Ethics Reform Act, a series of amendments to the 1978 legislation. On either side of the border, then, serious governmental discussion of public-sector conflict of interest recurred throughout much of the 1970s and 1980s. More generally—as one prominent scholar of government ethics has noted—by the early 1970s, there already had emerged within the political culture of both countries a broad level of agreement as to the nature and harmfulness of a variety of government ethics problems. This consensus, Kenneth Kernaghan observes, arose in no small part as a result of the international publicity accorded the Watergate affair.

Notwithstanding the historical and cultural commonalities between the two countries' recent experiences with public-sector conflict of interest, important differences remain. In many other areas of administration and policy—from public-service morale to health care—scholars continue to explore the ways in which structural differences between the two forms of government have led to divergences in understanding and approach.[1] In this chapter I shall examine the ways in which differences in the structural configuration of the two governments have issued forth in different cross-border understandings of and approaches to public-sector conflict of interest at the federal level. Several of these government structure–induced differences persist, even as a convergence in the substance and extent of public and media concern may have occurred at the political-cultural level.

Specifically, I will initially discuss four areas in which structural differences between the Canadian and American governments have led to divergence in the two countries' approaches to public-sector conflict of interest: (a) the circumstances under which each government has attempted to use statutory as against nonstatutory conflict regimes; (b) their differing understandings of the postemployment questions raised by the activity of former cabinet members; (c) disparities between the two countries' approaches to remedies and penalties for conflict; and (d) the divergent fashion in which the two countries handle representations that legislators make before the executive on behalf of paying clients. I will then discuss a fifth, more historical and philosophical, difference between Canadian and American approaches to public-sector conflict of interest, one also attributable to the structural differences between the two countries' governments. This particular difference, it should be noted, has to a large degree been neutralized by the recent cultural convergence that has taken place in the two countries' attitudes toward conflict of interest. In fact, it represents less a structural difference between the American and Canadian governments per se than one between the U.S. presidential system and the British parliamentary system. Nevertheless, since this difference has not been explicitly addressed in analyses of public-sector conflict of interest in Britain, and since to my knowledge it has never been explored in the case of Canada, I examine it in general terms in this essay's final section.

Statutory versus Nonstatutory Conflict-of-Interest Regimes

Statutory Regimes

One of the most critical, thorny, and recurrent issues faced by both governments in the area of conflict-of-interest regulation has been raised by the need, at any given juncture, to decide whether to embody the substance of proposed conflict-of-interest regimes in statutory or nonstatutory form. Two questions have been key: How extensive should statutory regulation be? To whom should it apply? At the most general level, the disposition of these questions in the United States has been determined by two structural features of the presidential system: Because the executive and legislative branches are constitutionally separate, Congress historically has had a considerable degree of relatively independent control over the content and disposition of statute law. And because the two branches share the power of appointment, Congress participates, through confirmation as well as oversight, in determining the makeup of and imposing operating requirements on several layers of senior executive branch officeholders. As a result of both its independent power to legislate and its prerogatives of confirmation and oversight, Congress has been able to impose upon cabinet and subcabinet-level executive branch officeholders significant *statutory* strictures in the areas of postemployment, divestiture, recusal, gifts, and hospitality without encumbering itself in the same fashion.

In Canada, by contrast, the executive and legislative branches overlap—cabinet sits in Parliament, controlling and disposing of the legislative agenda—but the two do not significantly share the power of appointment and oversight: these powers belong essentially to the executive and to the prime minister in particular. As one senior Canadian civil servant succinctly put this latter point, "[t]he essence of parliamentary government is that it depends for its effectiveness on those constitutionally responsible for the exercise of delegated authority, rather than detailed parliamentary control of the executive" (Osbaldeston 1987, 6).[2] Two important considerations with regard to the disposition of statutory conflict-of-interest regimes in Canada follow from the fact that cabinet sits in Parliament, providing the only medium for legislative monitoring of the subcabinet executive, and itself controlling the legislative agenda. First, Parliament has never been asked to consider conflict-of-interest legislation that applies to the subcabinet executive—meaning that any direct conflict-of-interest strictures on the subcabinet executive will remain nonstatutory.[3] Second, Parliament is unlikely ever to be given the opportunity to consider conflict-of-interest legislation (whether stringent or relaxed) that treats members of cabinet significantly more severely than it treats members of Parliament—at least by comparison with the statutory disparity between legislative and cabinet-level strictures that has prevailed in the United States.[4] In other words, this difference in structure between the two federal governments means that Canadian attempts at statutory conflict-of-interest regimes have excluded the public service while they have minimized any differences in the treatment accorded cabinet ministers and M.P.s. And it means that U.S. statutory regimes have embraced the civil service while they have maintained a wider differential in the burden placed on cabinet secretaries, and the executive branch broadly, as against that placed on congressmen.

Consider the two occasions on which Canadian governments have introduced statutory regimes: the *Green Paper on Members of Parliament and Conflict of Interest* in 1973 (which led to the introduction of Bills C-62 and C-6 in 1978) and Bill C-114 in 1988 (which was reintroduced without substantive changes as Bill C-46 in 1989). Both, to the extent possible—but in very different ways given the different climates of the times—confined themselves (in one case completely, in the other, notably) to strictures the violation of which their drafters saw as equally objectionable, whether committed by a cabinet minister or an ordinary member. The 1973 *Green Paper* took a minimalist approach, containing as it did only two statutory proposals: that members and ministers not be allowed to hold contracts with the government and that they not be permitted to hold "incompatible offices," that is, offices in the federal, provincial, or municipal governments. Any further strictures that one might have thought ought to apply to cabinet members, but not to ordinary members because of the great differential in their power, did not see the light of day—precisely because of the great differential in their power: cabinet simply refused to introduce or accept them in the form of amendments.

Both in the House and in committee, government members advanced a doctrinal substructure for the equal statutory treatment the *Green Paper* proposed to accord M.P.'s and ministers, denying as they did that ministers display a greater tendency or capacity for conflict than do ordinary members. One government member, for example, argued that "members of the opposition have a[n even] greater capacity to put themselves into conflict of interest than [does] a minister, whose time tends to be taken up with day-to-day administration" (Canada 1975, 10). Another government M.P. claimed that it is contrary to moral reasoning to draw distinctions between the harm posed by ministerial conflict and that posed by ordinary-member conflict—turpitude is turpitude, after all—and urged his colleagues in the House "to first look at ourselves, every single one of us, and stop talking as if the situation is serious if it is big, and not too serious if it is small. . . . It is darned nigh time that we started discussing the activities of members of this House before we start worrying about ministers of the Crown" (Canada 1974, 2123–24).[5] (Not surprisingly, opposition members responded to this attempted minimization of the pertinent differences between members and ministers by declaring that the gov-

ernment was patently starting "at the wrong end of the power structure by beginning with members of Parliament" [Canada 1974].)

The statutory recommendations of the 1973 *Green Paper*, though embodied
in Bills C-62 and C-6 (1978), never became law; they died on the order paper at
session's end. The only other occasion on which a Canadian government has
introduced a statutory conflict-of-interest regime was with Bill C-114 in February 1988 (reintroduced with minor modifications as Bill C-46 in November
1989). Without descending to the "lowest common denominator" doctrine
adopted by its predecessors, C-114/C-46 nevertheless represents an approach by
which differences in statutory treatment to be accorded members of the legislature and the cabinet are notably smaller than they are in the American case.
Before exploring how this is so in particular, it must be noted that the U.S. Ethics
Reform Act, passed in November 1989, did introduce some long-sought-after
parity into the regulatory treatment accorded the U.S. executive and legislative
branches. Officers and employees of both branches are now subject to equivalent
postemployment, disclosure, and gift-receipt regimes. Yet Title X of the Ethics
Reform Act stipulates that all provisions of the act applicable to Congressmen
and their employees result from an exercise of the rule making, as distinct from
the legislative, power of the two Houses. As such, these provisions can at any
time be altered—insofar as they apply to each House—by either House in the
same manner as each changes its rules, a procedure far different from the one
necessary to amend legislation. For all intents and purposes, although the Ethics
Reform Act did bring greater substantive parity to ethics treatment of the two
branches, it brought no statutory parity. The differences between the statutory
strictures governing the executive branch and those governing the legislative
branch remain as great as they were before.

Even if the disclosure, postemployment, and gift provisions of the Ethics
Reform Act were to have applied as statute to Congress as they do to the cabinet
and the rest of the executive branch, Canada's Bill C-46 would bring legislators
and cabinet members a crucial step closer in terms of common statutory governance or parity. As Robert N. Roberts suggests in *White House Ethics*, the heart
of conflict-of-interest regulation lies neither in disclosure nor in postemployment
strictures but in the prohibition of contemporaneous conflicts between public
duties and private interests. The Canadian bill would provide equal statutory
treatment for cabinet members and legislators in a way that would be difficult to
imagine happening in the United States. The Canadian bill's definition of conflict of interest is that which occurs whenever a cabinet member (including a
minister), or the member's spouse or dependent, has "significant private interests
. . . that afford the opportunity for the member to benefit, whether directly or
indirectly, as a result of the execution of, or the failure to execute, any office of
the member." The bill then requires both ministers *and* members to "arrange
[their] private affairs" to prevent "conflicts of interest from arising." More precisely, the bill empowers an independent three-person Conflict of Interest Com-

mission to "advise" ministers and members of "any action that the Commission considers to be required . . . to ensure that" the minister or member does not find him- or herself in a conflict of interest as the bill defines it. For example, "[w]ithout limiting" the commission's capacity to recommend other remedies, the bill specifically empowers the commission to "recommend the establishment of a trust on such terms, and subject to such conditions, as it considers appropriate," for the interests of ministers and members in conflict. As Ian Greene (1990) has noted, the commission "could also recommend the divestment of certain assets" by ordinary members as well as by ministers. Elsewhere, the commission is given the power to certify that a particular minister's or member's "private interest" is "permitted . . . for the purposes of this Act."

In other words, Bill C-46 would subject members of the Canadian legislature to statutory provisions that capture the spirit of 18 U.S.C. 208, the central conflict-of-interest law in the United States, which applies only to members of the executive. While Congress has been willing to impose upon itself statutory disclosure, postemployment, and gift provisions, it has never imposed upon itself statutory requirements for recusal or divestiture, that is, legally required remedies for contemporaneous conflicts between private interests and public duties. As numerous congressmen have declared in debate over the years, if legislators were required to recuse themselves in conflict situations, they would disenfranchise their constituents—an intolerable evil, and one that does not apply when executive branch members are required to recuse. Unlike executive branch employees, whose specialized public activities in most cases impinge only on a select class of private interests, the public acts of legislators can, over time, affect every conceivable private interest. To statutorily require divestiture of legislators, it is argued, is thus a far more draconian proposition than to require it of most executive branch employees, including cabinet members.[6] Such arguments suggest that *statutory* requirements dealing with conflict of interest per se will continue to apply to U.S. cabinet members, while members of Congress will persist in remaining free of them. The Canadian legislation, by contrast, would subject both cabinet members *and* ordinary members to statutory prohibitions on conflict of interest per se—a proposal that is testimony to the relative lack of independence of the legislature under the Canadian parliamentary system and to cabinet's power to pass on to members many of the strictures that the public seems to require of ministers.[7]

One reasonably might have expected that in Canada the inequity in power between the cabinet and the legislature would, over time, have justified the placement of significantly heavier conflict-of-interest strictures on the former. Yet Canada's brief history of experimentation with proposed statutory conflict-of-interest regimes suggests that precisely because of that inequity the differential in statutory strictures attempted has, by comparison with U.S. law, been relatively modest. Conversely, the formal equity in power between the U.S. legislature and executive has suggested to many observers that there should be no substantial differential between most of the conflict-of-interest strictures placed on the two branches (Association of the Bar of the City of New York 1960). Yet it is precisely because of the particular structure of that interbranch balance of power that Congress has been able to control the content and disposition of conflict legislation and also has been able to impose a more significant burden of statutory strictures on the executive while in effect exempting itself.

Nonstatutory Regimes

Though there is a discernible tendency toward *relatively* equal statutory treatment of legislators and cabinet members in Canada, when it comes to nonstatutory regimes there is a marked inequality between the progress made by the two branches. This is the case simply because in the nonstatutory instance the inequity in power between cabinet and Parliament has worked the other way: precisely because the Canadian executive is relatively untrammeled in power and responsibilities, a recognized need for extensive self-regulation has arisen. Thus, the last twenty years have seen the development of detailed nonstatutory codes of conduct and bodies of precedent covering all executive officeholders. Nonstatutory controls in the Canadian legislative branch, by contrast, are comparatively scanty. That Parliament has escaped such controls, and has not been subjected to any great pressure to introduce them, is largely attributable to the relatively circumscribed power of the average member and the virtually nonexistent power of parliamentary staff. Thus, the Canadian House of Commons' *Conflict of Interest Rules* volume is only eleven pages long, and much of it deals not with the private interests of members but with ways a member may be compromised by holding other public offices or contracts with public entities. In the United States, by contrast, the relative balance in power between the two branches explains in part why both have developed comparably extensive nonstatutory rules, regulations, and bodies of opinions. The Senate Ethics Committee's *Interpretive Rulings*, for example, is a 275-page volume of detailed rulings, and the House *Ethics Manual* has 264 pages. Both manuals deal largely with conflict-of-interest questions. Over the past ten years the Office of Government Ethics has built a correspondingly detailed body of advisory opinions to cover the U.S. executive branch—opinions that augment the detailed regulations that have been promulgated government-wide and for each department and agency.

Statutory regimes in the United States have generally tended to result in inequity between the legislature and the executive, to the legislature's "advantage." A rougher relative parity has been reached between the two branches in the extensiveness of their nonstatutory regimes. In Canada, by contrast, statutory regimes have always pushed in the direction of equal treatment of legislators and ministers—whether that treatment is light, as it was with C-62 and C-6, or heavy, as it is with C-114/C-46. Conversely, nonstatutory regimes—rules, regulations, codes, and guidelines—show a relative inequity between the two branches, also to the legislature's "advantage." And this particular pattern of statutory/nonstatutory approaches reflects underlying configurations in the relative powers of the executive and the legislature in each country.

Postemployment Provisions

In the area of the regulation of officeholders' postemployment activities, the most fruitful points of contrast between the two countries' approaches are not to be found in the postemployment situations of former members of the legislature or in those of former subcabinet members of the executive, but in postemployment situations faced by former cabinet members. On one hand, there is a far greater turnover in legislative membership in Canada after each federal election than there is in the United States, on the other, there is a far greater turnover of senior subcabinet executive branch personnel in the United States after each election than there is in Canada, where the civil service is permanent and nonpartisan. Because of the relatively low level of legislative turnover in the United States, and of senior subcabinet executive branch personnel in Canada, the class of officeholder for which turnover in the two countries is most nearly proximate is that of cabinet member. And yet, although both Canadian and U.S. cabinets experience over time a relatively comparable measure of turnover, the postemployment circumstances that surround the two types of turnover, and hence the postemployment strictures that govern them in C-46 and the Ethics in Government/Ethics Reform Acts, respectively, differ markedly and instructively.

Generally speaking, in Canada cabinet ministers are career politicians with uncertain tenure, in contrast to their U.S. counterparts who are drawn largely from the private sector and are called upon to serve a fixed term. In the Canadian debate over conflict of interest, the fact that cabinet members are not preponderantly drawn from an immediate private-sector background has given rise to fewer suspicions that they would be likely to exercise certain kinds of favoritism while in office and to a common acceptance that they are less readily marketable upon leaving office.[8] Because Canadian cabinet ministers face an uncertain tenure—they often depart the ministry after a government-wide political defeat at a juncture they cannot predict beforehand—they are both more financially vulnerable while in office and less likely to be able to exercise political influence upon departure than are their American counterparts. In the words of former cabinet ministers Mitchell Sharp and Michael Starr, authors of *Ethical Conduct in the Public Sector*, a 1984 task-force report prepared at the request of Prime Minister Trudeau, "[f]ormer ministers . . . seldom resign voluntarily in order to take private employment; [a] high proportion of them, in one way or another, are forced out of office and have to look for a job." Moreover, "[t]he ability of a former minister to influence government decisions to his or her advantage depends upon which party is then in office." If, as is likely the case, the former minister finds himself in a postemployment situation in the first place because his "party has been defeated, he is not likely to receive preferred treatment and [permanent] officials are likely to be very circumspect in dealing with him" (Starr and Sharp 1984).

Cabinet members in the United States have not been deemed to be in an analogous situation in any of these respects. When compared with their Canadian counterparts, they are commonly treated as if they are both more capable of survival under a stricter postemployment regime and more deserving of one. Since they are more often drawn from the private sector, former U.S. cabinet members are, in comparison with their Canadian counterparts, generally seen to be more vulnerable to certain kinds of influence while in office (particularly that exerted by previous employers and clients), and more marketable when they leave. Because of the greater degree of knowledge and control they possess concerning the timing of their departure, cabinet members in the United States generally are deemed to be more protected from sudden job loss while in office and more capable of exercising "influence" with their former colleagues and subordinates upon departure.

These differing, structurally rooted career contexts of U.S. and Canadian cabinet officers, along with the relevance of those career situations for the purposes of conflict of interest regulation, were neatly brought to the fore during a 1983 Canadian parliamentary debate on the postemployment activities of cabinet ministers: In the United States, one of the main evils that critics associate with an overly severe postemployment regime is its tendency to deter competent private-sector individuals from becoming cabinet secretaries. In the 1983 Canadian debate, by contrast, the main evil associated with the idea of an overly severe post employment regime was its perceived tendency to cause cabinet ministers to cling "inordinate[ly]" to office (Canada 1983). The fact that American cabinet secretaries are drawn primarily from business backgrounds has led some observers to conclude that the main casualty of a more stringent U.S. postemployment regime would be the quality of cabinet-level knowledge and skill and, in particular, cabinet's accessibility to private-sector insights and aptitudes. That Canadian cabinet ministers are drawn primarily from political backgrounds evidently suggests that the main casualty of a stringent postemployment regime would be the quality of cabinet-level courage and political independence and, in particular, cabinet's willingness to take the sorts of unpopular or impolitic actions that could hasten their leaving office.

These differences in perceived postemployment situations are reflected in dissimilarities between the postemployment provisions in C-114/C-46 and the Ethics in Government/Ethics Reform Acts. To be sure, former Canadian cabinet ministers under C-114/C-46 would be subject to certain restraints that do not fall on former U.S. cabinet secretaries. For example, for a period of one year after leaving office, Canadian ex–cabinet ministers would not be able to counsel companies that deal with their former departments, and would not be permitted to accept employment from any entity with which they dealt while in government. Ex–cabinet secretaries in the United States, by contrast, are not subject to such strictures. Another section of the Canadian bill would empower the three-person Conflict-of-Interest Commission to waive any or all postemployment strictures in situations in which "the public interest in ensuring reasonable employment for former ministers outweighs the public interest in prohibiting contacts between the ex-minister and the government." Moreover, should the commission find that these two conceptions of the public interest are in implacable tension, it would be free to grant the ex-minister a "hardship allowance." Specifically, beyond the six months' severance to which the ex-minister is normally entitled, the commission would have the capacity to authorize payment of another six months' salary to bring the ex-minister to the end of the year-long cooling-off period. Neither such a waiver nor the hardship allowance is available to the former U.S. cabinet secretary. The possibility of the waiver, and the justification for it, reflect the less significant nefarious political influence that the Canadian excabinet member is seen to be capable of exercising, at least compared with his or her U.S. counterpart. The hardship allowance reflects the ex-minister's arguably more significant economic vulnerability.

The Starr–Sharp report, which has become the Talmud of public-sector conflict-of-interest regulation in Canada, provides the rationale for yet another difference in the postemployment provisions mandated under the Canadian and U.S. acts. On those occasions when "rules regarding contacts between former [cabinet ministers] and the government . . . [are] breach[ed]," Starr and Sharp ask, "[w]ho should be 'responsible'—the excabinet minister or those public servants whom the excabinet member contacts?" (Starr and Sharp, 1984, 224). The U.S. Ethics in Government Act is clear in its answer to this question: The responsibility for obeying the law and the penalty for breaching it fall exclusively on the ex–cabinet member. In the case of Canada, though, Starr and Sharp write,

> . . . it may be quite unfair to place the primary responsibility upon the former [minister]. He or she is bound to be at a disadvantage when allegations are made about the impropriety of his or her contacts with the government. Every contact made, however innocent, becomes suspect and he or she cannot defend himself or herself when charges are made in the House of Commons. The [current] minister [by contrast] can answer for himself or herself and his or her officials.
>
> The rules pertaining to postemployment activities should [therefore] not be drawn up in such a way that the onus is on the former minister to prove that he or she did not break them. We believe that former Cabinet ministers in Canada are entitled to the benefit of the doubt in terms of questions of ethical conduct. To put it any other way is an invidious basis on which to establish public policy. [Starr and Sharp 1984, 224-25]

The courtesies here extended to the excabinet member/lobbyist would sound strange to American ears. For Starr and Sharp, the ex-minister who comes under a cloud is apparently defenseless politically if not legally. Moreover, the ex-minister is entitled not to be judged according to the higher moral standards of public life, but rather is to be extended the latitude that traditionally accompanies more mainstream standards of legal justice: he or she must always be given the benefit of the doubt. Starr and Sharp thus conclude that the onus for any wrongful contact between an ex-minister and his or her former officials should lie on those former officials, who operate with less political vulnerability and labor under a greater public obligation: "We believe," Starr and Sharp write,

> that the only effective means of dealing with this problem of representations made to government is to lay the responsibility on current office holders to avoid giving preferential treatment to former public office holders. . . . The fact that a former public office holder makes representations to the department of which he had been minister . . . is not *per se* abhorrent. What matters is whether he or she receives treatment more favourable than might be accorded anyone else in similar circumstances. [Starr and Sharp 1984, 230]

In this passage, Starr and Sharp provide the rationale for one other important distinction between C-114/C-46 and the Ethics in Government/Ethics Reform Acts. To be sure, the Canadian bill does not go so far as do Starr and Sharp in relieving the ex-minister of any postemployment culpability. As with U.S. law, it would place an affirmative requirement on the ex-cabinet member to observe the postemployment rules, and criminal penalties would attach to him or her for violation. Unlike the U.S. act, and along the lines of Starr and Sharp, the Canadian bill places a positive statutory onus on current officers or employees not to grant contracts or benefits to ex-cabinet members under circumstances in which the ex–cabinet member would be violating postemployment restrictions. The implication clearly is that the most junior executive branch employee is more powerful and protected than is his or her ex-ministerial boss and should be considered capable of, and held responsible for, resisting the ex-minister's blandishments.[9] Such a doctrine has no analogue in the U.S. Ethics in Government/Ethics Reform Acts or in the debates surrounding them, which often explicitly assume an inability on the part of the former secretary's inferiors to be indifferent to his influence or to the nature of their previous relationship (U.S. Senate 1987). The ex-minister in Canada is seen to be less politically powerful and more politically vulnerable than counterparts in the U.S. cabinet and former subordinates in the Canadian executive branch. The postemployment provisions of C-114/C-46 reflect these relative differentials in perceived power and vulnerability.

Remedies and Penalties

Another notable set of structurally induced differences between the Canadian bill and American law lies in the area of remedies and penalties for legislative and cabinet-level conflict of interest. Consider first remedies—measures such as disclosure, divestiture, trust arrangements, and recusal. Under the U.S. Ethics in

Government Act and other statutes, some remedies must rely for their effectiveness on direct democratic sanction (in particular, full public disclosure for congressmen and senior executive branch officeholders) or on indirect democratic sanction (as when various divestiture or recusal arrangements are imposed on senior executive branch employees by the people's representatives in the Senate). Other remedies—stipulations regarding the use of the trust instrument for executive branch officeholders, for example, and certain requirements regarding recusal or divestiture—are to be found in the act itself or in organic departmental and agency statutes and pursuant regulations.

Under the Canadian bill, by contrast, remedies are more exclusively an administrative matter. The extent to which the member's or minister's disclosure would be made public is left to the discretion of a registrar appointed by the three-person commission, and arrangements for divestiture, trusts, and recusal would be left to the discretion of the commission itself. In the United States remedies for legislative and cabinet-level conflict fall to some considerable extent within the province of democratic politics, and cabinet-level conflict is governed by statute law and regulations. Under the Canadian bill remedies for legislative and cabinet-level conflict fall largely under the administrative discretion of an independent body.

Penalties fall under the rubric of different types of institutions in the two countries. In the United States, if a putative contravention of the applicable conflict-of-interest, disclosure, or postemployment statutes is sufficiently serious, it falls for prosecution to a branch of government independent of that which houses the alleged offender. Thus, while each house of Congress is responsible within bounds for policing the provisions of the law as they apply to its own members, criminal breaches committed by members of Congress fall to the executive branch, specifically the attorney general, to prosecute, and to the courts to judge. And while the Office of Government Ethics and the attorney general are initially responsible for following up any putative contraventions of the conflict-of-interest statutes by fellow employees of the executive branch, serious alleged criminal infringements by senior executive branch personnel are referred for prosecution outside the executive branch to a judicially appointed independent counsel and then to the courts for judgment.

By contrast, the Canadian bill expressly states, "failure to comply with any provision of this Act does not constitute an offence punishable . . . under the criminal code." Instead, upon its receipt from the commission of an adverse report regarding a member's or a minister's activities, it is only the parliamentary chamber in which the member or minister holds his seat that is empowered to apply a penalty: reprimand, fine, the payment of compensation, or permanent removal/request for resignation from the chamber. Thus, while under the U.S. act, the adjudication of offenses and the application of penalties of a certain severity are taken out of the hands of the legislature and the executive and given to independent branches to apply, in the Canadian bill they are ultimately levied by the legislature, which means, assuming a majority government, that they are levied by the executive in part if not in whole. (The only exception here is the penalty for the postemployment provisions that apply to former cabinet ministers, and these are left to the executive branch to prosecute, because the alleged offender is necessarily no longer a member of the legislature.)

In sum, under the Canadian bill, remedies for legislative and cabinet-level conflict of interest would fall more under the rubric of a discrete, discretionary, and independent body and less under the direct strictures of statute law or democratic politics. This difference reflects the great weight that Canadian governance places on the independent tradition and embodied wisdom of permanent public service bodies and the great weight American governance places on the ideals of popular sovereignty and a government of "laws, not men." Under U.S. law, penalties for serious legislative and executive-branch conflicts of interest fall more under the auspices of bodies independent of the legislature and the executive whereas under the Canadian bill they would be the responsibility of the legislature and the executive. This difference is straightforwardly reflective of the doctrine of separation of powers in the United States, and the constitutional supremacy of Parliament in Canada.

Rules Governing Legislative-Executive Interaction and Conflict of Interest

Another major difference between the two countries' understanding of public-sector conflict of interest concerns the permissibility of a member of the legislature's representing a paying client before an executive agency or department. Statute law in the United States proscribes the receipt of compensation by members of Congress for advocatory services rendered on behalf of clients before federal agencies or departments in matters in which the United States is interested. According to Justice Harlan, the "main object" of such a law "is to secure the integrity of executive action against undue influence" exerted by "members of [the legislative] branch . . . whose favor may have much to do with the appointment to, or retention in, public position of those [executive branch officeholders] whose official action it is sought to control or direct" (United States 1906). Others have argued that the quality of executive branch decision making could be compromised whenever a congressman—who by virtue of his or her office may possess some considerable control over a given department's or agency's budget—makes representations, whether for a paying client or a nonpaying constituent, before that department or agency.[10] Because senior executive branch officeholders come under official political and financial control by Congress, they must be protected from any unofficial ex parte and pecuniarily motivated representations made by individual congressmen.

In Canada there is no equivalent law. Nor does the U.S. rationale for one apply with equal force: Parliament has no independent control over executive appointments, and no independent power of the purse. This is not to say that

Canadian legislators have been entirely sanguine about M.P.s' representing paying clients before executive agencies and departments. The evil such interventions have been seen to portend is less an impairment on the impartial judgment of the executive officer being lobbied than an encumbrance on the representational capacity of the legislator doing the lobbying. The *Green Paper*, for example, did include a nonstatutory proposal to prohibit any member from "advocating any matter or cause related to his personal, private or professional interests . . . before any Government boards or tribunals for a fee or reward" (Canada 1975). Those few members who saw merit in the proposal, though, generally qualified their support along lines that make clear that they were concerned not to preserve untainted executive branch judgment but rather to protect unhindered legislative branch advocacy. One M.P. claimed that a prohibition against a member's representing a paying client before the executive should apply only when the client is also a constituent—because a constituent has the right to his member's representational talents gratis—but not if the member is representing someone other than a constituent, who has no such similar right (Canada 1975, 16). Another M.P. argued that as long as the cause a given parliamentarian represents for a paying client is compatible with the interests of his constituents, he is entitled to charge a fee for advocacy before government tribunals (Canada 1975, 21). Still another argued that a legislator should be allowed to charge a fee for representation even to a constituent, as long as no other constituent has a competing interest (Canada 1975, 22). None of these Canadian parliamentarians, in their ruminations on the propriety of paid legislative representation before the executive, is concerned with protecting "the integrity of executive action," as Justice Harlan put it, but rather with preserving the integrity of legislative representation. In any case, the *Green Paper* proposal was never acted upon, and to this day there are no restrictions on a Canadian M.P. (or senator) representing a paying client before an executive department or agency. (The Parliament of Canada Act, though, does prohibit compensation to a member or senator for services rendered in the attempt to influence other members of his or her particular chamber.)

**Independent Political Judgment: A Historical Example
of Structurally Induced Canadian-American Differences
in Approach to Conflict of Interest**

One final structurally induced difference between the two countries' approaches to public-sector conflict of interest is worthy of mention and explication—it is in three respects slightly different than that discussed above. In the first place, this particular difference arises not simply between the U.S. and Canadian approaches per se, but between the American approach and the British parliamentary approach broadly construed. It is necessary therefore to look at British as well as Canadian experience. In the second place, this particular difference is perhaps more philosophical than legal in nature; one finds evidence of it as much in debates and discourse as in laws and codes. Finally, this particular difference is more historical than contemporary in nature, although many signs of it still survive.

This final difference can be described in the following terms: In the United States, a congressman's possession of private interests is generally regarded as an encumbrance on the capacity to exercise unfettered political judgment, while the only widely accepted argument in favor of significant public emolument for legislators is that a large enough public salary might bring freedom from reliance on what are seen as more compromising means of private support.[11] Because of the relatively greater power exercised by the executive over the legislative in parliamentary systems, the conception of conflict of interest prevalent in both the Canadian and British traditions has been skewed toward the idea that legislators who rely on income from private interests are relatively more likely to retain independence of mind and integrity of judgment—that is, they are relatively more likely to serve the public interest in a faithful and unencumbered way. As something of a corollary, those legislators in Canada and Britain who receive their remuneration solely from the public treasury have, historically, been thought more likely to find their judgment compromised in some fashion— whether by a debt to the crown, the prime minister, the party in power, or the executive broadly construed.

Consider the corollary first: Even on the eve of the British House of Commons' first vote in favor of paying salaries to members of Parliament in 1911, there were still many M.P.'s who "defended" their unsalaried status "as a sign of their disinterestedness" (McGill 1959, 809). Indeed for the previous century and a half, according to one observer, "independence [of political judgment in Britain had] . . . mean[t] only independence from the crown" (McGill 1959, 808, 809),[12] that is, independence of executive patronage and royal pensions, not independence of private interests or personal retainers. As recently as the late 1970s, British M.P.s, in debating new proposals to raise members' salaries, expressed the view that members' pay should not be so substantial as to make them feel beholden to the government of the day (with its power of dissolution) for their livelihood, nor should ministerial pay be such that ministers would feel financially inhibited from resigning on a matter of principle. As one member urged, "the genuine and individual, independent judgment that is so vital to the successful working of the House . . . would be jeopardized to some extent if being an honourable Member represented a person's only livelihood."[13] While such a line of argument can be found from time to time in the American debate, it is relatively muted. Certainly the dominant chord governing the recent U.S. proposals for congressional pay increases had it that a member's independence of judgment would be jeopardized *unless* his being a congressman came to represent his only (earned) livelihood.

In the case of Canada, one can also find examples of this particular structurally rooted parliamentary understanding of conflict of interest. Up until the first few decades of this century, Canadian statute law held that any member of Parliament appointed to the cabinet had to resign his seat and seek again in a by-election the approval of his constituents. This idea, which followed a British parliamentary tradition of long standing had its origins in the need of constituents "to guard against members being brought under sinister executive control" by virtue of their receipt of public emolument as cabinet members (Dawson 1970).[14] Notably, the only two types of conflicts of interest that the Canadian *Green Paper* and Bills C-62/C-6 sought to prohibit were those posed by a member's receipt of public sources of income: namely, other government offices and federal government contracts.[15] A latter-day variation on this strand of parliamentary doctrine lay behind the recent decision of one of Canada's former environment ministers to recuse himself from his ministerial responsibilities in all decisions respecting the environmental impact of a proposed crossing to be built between his island constituency and the Canadian mainland (as the local M.P., the minister vigorously supported the link). The minister termed his situation a "conflict of interest"; but it is important to note that the conflict in question was not the generic sort that arises in representative democracy between the legislator's twin roles as a delegate for his constituents and a trustee for the broader national interest. Rather, it was of a more specific type that arises in a parliamentary democracy between a minister's twin roles as a representative in the legislature and a member of the executive with departmental imperatives. The minister argued that there was an encumbrance placed on his ability to act and to exercise his judgment as an independent member of Parliament, not by virtue of any private employment he held but by virtue of his public employment as a member of the cabinet. The minister believed that his first obligation was to function as a representative, and in order to fulfill that obligation unencumbered he felt compelled to free himself from the obligations under which he labored as a member of the executive.[16] For his trouble, the minister lost his seat in the subsequent general election.

Historically, then, parliamentary tradition displays a strand of argument on which a seat in cabinet, and public remuneration more generally, can place the legislator in conflict. Conversely, it also displays a strand according to which independent pursuits, private interests, and private sources of income are all deemed fundamental to ensuring the legislator's uncompromised political judgment. In the early 1980s, the British House of Commons debated the question of whether sitting members should be permitted to retain outside interests and employment. A survey of members at the time revealed that the minority who were in favor of some form of prohibition on outside private interests were generally concerned less with abating conflict of interest than with diminishing encroachments on members' time—that is, if private interests were seen to pose a threat at all, it was a threat to members' undivided attention, not to their unencumbered judgment (Williams 1984).[17] Conversely, the majority of M.P.s, who had some difficulty with prohibitions against members' holding outside interests, felt that such prohibitions would not only serve to deprive the House of "valuable experience and expertise," but that they would actually "erode the independence of MPs" (Williams 1984, 34).

In a recent study, Michael M. Atkinson and Maureen Mancuso (sic) offer another explanation for the British parliamentary system's greater tolerance for legislators who hold private interests and sources of income. Specifically, Atkinson and Mancuso argue that the British parliament enshrines as "Burkean" philosophy of representation in which members are explicitly meant to represent pure interests. The U.S. Congress, by contrast, embodies a more classically liberal philosophy, in which "representation has always been of persons [and therefore of constituencies]; the representation of interests has been viewed as an intolerable evil, to be tamed by a well-constructed government" (Atkinson and Mancuso 1991). Because their institutional culture thus impels them, or at least allows them, to represent broad interests (agricultural, banking, labor), British M.P.s have much greater latitude to engage in consultancies and receive retainers for "promoting interests that are not attached to [their] constituencies or to persons as such" (p. 481).

British M.P.s are thus viewed as advocates for, or representatives of, more than just a constituency: this is a useful observation, and it helps explain why British legislators' retention of private interests is seen to be compatible with their capacity to engage in effective representative advocacy. Answering the question as to why British legislators' retention of private interests should also be seen to promote their capacity to exercise independent legislative judgment, however, requires us to look at a different strand in the parliamentary tradition— the one in which a member's private interests, whether shared with or contrary to those of his constituents, help him retain his independence of the crown, the executive, and the party.

It is worth noting that this particular strand in parliamentary doctrine on conflict of interest—according to which private interests and income are seen as less troublesome and public emolument as more—has surfaced in Canada in connection with executive branch employees as well as with legislators. For example, there was no enduring controversy in Canada, comparable to that in the United States, over the use of dollar-a-year men—government executives whose salaries were paid by private-sector companies—during World War II.[18] More generally, in the United States, 18 U.S.C. 209 criminalizes private supplementation of the salaries of executive branch employees other than special government employees. In Canada, by contrast, neither the current nonstatutory code governing executive branch employees nor the proposed Canadian legislation prohibit executive-branch employees from accepting salaries from private sources for their work as public officials. Conversely, in Canada there is no positive legal requirement that executive branch employees receive remuneration for their official services from the public treasury. The U.S. Anti-Deficiency Act, which enjoins the executive from engaging the services of personnel for whom Congress has not voted public remuneration, is at once a method of protecting against the conflicts that may arise when executive employees rely on sources other than the government for their salaries, and a means of preserving Congress' constitutional ability to control the executive through its power of the purse. As such, it rests on a principle different from that historically operated within the parliamentary system, in which the conflict of interest more to be guarded against is the one that arises when public officials come to rely on the public treasury for their salaries, thereby coming under the compromising control of the executive. Hence, in Canada, there is no Anti-Deficiency Act that requires executive branch officials to receive public remuneration for their official services, just as there is no 18 U.S.C. 209 that prohibits them from receiving private remuneration for their public services. Of course, in practice executive branch employees in both countries remain on the public payroll; the pertinent difference is that in Canada there is no legal tradition that requires this.

It is perhaps not surprising, as a study of "Conflicts of Interest in England" found fifteen years ago, that none of the century's four British Royal Commissions on the Civil Service has given significant attention to the conflicts of interest posed by public officials holding private interests and pursuing outside activities (Wilson 1969). Nor is it surprising that "conflict of interest guidelines [to say nothing of legislation] were not addressed in Canada until the late 1960s, and were only reflected in actual orders in council in the early and mid-nineteen seventies" (Starr and Sharp 1984, 75). In the United States, by contrast, legislation dates back to the nineteenth century. More recently, though—and as a result of the convergence in concern with conflict of interest which, as Kenneth Kernaghan has noted, has arisen in the political culture of all three countries—this particular structurally induced parliamentary/presidential difference has become muted. In Canada, the recent public consternation over federal cabinet ministers who continue to pursue conflicting private interests while in office, as well as comparable offenses at the provincial level, suggests that this strand of parliamentary doctrine has largely lapsed into history. In Britain, the recent case of John Browne, M.P., in which Browne was found guilty by a House committee of failing to declare his interests under House rules, suggests that the forces of cultural convergence may be making some headway in Great Britain. Still, as one scholarly observer of the British scene notes, notwithstanding the Browne affair many of the issues that raise concern in the United States still "are not seen as ethical or moral problems" in Great Britain; indeed, "the House of Commons still debates now and again whether the Register of Interests should become compulsory, which is perhaps an indication of how unserious a problem [conflict of interest] is"—or is seen to be—in Britain (Dunsire 1990).[19]

There is a certain irony to this last, somewhat historical and philosophical, distinction between the parliamentary and presidential conflict-of-interest traditions. For decades, comparative political scientists have argued that Canadians and Britons live in nations built by big government and sustained by the welfare state and that their political cultures place a premium on the reliability and trust that comes from being able to depend on the crown and the public purse. Americans, by contrast, are said to live in a land built by individual enterprise; they are depicted as partisans of the independence of spirit that comes from relying on private means and wherewithal.[20] This distinction may very well be true, at least to some extent, of Canadian, British, and American political culture as a whole. Yet when it comes to the ways in which citizens who live under the parliamentary and presidential systems like to see their officeholders behave, the reverse seems to be the case: In a variety of ways, Canadians and Britons have displayed a relative tendency to prefer officials who embody the independence that comes from relying on private means and wherewithal. Americans, by contrast, seem to feel more comfortable with officials who are dependent solely on the public purse. Given the reported tendency of the political culture of citizenship to tack in the opposite direction within the three countries, this particular parliamentary-presidential difference should be taken as testimony to the importance of governmental structure and to its role in shaping traditional understandings of official morality.

Conclusion

In summary, differences in governmental structure have led Canada's recent conflict-of-interest tradition to differ in important respects from the American tradition. In the first place, three factors have given rise to very different histories of the attempts to use both statutory and nonstatutory regimes in the two countries. These factors are (a) the dual status of the cabinet member as a minister and a legislator in Canada (which means that in Canada—as distinct from the United States—the attempt is made to subject legislators to many of the statutory controls proposed for cabinet members); (b) the relative isolation of the Canadian subcabinet executive branch from legislative control (which means that, as distinct from the United States, the subcabinet executive is not subject to statutory controls); and (c) the comparably limited powers possessed by the individual Canadian legislator (which means that in Canada legislators are not subject to particularly extensive nonstatutory controls). In the second place, the Canadian ex-minister's relative vulnerability and eclipsed power have given rise to a more liberal proposed postemployment regime for former cabinet members in Canada than obtains in the United States. Third, the independence of Canadian public-service bodies and the supremacy of the executive-in-Parliament mean that under the proposed Canadian conflict-of-interest regime, remedies and penalties respectively rest rather more in those two institutions than they do in their U.S. counterparts. Instead, in the United States, democratic forums and legal strictures are more relied upon for remedies, and branches independent of the legislature and the executive are more readily called upon for penalties. Fourth, because the Canadian legislator commands a relatively circumscribed degree of control over the executive, unofficial paid legislative representations before government agencies and departments are not prohibited in Canada, while they are in the United States. (And, to the extent that they are found objectionable in Canada, they are deemed to be so for different reasons.) Finally, and more historically, because of the greater power exercised by the executive over the legislature in British parliamentary systems, Canadian political history shows signs of a marked "British" lack of concern over officeholders who have private interests and incomes, and a worry about officeholders dependent on the public treasury—an attitude largely foreign to U.S. debate.

The two countries' comparative experiences in dealing with public-sector conflict expand on O.P. Dwivedi's suggestion that the idea of government ethics (indeed, the very term itself) embodies a certain tension. For while ethics is often supposed to evince the character of a timeless and universal "higher law" or set of "broad principles," governments themselves "assess complex social and political issues less according to the fundamental truths they proclaim [than] from the standpoint of changing directions and evolving public agenda. For is it not self-evident that some of yesterday's morally accepted issues have become today's immoral acts?" (Dwivedi 1987, 12, 13). If over the course of time, as Dwivedi suggests, evolving government agendas issue forth in different understandings of administrative rights and wrongs, then across geographical space varying government structures can also issue forth in different understandings of administrative rights and wrongs. As we have seen, (a) the same types of officials (legislators, cabinet members, public servants) are seen, in the two countries' approaches, to be amenable to very different types of regulatory schema; (b) the same situations are regarded as giving rise to divisions of responsibility among participants for regulatory transgressions (as between ex-cabinet members and the public servants they approach); (c) the same institutions (the public service, the legislature, and the executive branch) are seen to possess different degrees of competence in the ability to prevent or judge wrongdoing; (d) the same types of activities (paid legislative representations before the executive) are for different reasons classified as wrongdoing; and (e), more historically, an officeholder's possession of the same types of interests and income are seen to have different consequences for the creation of conflict. These are all differences in ethics and yet they are all directly attributable to differences in governmental structure. If government ethics is often agenda driven, as Dwivedi suggests, then it is also structurally determined.

Notes

An earlier version of this essay was presented at the Conference on the Study of Government Ethics, Park City, Utah, June 1991, organized by the American Society for Public Administration Section on Public Administration Research. The author is grateful to several conference participants for helpful comments. As well, the author wishes to express his thanks to Stephane Dion, Stuart Gilman, Jean-Pierre Kingsley, John Langford, Mary Ann McCoy, and Iris M. Young for reading a previous version of the chapter and offering important suggestions.

1. See, for example, Bert A. Rockman, and R. Kent Weaver, eds., *Do Institutions Matter?* Washington, D.C.: Brookings, forthcoming, 1993.

2. It should be noted that a minority school of thought within Canadian politics and political science has, for the past fifteen years, pushed for greater direct parliamentary control over the executive. For a decisive critique of this doctrine, see S.L. Sutherland, 1991, "Responsible Government and Ministerial Responsibility: Every Reform Is Its Own Problem," *Canadian Journal of Political Science* 24: 91-120.

3. See, for example, the remarks of the Honorable Gerald Regan, in Canada, *House of Commons Debates* March 21, 1983. See also Kenneth Kernaghan, 1973, "The Ethical Conduct of Canadian Public Servants," *Optimum* 4: 16. Kernaghan has additionally made this point more broadly about Canadian provincial governments in Kenneth Kernaghan, 1974, "Codes of Ethics and Administrative Responsibility," *Canadian Public Administration* 17: 529; and 1980, "Codes of Ethics and Public Administration: Progress, Problems and Prospects," *Public Administration* 58: 210. More recently, as Kernaghan and Langford note in their book on ethics for Canadian public servants, "[r]ather than resort to legislation, most Canadian governments have been inclined to write down rules for responsible administrative behaviour in the form of guidelines, directives . . . or codes of conduct." See Kenneth Kernaghan and John W. Langford, *The Responsible Public Servant* (Halifax: Institute for Research on Public Policy, 1990), 184; see also, generally, *Conflict of Interest in Canada: A Federal, Provincial, and Territorial Perspective* (Ottawa: Office of the Assistant Deputy Registrar General, 1990). None of this is to say, of course, that the civil service in Canada is not subject to some statutory controls on ethical behavior: the Canadian Criminal Code covers bribery, fraud, breach of trust, and influence peddling among public servants, and the Public Service Act governs issues of political neutrality. Yet most scholars of the subject recognize that these statutes deal with problems other than those that conventionally fall under the rubric "conflict of interest," for which there has never been a statute proposed that would apply to federal public servants. See, for example, Kernaghan and Langford, *The Responsible Public Servant*, 184, 139. See also, generally, Kernaghan (1980, 209-11 *passim*.); Michael M. Atkinson and Maureen Mancuso 1985, "Do We Need a Code of Conduct for Politicians? The Search for an Elite Political Culture of Corruption in Canada," *Canadian Journal of Political Science* 18: 461; and Jean-Pierre Kingsley 1989, "Conflict of Interest as a Part of Political Ethics: The Canadian Federal Government Experience," Paper presented to the Conference for Business and Public Sector Ethics, Cambridge, U.K., July 13.

4. Ian Greene (1990, 251), for example, has observed generally of Canadian statutory strictures both federal and provincial that "[w]hen legislation came, it was inevitably drafted so as to cover both ministers and other legislators, with little apparent recognition that the appropriate standards of impartiality for these two groups might be different."

5. Canada, *House of Commons Debates*, December 10, 1974. See also *Minutes and Proceedings* no. 21. Similar sentiments were expressed by ministers and government members in the debate of March 1983; see Canada, *House of Commons Debates*, March 21, 1983.

6. See, for example, the arguments against including congressmen under the ambit of 18 U.S.C. 208 in The President's Commission on Ethics Law Reform, *To Serve with Honor: Report and Recommendations to the President* (Washington, DC: U.S. Department of Justice, 1989).

7. It should be noted, though, that in one respect the Canadian bill would place on

cabinet members statutory requirements more onerous than those imposed on members of the legislature: cabinet members, as distinct from ordinary members, would not be allowed to engage in outside employment, carry on businesses, or hold directorships in other than charitable organizations, social clubs, religious organizations, or political parties.

It is important to note that a committee of M.P.s and senators, reporting on C-43 in 1992, endorsed and in some respects suggested making more explicit divestment and recusal remedies for M.P.s (the latter would be made an obligation in some instances), even though acknowledgment was made both of the need not to deter individuals from serving in the legislature, and the importance of not interfering with a member's representative functions (Special Joint Committee on Conflicts of Interest. 1992. *Report to the Senate and to the House of Commons*. Ottawa, ON: Supply and Services Canada, 15, 24, 12).

8. See, for example, Brenda Zosky Proulx, "Life in the Slow Lane," *Montreal Gazette*, October 26, 1985—a report on the subsequent job problems faced by five cabinet ministers who were not re-elected in the 1984 general election. One cabinet minister told Proulx: "Finding work can be a problem for an excabinet minister. The myth is that . . . the job offers run after you. That's not the way it works."

9. This notion of placing a smaller relative onus on ex-ministers—and a greater relative responsibility on incumbent officialdom—for ex-ministerial transgressions appears elsewhere in Canadian discussion. See, for example, *House of Commons Debates*, March 21, 1983.

10. See Erwin J. Krasnow and Richard E. Lankford, 1964, "Congressional Conflicts of Interest: Who Watches the Watchers?" *Federal Bar Journal* 24: 272. See also "Communications with Administrative Agencies," in *Ethics Manual for Members, Officers and Employees of the U.S. House of Representatives*, 100th Congress, 1st Session (Washington, DC: 1987).

11. See, for example, U.S. House of Representatives. *Presidential Pay Recommendations: Hearings before the Ad Hoc Subcommittee on Presidential Pay Proposals of the Committee on Post Office and Civil Service*, 95th Congress, 1st Session, 1977; *Congressional Record*, 95th Congress, 1st Session, February 9, 1977; and *Debates and Proceedings in the Congress of the United States*, 15th Congress, 1st Session, December 1816.

12. See also, for example, United Kingdom, *Parliamentary Debates*, August 10, 1911; *Parliamentary Debates*, March 24, 1893; and *Parliamentary Debates*, August 10, 1911.

13. See United Kingdom, *Parliamentary Debates*, July 28, 1978. "If we think of independence," one member argued, "there is no one so independent of government and the Whips as an unpaid Member." "Independence" here is simply and naturally equated with financial independence of the public treasury, not with financial independence of private interests. See also *Parliamentary Debates*, July 21, 1980; and the *Daily Telegraph*, August 16, 1983, editorial: "it is not desirable that MPs should become wholly dependent on their parliamentary salaries [for] parliamentarians wholly beholden to their parties may lose some independence."

14. Even to this day in Britain when members become ministers, and consequently begin to draw salaries for their executive positions, their parliamentary pay is reduced, and for their services as members they receive less pay than do nonministerial members. This practice represents a vestige of the idea that the member's capacity to be both a delegate/spokesperson for the views of his or her constituency and a trustee espousing an independent view of the public interest is to some degree impaired when he or she becomes financially beholden to the pleasure of the government and the crown by becoming a member of the executive.

15. See also the discussion in Canada, Library of Parliament Research Branch, *Conflicts of Interest and Parliamentarians*, October 15, 1968. In addition, as noted above, the Canadian House of Commons *Conflict of Interest Rules* are concerned not with the conflicts that may arise when members hold various private interests, but with those that arise when members hold other public offices or contracts with the crown.

16. The prime minister, it should be noted, refused the minister's offer of recusal, and he did so, according to the minister, because the prime minister "thought the interests of Islanders would not be advanced by a diminution of my status as Minister of the environment." In other words, the prime minister's first concern appeared to be reassurance of the minister's constituents that his representational capacities would not be harmed were he to continue to serve as a member of the executive on this matter. The prime minister notably did not attempt to reassure environmental groups that his environment minister's executive decision-making capacities would not be compromised by his continuing representational responsibilities. See *Charlottetown Guardian*, January 28, 1988.

17. The concern that private interests would encroach on a member's time holds primacy over the concern that they might impede the member's judgment. This is evinced at various points in the history of the British debate. See, generally, D.C.M. Platt, 1961, "The Commercial and Industrial Interests of Ministers of the Crown," *Political Studies* 9: 279, 280, 284. When, in 1971, the Review Body on Top Salaries considered banning honoraria for U.K. Commons Committee chairmen, it did so because the events giving rise to such honoraria impinged on the time chairmen should devote to committee work, not because the honoraria were thought to compromise their judgment (see *Review Body on Top Salaries, First Report: Ministers and Members of Parliament.* London, 1971). By contrast, the need to avoid conflicts of interest is quite explicitly elevated over the need to avoid encroachments on time in U.S. congressional argumentation in favor of restricting outside earned income and honoraria. See, for example, U.S. House of Representatives, *Presidential Pay Recommendations*, and *Congressional Record* October 28, 1981.

18. Starr and Sharp (1984, 77) describe a "period of quiet" in conflict-of-interest activity at the federal level between the 1930s and 1951. By contrast, see Michael Reagan, "Serving Two Masters: Problems in the Employment of Dollar-a-Year and Without-Compensation Men (Ph.D. diss., Princeton University, 1959).

19. These are the words of Andrew Dunsire, Professor of Political Science Emeritus, the University of York, England, in a letter to the author dated February 23, 1990. In a recent study of the considerable extent to which parliamentary conflict of interest is now a concern in the United Kingdom, Malcolm Shaw notes several practices still operative in Parliament, which would not be permitted for U.S. Congressmen. For example, British "[m]embers may work for, or even form, a public relations or political consultancy firm which has clients with a stake in public policy outcomes." See Malcolm Shaw, "Members of Parliament," in *Parliament and Pressure Politics*, edited by Michael Rush (Oxford: Clarendon, 1990), 85-116. Also noteworthy is Anthony King, in his seminal "The Rise of the Career Politician in Britain—and Its Consequences." 1981, *British Journal of Political Science* 11: 249-85. King explicitly states that even the typical British "career politician" he analyzes may well "live 'for' politics . . . But he does not necessarily live off politics. He may have a large private income; he may earn substantial sums, possibly more than his parliamentary salary, by writing for newspapers or practising at the bar. . . . " (p. 250). In the United States, such an individual would not be considered a "career politician."

20. See, most recently, Seymour Martin Lipset, *Continental Divide: The Values and Institutions of the United States and Canada* (New York and London: Routledge, 1990), xiii, 7.

References

Association of the Bar of the City of New York. 1960. *Conflict of Interest and the Federal Service*, 13. Cambridge, MA and U.S. Senate, Committee on Governmental Affairs 1987. *Post-Employment Lobbying Restrictions*. 100th Congress, 1st Session.

Atkinson, Michael M., and Mancuso, Maureen. 1991. "Conflict of Interest in Britain and the United States: An Institutional Approach," *Legislative Studies Quarterly* 16: 483.

Canada. 1973. President of the Privy Council, "Members of Parliament and Conflict of Interest." Ottawa.

Canada. 1975. *Minutes of Proceedings and Evidence of the Standing Committee on Privileges and Elections of the House of Commons*, First Session, Thirtieth Parliament, 1974-75, no. 12 and no. 13.

Canada. 1974. *House of Commons Debates*, December 10, 1974.

Canada. 1983. *House of Commons Debates*, March 21, 1983.

Dawson, R. MacGregor. 1970. *The Government of Canada*. 5th ed. Toronto: University of Toronto.

Dunshire, Andrew. 1990. Letter to the author from Andrew Dunsire, Professor of Political Science Emeritus, the University of York, England, February 23, 1990.

Dwivedi, O.P. 1987. "Moral Dimensions of Statecraft: A Plea for an Administrative Theology." *Canadian Journal of Political Science* 20: 12, 13.

Greene, Ian. 1990. "Conflict of Interest and the Canadian Constitution," *Canadian Journal of Political Science* 23: 249, 251.

Kernaghan, Kenneth. 1980. "Codes of Ethics and Public Administration: Progress, Problems and Prospects." *Canadian Public Administration* 58: 208, 213.

McGill, Barry. 1959. "Conflict of Interest: English Experience 1782–1941," *Western Political Quarterly* 12: 809.

Osbaldeston, Gordon. 1987. "The Public Servant and Politics." *Policy Options* (January): 6.

Roberts, Robert N. 1988. *White House Ethics: A History of the Politics of Conflict of Interest Regulation*, 162. Westport, CT: Greenwood.

Starr, Michael, and Sharp, Mitchell. 1984. *Ethical Conduct in the Public Sector: Report of the Task Force on Conflict of Interest*. Ottawa: The Government of Canada.

United States. 1906. *Burton v. United States*, 202 United States 344 (1906).

U.S. Senate. 1987. *Post-Employment Lobbying Restrictions*. 100th Congress, 1st Session.

Williams, Sandra. 1984. *Conflict of Interest: The Ethical Dilemma in Politics*. Aldershot, Hants, England: Gower.

Wilson, Geoffrey. 1969. "Conflicts of Interest in Public Law . . . In England." *Proceedings of the Sixth International Symposium on Comparative Law*. Ottawa: University of Ottawa Press.

Part Two

Ethics as Control

4

Whistleblowing, Organizational Performance, and Organizational Control

James L. Perry

Recent headlines tell a story of a rising tide of conflict within organizations: "NASA Critic Says Job Binds Him to Truth, Not Agency," "Tennessee Valley Authority Stung by Critiques of its Nuclear Program," "Troop Carrier's Flaws Masked, Memos Say," "Weapons Costs Underestimated for 30 Years, Official Charges," "Maverick at USDA Attacks Inspections." The headlines reveal the growing incidence of disputes between individuals and their organizations, often about matters with substantial implications for groups not party to the dispute. Headlines have also given a name to this phenomenon: Whistleblowing.

Although whistleblowing is like other types of organizational disputes (for example, those between departments or between labor and management), it also has distinctive attributes. It may be characterized by three procedural and substantive properties that collectively distinguish it from other types of organizational disputes: (1) apparent altruistic behavior on the part of the initiator of the dispute; (2) asymmetric distribution of power; and (3) absence of well-developed, neutral dispute resolution mechanisms.

Whistleblowing is unique in that it involves individuals initiating disputes apparently on behalf of third parties not directly involved in the employment or contractual relationship—for example, taxpayers or stockholders. The disputes are *apparently* on behalf of third parties because the actual motivations for whistleblowing may reveal that self-interest rather than altruism (Mansbridge 1990) is the driving force behind a whistleblower's claim. Personal vindictiveness toward a supervisor or an organization could plausibly be the trigger for charges about organizational wrongdoing or illegitimate activity. The important point is that the claim could appear outwardly to be altruistic, regardless of an individual's motivation.

Another feature of whistleblowing is that it typically involves conflict between two parties with unequal power. Weinstein (1979, 2) suggests that whistleblowing involves "attempts to change a bureaucracy by those who work within the organization but who do not have authority." The whistleblower also is likely to be at a power disadvantage because the resources that can be brought to bear in any conflict are asymmetrically distributed. Whistleblowers can rely on their personal resources and whatever additional resources they can persuade others to commit to the conflict. In contrast, any organization that chooses to ignore the claims of a whistleblower and contest the dispute can readily mobilize organization members, legal services, and its network of external supporters to resist responding to legitimate claims. Thus, the whistleblower can expect to face an opponent who is structurally guaranteed a power advantage, often of immense proportions.

A third distinguishing characteristic of whistleblowing is that it usually occurs in the absence of well-developed, neutral dispute resolution mechanisms. Third-party procedures are now used to resolve a variety of disputes, ranging from labor–management interest disputes, commercial contract disputes, consumer claims, and conflicts between community groups. The claims of whistleblowers seldom are afforded opportunities for third-party review and resolution. In some environments, such as the federal government, the whistleblower may have some organizational mechanisms for third-party review of the evidence and disposition of the claim. Even with such procedures, the whistleblower is at a disadvantage when compared to other dispute contexts. The recency of procedures for whistleblower disclosure has prevented them from becoming fully institutionalized. One indicator of lack of institutionalization is that the procedures are not widely accepted by the parties affected by them. For example, after an analysis of survey data from federal employees, Miceli and Near (1984, 704) reported that "finding the right encouragements or inducements for whistle-blowers might be problematic and certainly will require long term, concerted effort." Another problem is that, despite good intentions, the procedures are sometimes poorly designed for protecting the whistleblower and assuring disclosure of wrongdoing (Devine and Aplin 1986).

Research on whistleblowing has grown significantly in recent years (Near and Miceli 1986; Graham 1986), but much of the research has focused on the individual whistleblower, particularly the whistleblower's motivations and cognitive and affective decision processes. Significantly less research has been devoted to putting the whistleblowing process into its larger social context (Johnson and Kraft 1989). This chapter begins to fill that void by analyzing organizational consequences of whistleblowing.

Theoretical Framework

In creating a theory about whistleblowing and its consequences, it is useful to start with an understanding of the scope of the phenomenon. Building from an earlier definition by Miceli and Near (1985), whistleblowing is conceived as the disclosure by individuals or groups of activities claimed to be illegal, immoral, or illegitimate. One implicit assumption underlying the definition is that the whistleblower is not a passive participant or bystander who merely initiates the process by reporting a claim of wrongdoing. Some scholars (Weinstein 1979; Zald and Berger 1978) have argued that the whistleblower has no legitimate authority to effect change but must instead work through unconventional channels. This contrasts with the situation in some organizations in which individuals who occupy specific roles are authorized to bring illegal or illegitimate activities to the attention of authoritative actors, thereby creating a prima facie case for change. The assumption of the present study is that whistleblowers will derive their power from both formal and informal channels within organizations, and the phenomenon should not be defined to preclude either source of power.

The definition does not presuppose the validity of the whistleblower's claim. Much of the literature on whistleblowing assumes or limits the domain to disputes that are grounded in matters of principle, that is, where dissent involves conscientious objection to violations of standards of justice, honesty, or economy (Bowie 1982; Graham 1986). From an organizational perspective, however, the substance of a whistleblower's complaint is a matter that involves some degree of uncertainty. Although the authenticity of a whistleblower's complaint may be irrelevant for the organization that chooses to ignore it or to retaliate against the whistleblower, it is clearly relevant to the organization that wishes to respond appropriately. Responsive organizations are faced with investigating the complaint to identify whether it is authentic or not.

Any theory of the consequences of whistleblowing must account for variations in the validity of claims that might potentially be brought by a whistleblower. Claims are likely to be of three types. The type that is most often assumed in the literature involves the reporting of wrongdoing that is accurately perceived by the whistleblower. At least two other types of claims, however, are likely to manifest themselves. One type of invalid complaint arises when the whistleblower's action is grounded in erroneous perceptions or incomplete information about an activity. Another, more serious, instance involves whistleblowing grounded in opportunistic self-interest, where the whistleblower fabricates a problem for self-protection or gain.

Because the validity of whistleblower claims may initially be uncertain, the content of the claim is not a given. Instead, the claim is subject to definition by the whistleblower, the targets of the claim, and other contending parties. It is conceptually inaccurate, therefore, to conceive of the claim as a "performance gap" or "problem" as Graham (1986) does with regard to the more limiting concept of principled dissent. This study, therefore, will use the broader concept of "issue," referring to the controversy initiated by a whistleblower. Following Cobb and Elder (1983, 82), an issue refers to a conflict between two or more identifiable parties over procedural or substantive matters.

Underlying this research are several assumptions about the behavioral predispositions of individuals and organizations. One assumption is that an organization will resist change attempts unless it has learned responses or designed itself in a way to facilitate positive or routine handling of disputes. Resistance to change is grounded in two general tendencies of individuals and organizations. The first of these tendencies involves what Staw, Sandelands, and Dutton (1981) term the threat–rigidity effect. The general thesis of Staw et al. is that "a threat to the vital interests of an entity, be it an individual, group, or organization, will lead to forms of rigidity" (p. 502). The two most prominent processes that contribute to rigidity in the face of threat are restriction of information processing and constriction of control. Whether these responses to threat are functional or not depends on the magnitude of the threat itself. Rigidity in response to potentially radical environmental changes is likely to be maladaptive, but response rigidities to incremental changes may be quite functional.

A second, related tendency may be described in terms of how people respond to different accountability mechanisms (Jos 1990). Staw (1980) has argued that individuals exhibit different forms of rationality in response to different accountability mechanisms. Decision makers exposed to predecisional accountability are likely to exhibit prospective rationality, in which the decision maker devotes considerable effort to finding the most defensible options. However, when people are accountable only after a decision has been made, they are likely to resort to retrospective rationality—to cope by trying to justify their actions. These justification processes may range from simple verbal rationalizations to elaborate excuses designed to minimize damage to their social images (Tetlock 1985). Thus, whistleblowing, because it represents a type of postdecisional accountability, is likely to set into motion countervailing forces that motivate its targets to bolster previous decisions (Tetlock 1985).

Whistleblowing and Organizational Consequences

The organizational consequences of whistleblowing may be conceived in both micro- and macro-organizational terms. Outcomes at the micro level focus on the reactions of the organization to the whistleblower's claim and its resolution (Graham 1986). At the macro level, several studies, most of them outside the whistleblower literature, are suggestive of the possible linkages between whistleblowing and more general processes of organizational change and stability. This study focuses on the latter consequences of whistleblowing.

Some insight about salient macro-level outcomes is provided by Zald and Berger (1978). Their central thesis is that much conflict in organizations, including whistleblowing, occurs outside normal channels and such "unconventional opposition" may appropriately be understood using social movement analysis. They contend that phenomena resembling social movements are important because they affect major outcomes in organizations, including the control of organizational resources and organizational survival. The Zald and Berger analysis suggests that the whistleblowing process and its aftermath might influence a broad range of outcomes, two of which are particularly salient: organizational control (Pfeffer and Salancik 1978) and organizational performance (Hirschman 1970).

The resource-dependence perspective (Pfeffer and Salancik 1978) suggests that organizational choice is socially controlled. The organization's dependence on the environment for resources creates the conditions under which external entities have power over the organization. This power permits environmental elements to constrain and control organizational action. The likelihood of control, however, is not deterministic. It is contingent on the presence of conditions that encourage an organization to comply with the demands of external entities. The crucial point of the resource-dependence perspective for this research is that the actions of the whistleblower affect the stability of patterns of exchange in the markets of influence and control within the organization, which, in turn, affect environmental dependence.

A second macro-level outcome can be tied directly to the whistleblower phenomena using Hirschman's (1970) theory of exit, voice, and loyalty. Hirschman sought to explain member responses to declines of performance in organizations and administrator responses to members' attempts to influence the organization. He reasoned that declines in the rationality of organizations are likely and that the behaviors of members as responses to these declines can lead to corrections in inefficiencies or ineffectiveness.

The member response to performance decline that has typically been the focus of traditional economic analysis is exit, in which a member leaves an organization or ceases to buy a firm's product. Hirschman identified a second generic form of member response—voice—which represents a political response. Voice involves the direct expression of dissatisfaction to management or to some other authority. Although Hirschman treats exit and voice as essentially mutually exclusive, Kolarska and Aldrich (1980) have argued that they represent four responses if they are considered jointly: (1) stay and be silent; (2) stay and be vocal; (3) exit and remain silent; and (4) exit vociferously.

It is obvious that the act of blowing the whistle indicates a choice between one of two of Kolarska and Aldrich's four responses. Whistleblowers opt to stay and be vocal or they exit vociferously. In some instances, the behavioral options will be used sequentially if the organization is not responsive to an employee's efforts to effect change from within. The important conceptual point is that these responses are intended to correct declines in organizations and should, therefore, be linked to organizational performance.

Hypotheses

A basic premise of this research is that organizations will resist change attempts unless the organization has learned responses or designed itself in a way to facilitate positive or routine handling of disputes (Staw, Sandelands, and Dutton 1981). The veracity of whistleblower claims will vary greatly, with some whistleblowers raising legitimate claims and others raising false issues to punish co-workers or superiors (Westin 1981). How the organization is designed to respond to these different types of claims is important. Does the organization make type I (rejecting true claims) or type II (accepting false claims) errors? Does it reward illegitimate claims? Does it punish legitimate claims? An organization cannot know in advance the mix of legitimate/illegitimate claims, but it can make strategic choices with respect to acceptable levels of error for each type. Hirschman (1970, 42) suggests that institutions may be designed to lower the costs of voice and increase its rewards as a means for taking advantage of the recuperative powers of voice. Thus, the design choices that organizations make are likely to influence organizational consequences, which suggests the following hypothesis:

> **Hypothesis 1.** The more organizational policies tend to punish legitimate claims and reward illegitimate claims, the more likely organizational performance will suffer.

O'Day (1974) suggests that superiors in organizations are likely to engage in intimidation rituals to discourage reform-minded individuals from continuing to seek reform. According to O'Day, the increasingly oppressive rituals have two purposes. First, the rituals are intended to control reformers so that they do not succeed in recruiting others to their cause. Second, the rituals are designed to maintain the image of authorities. The most direct manifestation of these rituals is the organization's hostility toward the whistleblower, under the guise of informal reprimands or more formal disciplinary action. Ultimately, the rituals shift the focus from the whistleblower's claim of alleged immoral, illegal, or illegitimate activity to the whistleblower's deviance from or noncompliance with organizational norms (Harshbarger 1973). By obscuring the facts, the conflict diminishes the organization's capacity to make rational judgments. Thus:

> **Hypothesis 2.** The greater the hostility toward the whistleblower, the less likely whistleblowing will improve organizational performance.

Another important dimension of the whistleblowing process involves whether the issue created by the whistleblower's claim is resolved. In some cases, closure will occur when an authoritative source vindicates the whistleblower's position and punishes wrongdoers. Various other scenarios are possible as well, among them that the issue will not be resolved and the controversy will continue or dissipate without any formal resolution. Even if the whistleblower's claim has no merit, it is unlikely to be to the organization's advantage to let the controversy hang fire so that it is a continuing distraction and irritant to the whistleblower and other organizational participants, such as co-workers and supervisors. It can be concluded, therefore:

> **Hypothesis 3.** The more able the organization is to resolve issues, the greater the likelihood that whistleblowing will improve organizational performance.

Organizations will strive to maintain their autonomy. The exercise of voice (Hirschman 1970) by the whistleblower threatens organizational autonomy. If the organization is sensitive to voice as a recuperative mechanism, the organization is more likely to act upon the claims of the whistleblower and is less likely to lose any of its autonomy over goal setting or resource allocation. On the other hand, if an organization ignores the whistleblower or reacts with hostility, then the organization risks the intervention of third parties, possible imposition of a solution, and public disapproval and sanctions.

The extent to which whistleblowing affects organizational control is a function of the arena in which the whistleblower's claim is resolved. Externally derived solutions are likely to involve the imposition of mandates upon the organization to comply with certain modifications of organizational policies or practices. Even if externally derived solutions do not prescribe specific organizational changes, they are likely to increase an organization's vulnerability to external control (Pfeffer and Salancik 1978). This implies the following:

> **Hypothesis 4.** Externally derived solutions to whistleblower claims are likely to reduce organizational control.

Another influence upon the extent to which whistleblowing affects organizational control is the power of the organization to defend itself against the whistleblower's claims. If organizations are driven to maintain autonomy, their ability to overcome threats to their control is dependent on the amount of power they wield. Therefore,

> **Hypothesis 5.** The greater an organization's power, the more capable it will be of defending itself against a whistleblower's claim and the less the effect on organizational control will be.

Hirschman's theory has implications for predicting organizational consequences under varying assumptions about the responsiveness of organizations to member voice during declining performance. For instance, Hirschman suggests that an organization's recovery from performance decline depends on its responsiveness to whatever recuperative mechanisms it is equipped with. One implication is that organizations that are equipped with voice mechanisms but are responsive to exit are less capable of recovering from performance declines and more likely to suffer permanent decrements to performance.

Organizations that discourage dissent are prone to the most serious consequences when whistleblowing does occur. Although an organization may successfully discourage voice, it does so by sacrificing opportunities to correct performance declines. In so doing, however, it assures that should a whistleblower succeed, the magnitude of any potential correction is likely to be greater than if a small number of corrections had been made incrementally. Thus,

> **Hypothesis 6.** Organizations that discourage dissent will suppress internal and external whistleblowing, but when whistleblowing does occur it is likely to lead to reductions in organizational control.

Methods

The research used the case survey approach first described in Yin and Heald (1975) and further developed by McClintock, Brannon, and Maynard-Moody (1979) and Yin (1981a, 1981b). As described by Yin and Heald (1975, 372): "The case survey calls for the reader-analyst to answer the same set of questions for each case study. The questions are close-ended, so that the answers can be aggregated for further analysis." The quantitative evidence derived from each case study permits the computation of statistical measures of association, overcoming one of the shortcomings of case studies—the inability to aggregate across cases. Thus, the case studies can be reviewed with scientific rigor.

Sample

The sample of cases was drawn from agencies of the federal government. In order to obtain a sample that was representative with respect to the intensity of the dispute, it was necessary to stratify cases (Kish 1965) by whistleblowing channel. We originally set out to sample cases from three strata: intraorganizational/informal channels (the management hierarchy, co-workers, unions, and personnel offices); formal channels (inspectors general, hotlines, office of the special counsel); extraorganizational/informal (Congress, media). After initiating contacts with various sources to identify cases, we found that very few cases could be identified for the first stratum, intraorganizational/informal channels. There appeared to be several reasons for this difficulty. First, we found that few informants considered disputes that were settled within the management hierarchy to be whistleblowing. Informants implicitly associated whistleblowing with disloyalty to the organization or with violation of the norms of commitment to the organization or co-workers. Informants were probably also less likely to recall incidents occurring within intraorganizational/informal channels because these disputes might have involved low levels of conflict, been quite routine, and produced few, if any, artifacts (for example, case reports of adjudicators). Second, because whistleblowing in the federal government is highly formalized, many individuals who seek to report illegal, illegitimate, or immoral activities prefer to use formal channels rather than the organizational chain-of-command. Even in field installations, most complaints are processed through formal whistleblowing channels.

Because of the difficulties encountered in identifying cases from the intraorganizational/informal stratum, the sample that was finally selected was composed of cases from only two of the originally defined strata. Although this resulted in a sample that was less diverse than anticipated, it was consistent with the realities encountered in the field research. A summary of characteristics of the sample is provided in Table 4.1. The sample of cases represents a wide spectrum of the organizational hierarchy, with relatively equal representation from top management, middle management, and nonmanagement positions. About one-third of the sample suffered some form of reprisal; about half of these had been fired. Most cases for which information was available were resolved (78.5 percent), but a noticeable proportion (12.1 percent) went unresolved. One-third of the cases involved anonymous whistleblowers, mostly hotline users, whose identity was not known to the investigators. About 27 percent of the overall sample involved hotline reports. Another 40 percent and 20 percent came from public and Merit Systems Protection Board (MSPB)/Office of the Special Counsel (OSC) sources, respectively.

These statistics indicate that the sample is quite diverse. It is probably more representative than samples used in previous research by Glazer and Glazer (1989), Soeken and Soeken (1987), and Jos, Tompkins, and Hays (1989), which primarily involved principled dissenters whose cases were highly visible. At the same time, the cases selected were probably not entirely representative of the population of whistleblowers because cases involving grievances and anonymous whistleblowers were undersampled. The undersampling of anonymous whistleblowers was unavoidable because of the data collection requirements of the research. Although some types of cases were undersampled, the overall sample was diverse and acceptable from the perspective of providing data that could be used to disconfirm the hypotheses.

Data

Data were collected on each case from archival records (memoranda, court cases, agency records, budgets), secondary sources, interviews, and a self-administered survey. An effort was made to build redundancy into the data collection procedures so that if information were not available from one source it could be obtained from another. The self-administered survey requested information (for

Table 4.1

A Comparison of Federal Government Whistleblowing Cases and the Effects of Several Organizational and Personal Variables on Outcomes

Variables/Categories	Frequency	Percent	Valid Percent	Valid Cases
Whistleblower's Position				87
Top Management	17	13.1	19.5	
Middle Management	22	16.9	25.3	
Supervisory	15	11.5	17.2	
Nonmanagement/Nonsupervisory	33	25.4	37.9	
Missing	43	33.1	—	
Was Reprisal Taken				130
Yes	44	33.8	33.8	
No	74	56.9	56.9	
Unable to Ascertain	12	9.2	9.2	
Organization Fired Whistleblower				109
Yes	24	18.5	22.0	
No	85	65.4	78.0	
Missing	21	16.2	—	
Claim Resolution				107
Resolved	84	64.6	78.5	
Partially Resolved	10	7.7	9.3	
Not at all Resolved	13	10.0	12.1	
Missing	23	17.7	—	
Was Whistleblower Anonymous				128
Yes	43	33.1	33.6	
No	85	65.4	66.4	
Missing	2	1.5	—	
How Long to Conclude Case				87
0–1 year	41	31.5	47.1	
1–2 years	16	12.3	18.4	
2–3 years	10	7.7	11.5	
3–4 years	8	6.2	9.2	
4–5 years	3	2.3	3.4	
More than 5 years	9	6.9	10.3	
Missing	43	33.1	—	
Was Address Obtained				130
Yes	105	80.8	80.8	
No	25	19.2	19.2	
Was a Survey Returned				130
Yes	57	43.8	43.8	
No	73	56.2	56.2	
Source of Case				130
Public Case	53	40.8	40.8	
MSPB/OSC	27	20.8	20.8	
GAP (Government Accountability Project)	8	6.2	6.2	
HHS (U.S. Department of Health and Human Services)	7	5.4	5.4	
Field Office Hotline	16	12.3	12.3	
HQ Office Hotline	19	14.6	14.6	

example employee demographics) that was also obtained from other sources such as court cases or newspaper reports. The redundancy assured that if one piece of data were not available it might still be obtained using the alternative source. The data were used to create three data files for each case: (1) the case survey file, containing analyst-coded information based upon archival records; (2) the self-administered survey file, containing the responses from the self-administered survey; and (3) the secondary data file, containing budgetary and survey information on the organization that employed the whistleblower.

Operational Definitions

The three data files were used to create the measures for the variables in the study. Each of the measures used to test the hypotheses is discussed briefly below and in greater detail in the Appendix. To maximize the number of cases available for analysis and to reduce the amount of missing data, we used one general rule for combining measures from the case survey and self-administered survey. The general rule was to create indicators for the data available from each data collection method. A combined indicator was created by standardizing the scores for the two indicators and substituting the self-administered survey measure in those cases for which the data were missing for the case survey. This procedure was used for all variables in the Appendix for which both case survey and self-administered data were available.

Hostility toward the whistleblower reflects the behavioral response of the organization toward the whistleblower, ranging from supportive to nonsupportive. It was measured by a simple count of the number of "yes" responses to retaliation items in the case survey and self-administered survey.

Issue resolution is the extent to which the issue created by the whistleblower's claim was resolved. Cases were sorted into three categories: "resolved" to "not resolved."

Organizational control is the extent to which the organization maintained control over decisions and resources following the whistleblowing incident. The indicator was created from case survey responses to the following question: "Did the organization lose control over any of its authority?"

Organizational performance is the extent to which the organization was perceived as being more efficient or effective as a result of the whistleblowing episode. A measure was created by use of standardized scores from the case survey and self-administered survey.

Organizational policy's punishment of legitimate claims refers to the extent to which the organization responded favorably to previous whistleblower claims. An agency index was created from aggregated employee responses to an item from the 1980 MSPB Whistleblower Survey that was repeated in the 1983 Merit Principles Survey.

Organizational policy's reward of illegitimate claims represents the extent to which the organization acquiesced to dubious claims in past whistleblower cases. An agency score was created from responses to an item from the 1983 Merit Principles Survey.

External whistleblowing channels refers to those formal and informal channels that lie outside an organization. This item was created from responses to items in the case survey and self-administered survey.

Externally derived solutions are solutions to the whistleblower's claims that are imposed by external authorities. Solutions were categorized according to whether the party was internal or external.

Organization power is the extent to which the organization possesses resources that may be used to persuade other actors of its position on an issue. The indicator for this concept was the size of the budget for the parent organization measured in constant dollars in the year in which the whistleblower claim was made. The data were taken from published budget documents.

Suppression of whistleblowing is the extent to which the organization takes actions to prevent whistleblowers from pursuing their claims both inside and outside the organization. It was measured using agency-level indicators of perceived reprisal created from items in 1980 and 1983 MSPB surveys.

Results

Multivariate statistical techniques were used to test the hypotheses. The regression results are presented in Tables 4.2 and 4.3. Table 4.2 presents three regressions. The first regression includes only the indicator for punishment of legitimate claims, the second includes only the indicator for reward of illegitimate claims, and the third incorporates both measures.

The organizational performance regressions provide little support for the hypotheses. The relationships for hostility and issue resolution are in the predicted directions, but none of the relationships reach the 0.05 level of significance in any of the three regressions.

The F-statistic is significant at the 0.05 level for only one of the three regression equations. The adjusted R^2 ranges from 2 percent to 6 percent for the three equations, which also suggests that the variables are relatively poor predictors of organizational performance.

Table 4.3 provides a contrasting picture for the predictors of organizational control. The F-statistics for two of the three independent variables and the overall regression were significant. Organization power was not significant in the regression. The results indicate that externally-derived solutions are more likely to be associated with reductions in organizational control. They also suggest that suppression of whistleblowing could be detrimental to organizational control.

Discussion

This study began with a theoretical model that was grounded in a basic assumption about organizational behavior. The assumption was that organizations will

Table 4.2

Multiple Regressions for Organizational performance

Independent Variables	Beta	Standard Error	t	Signifi- cance
Hostility	−0.16	0.13	−1.27	0.21
Issue Resolution	0.20	0.11	1.79	0.08
Punishment of Legitimate Claims	−0.02	0.12	−0.20	0.84

Adjusted R^2 = 0.06
F = 2.87
Significance = 0.04
N = 87

	Beta	Standard Error	t	Signifi- cance
Hostility	−0.19	0.12	−1.69	0.09
Issue Resolution	0.15	0.11	1.32	0.19
Reward of Illegitimate Claims	−0.05	0.11	−0.46	0.65

Adjusted R^2 = 0.04
F = 2.31
Significance = 0.08
N = 84

	Beta	Standard Error	t	Signifi- cance
Hostility	−0.17	0.14	−1.22	0.22
Issue Resolution	0.14	0.12	1.14	0.26
Punishment of Legitimate Claims	−0.04	0.13	−0.30	0.76
Reward of Illegitimate Claims	−.05	0.11	−0.48	0.63

Adjusted R^2 = 0.02
F = 1.48
Significance = 0.22
N = 80

resist change attempts unless they have learned responses or designed themselves in ways that facilitate constructive handling of disputes. Although the empirical research did not investigate this premise directly, it assessed a series of hypotheses that flowed from the basic logic of this assumption and the results of previous research on whistleblowing. The hypotheses attempted to predict the organizational consequences of whistleblowing. A statistical analysis of cases of whistleblowing in the federal government provided support for some aspects of the theory articulated in the hypotheses, but it also disconfirmed several of the hypotheses.

Contrary to one of the hypotheses, organizational performance was not affected by the extent to which organizational policies punished legitimate claims and rewarded illegitimate claims, as measured by aggregated perceptual mea-

Table 4.3

Multiple Regression for Organizational Control

Independent Variables	Beta	Standard Error	t	Signifi-cance
Suppression	0.38	0.10	3.92	0.00
Organizational Power	0.01	0.10	0.12	0.91
External Solution	−0.37	0.10	−3.56	0.00

Adjusted R^2 = 0.23
F = Statistic (Equation) = 9.46
F Significance = 0.00
N = 84

sures. Given the difficulty of measuring the concepts involved in this hypothesis, one reason for the absence of association may be shortcomings in indicators for the reward and punishment variables. Considering the retrospective nature of the study, however, the aggregated survey measures were the best sources of data available.

What do the results suggest about the voice–performance relationship derived from Hirschman's theory? Three potential inferences merit discussion: one involves the assumptions of Hirschman's theory, another involves the context in which this study was conducted, and a third involves the efficacy of individual action. These explanations cumulatively could account for the weak association between voice and performance.

The logic of the Hirschman framework is that organizations will be attentive to information about performance decline. This assumes, however, some commonality of interests between the organization (and perhaps, more appropriately, the various interests represented within it) and members who engage in exit or voice. The commonality of interests assumes that conflicts that arise are of the consensus variety, about means rather than ends. The disputes that arise from whistleblowing are often of the dissensus variety, fundamental disagreements about direction of the organization or its social role. The fundamental nature of some disputes may make them poor candidates to be resolved through the dynamics envisioned by Hirschman. Thus, the nature of some disputes may attenuate a voice–performance linkage. One whistleblower described the dilemma:

> While working as a contract librarian, I stumbled upon many illegal, fraudulent, abusive practices. When the administrator became aware that I knew of these practices, he terminated my position. The library has since become a shambles. Personnel are not given the benefit of up-to-date medical journals and articles. . . . Those who caused and condoned the illegal activities never answered for them at all. In fact, the chief offender is to this day drawing a large salary from the government.

Another factor that may influence the voice–performance linkage is the clarity of performance norms within an organization. Although Hirschman's theory was quite general, it relied predominantly on argumentation grounded in market-based organizations, where the benefit of success is profitability and the cost of failure is bankruptcy. In federal agencies the criteria of "good" performance are less clear. Federal agencies are responsible for accomplishing particular mission goals, but they are also under substantial pressures to satisfy political interests and conform to constituent and societal expectations. If good performance is ambiguous or is defined as conformity, then voice may be a relatively ineffective mechanism for correcting "performance declines." One whistleblower described the contrasting visions of performance that existed in a military installation:

> I spent two years in the DODDs school system. In that period of time I witnessed rampant abuse both on the job and on the army base. I was forced to throw away equipment that had never been used under threat of removal from my position. Bulk orders of supplies led to excess and shortages in teaching materials. A system of strict "chain of command" made resolution impossible. On the base, before inspection, hundreds of dollars of items were discarded so they would not come up on the supply sheet. Overall, I found the program of waste, fraud and abuse to be channeled toward petty things while major abuses were ignored.

Yet a third explanation for the absence of a voice–performance linkage is the sensitivity of performance to individual action. We know that individual exit over time—for example, customers who choose to discontinue use of a particular brand—can send a strong message to an organization about the need to improve its performance. It is not clear that the act of a single individual conveying the same message will be equally successful. Comparison with other individual action contexts is only suggestive, but Pfeffer and Salancik (1978, 12) note the limited explanatory power of leadership in research on administrative performance:

> Studies estimating the effects of administrators have found them to account for 10 percent of the variance in organizational performance, a striking contrast to the 90 percent of the intellectual effort that has been devoted to developing theories of individual action.

It is conceivable that the efforts of whistleblowers, even when they may be described as heroic, will have only small consequences for organizational performance.

To summarize, it appears that several factors may have operated to attenuate the voice–performance linkages inferred from general theory. Among these factors are the dissensus nature of some whistleblowing disputes, the ambiguity of performance norms in the sample of organizations studied, and the limited effects of individual action on organizational performance.

The results of the research are far clearer with respect to organizational control than to organizational performance. An organization's control of its resources and decision-making autonomy can be affected by a whistleblower's actions. The results indicate that issues that are resolved externally have a significantly greater probability of leading to reductions in organizational control than do those that are resolved internally. Although the relationship between suppression of whistleblowing and organizational control did not reach statistical significance, the size of the association suggests that organizations face a tradeoff between lack of responsiveness to internal reformers and loss of organizational autonomy.

The multivariate statistical results show that the amount of an organization's power does not immunize it from external control. What is pivotal in determining organizational control is whether the whistleblower engages in effective political behavior. Effective political behavior often involves some form of issue expansion as a means for moving the whistleblower's concerns to a formal governmental or systemic agenda (Cobb and Elder 1983). According to one observer interviewed for the study:

> As often as tradition and inertia win, it is also true that the powers that be fall frequently. . . . One needs to be very strategic within the organization and get the message to key constituents. Whistleblowers can succeed if they pursue significant matters—that is, politically appropriate constituencies.

The expansion to identification groups, attention groups, and the attentive public (Cobb and Elder 1983) is the primary means for arresting control from the organization.

Conclusions

In general, what can be concluded about the efficacy of whistleblowing? The results tend to reinforce some existing notions about the limitations of whistleblowing as a mechanism for organizational change. Although performance was not sensitive to organizational policies, the research indicated that appeals to external forces could decrease organizational autonomy and thereby increase accountability. Overall, one must conclude that whistleblowing, under existing institutional rules, has a very limited role to play in correcting specific abuses and promoting organizational change.

One of the difficult challenges encountered in this research involved identifying relationships between a whistleblower's actions and organizational consequences. The case survey methods used in the research dealt adequately with the problems of quantifying and comparing cases, but they did not address the criteria for attributing causality to the whistleblower's actions. Attributing causality is a risky endeavor even when available data are less constrained than they were in this research. Future research will have to employ different strategies to overcome the problem. One strategy might be to conduct a small number of prospective, in-depth case studies to develop more completely a theory of voice and organizational change. The in-depth case studies would be useful for observing cross-level (micro vs. macro) changes and the dynamics associated with them.

Appendix: Operational Definitions

Hostility toward the whistleblower is a count of the number of "yes" responses to retaliation questions in the case survey or self-administered survey.

> *Case survey*—A count of affirmative responses for the following items: poor performance appraisal; denial of promotion; denial of opportunity for training; assigned less desirable or less important duties in current job; transfer or reassignment to a different job with less desirable duties; reassignment to a different geographic location; suspension from job; grade level demotion; fired from job.

> *Self-administered survey*—A count of affirmative responses to "Did this occur?" for the following items: poor performance appraisal; denial of promotion; denial of opportunity for training; assigned less desirable or less important duties in current job; transfer or reassignment to a different job with less desirable duties; reassignment to a different geographic location; suspension from job; grade-level demotion; fired from job.

Resolution of the issue: the extent to which the claims of the whistleblower are resolved.

> *Case survey*—Responses to question (11).

> (1) resolved
> (2) only partially resolved; major aspects of the allegation were unresolved
> (3) not at all resolved

> *Self-administered survey*—*Responses to question (20), "What ended the controversy?" categorized in the following way:*

> (1) "I felt that my concerns had been completely addressed."
> (2) "I felt that my concerns were satisfactorily resolved by compromise."
> (3) "I stopped pursuing my claim because I became discouraged that any change would occur" or "I stopped pursuing my claim because I ran out of resources [e.g., money and time]" or "The controversy has not ended; it is ongoing."

Organizational policy's punishment of legitimate claims refers to the extent to which the organization has responded favorably to previous whistleblower claims. An agency index was created from aggregated employee responses to an item used in the 1980 MSPB Whistleblower Survey (item 22–8) and repeated in the 1983 Merit Principles Survey (item 20–6). The item asked respondents to indicate reasons for not reporting fraud, waste, or mismanagement. Affirmative responses to the option "I did not think that anything *would* be done to correct the activity" were taken as an indicator of this variable. The 1980 departmental score was used for all cases originating in 1982 or earlier. The 1983 departmental score was used for cases originating in 1983 or later. The department score was created by summing the responses of all respondents from the organization and dividing by the number of respondents.

Organizational policy's reward of illegitimate claims is the extent to which the organization has acquiesced to dubious claims in past whistleblower cases. It was measured using a departmental score created from responses to the following item from the 1983 Merit Principles Survey: "To what extent, if any, are the following an obstacle to taking disciplinary action against employees who do not improve their performance?" possibility of whistleblower complaint (ranging from "to no extent" to "a very great extent"). The department score was created by summing the responses of all respondents from the organization and dividing by the number of respondents.

Organizational performance is the extent to which the organization is perceived as fulfilling its mission.

> *Case survey*—Recorded responses to the following close-ended question: "Did the organization's performance improve or decline as a result of the whistleblowing episode?"
>
> (1) "The organization's performance declined (cost increases, decreases in efficiency) as a result of the whistleblowing episode."
> (2) "There is no evidence of changes (e.g., increases in efficiency, cost savings) in performance as a result of the whistleblowing episode."
> (3) "Improvements were made in internal control systems or procedures [e.g., accounting system changes, reporting requirements] but there were no visible changes in cost or efficiency," or "There was evidence of increases in efficiency or cost savings."

> *Self-administered survey*—Responses to the following item: "To what extent has the performance of the organization for which you worked at the time of the incident changed since you reported the incident?"

(1) The performance of the organization has improved significantly.
(2) The performance of the organization is unchanged.
(3) The performance of the organization has declined significantly.

External whistleblowing channels are those that lie outside the organization through which the whistleblower may present claims of illegal, illegitimate, and immoral activity.

Case survey—External channels equals "1" if "Office of the Special Counsel," "member of Congress," or "media" were checked "Yes"; external channels equals "0" if the three options above were not "Yes."

Self-administered survey—External channels equals "1" if respondent checked "Office of the Special Counsel", "member of Congress", or "media" for question (14); external channels equals "0" if these options were not checked.

Externally derived solutions are solutions to the whistleblower's claims that are imposed by external authorities.

Case survey—External solution equals "1" if the response to question "Was the resolution of the claim the result of action by someone outside the organization?" was scored 1 (courts), 2 (Congress), or 3 (other); "0" if scored 4 (no); "8" (not applicable) if scored 9 (not resolved).

Self-administered survey—External solution equals "1" if response to question (24) was "courts" or "Congress"; "0" if courts or Congress were not checked; "8" (not applicable) if respondent checked "The claim has not been resolved."

Organizational control is the extent to which the organization maintains control over major decisions.

Response to the following question in the case survey: "Did the organization lose control over any of its authority?"

(1) Yes, organizational authority was *revoked* by external authorities.
(2) Yes, organizational authority was *constrained* by external authorities.
(3) No.

Organizational power is the extent to which the organization possesses resources that may be used to persuade other actors. It was measured by the size of the parent organization measured in constant dollars (in the year in which the allegation was made).

Suppress internal and external whistleblowing is the extent to which the organization takes actions to prevent whistleblowers from pursuing their claims both inside and outside the organization. An agency index was created from aggregated employee responses to an item used in the 1980 MSPB Whistleblower Survey (item 28) and repeated in the 1983 Merit Principles Survey (item 23). The item was: "Within the last 12 months, have you personally experienced some type of reprisal or threat of reprisal because of an activity you reported?" The 1980 departmental score was used for all cases originating in 1982 or earlier. The 1983 departmental score was used for all cases originating in 1983 or later. The department score was created by summing the responses of all respondents from the organization and dividing by the number of respondents.

References

Bowie, Norman. 1982. *Business Ethics*. Englewood Cliffs, NJ: Prentice Hall.

Cobb, R.W., and Elder, C.D. 1983. *Participation in American Politics: The Dynamics of Agenda-Building*. Baltimore, MD: Johns Hopkins University Press.

Devine, T.M., and Aplin, D.G. 1986. "Abuse of Authority: The Office of the Special Counsel and Whistleblower Protection." *Antioch Law Journal* 4.

Glazer, Myron P., and Glazer, Penina M. 1989. *The Whistleblowers: Exposing Corruption in Government and Industry*. New York: Basic Books.

Graham, J.W. 1986. "Principled Organizational Dissent: A Theoretical Essay." *Research in Organizational Behavior* 8: 1–52.

Harshbarger, D. 1973. "The Individual and the Social Order: Notes on the Management of Heresy and Deviance in Complex Organizations." *Human Relations* 26: 251–69.

Hirschman, A.O. 1970. *Exit, Voice, and Loyalty: Responses to Decline in Firms, Organizations, and States*. Cambridge, MA: Harvard University Press.

Johnson, Roberta A., and Kraft, Michael E. 1989. *Bureaucratic Whistleblowing and Policy Change*. Washington, DC: United States Environmental Protection Agency.

Jos, Philip. 1990. "Whistleblowing, Accountability, and Professional Ethics." Paper delivered at the American Society for Public Administration Symposium on Public Administration Research, April 7–8, Los Angeles.

Jos, Philip H.; Tompkins, Mark E.; and Hays, Steven W. 1989. "In Praise of Difficult People: A Portrait of the Committed Whistleblower." *Public Administrative Review* 49: 552–61.

Kish, L. 1965. *Survey Sampling*. New York: John Wiley.

Kolarska, L., and Aldrich, H. 1980. "Exit, Voice, and Silence: Consumers' and Managers' Responses to Organizational Decline." *Organization Studies* 1: 41–58.

McClintock, C.C.; Brannon, D.; and Maynard–Moody, S. 1979. "Applying the Logic of Sample Surveys to Qualitative Case Studies: The Case Cluster Method." *Administrative Science Quarterly* 24: 612–29.

Mansbridge, Jane J. 1990. *Beyond Self-Interest*. Chicago: The University of Chicago Press.

Miceli, M.P., and Near, J.P. 1984. "The Relationships among Beliefs, Organizational Position, and Whistle-Blowing Status: A Discriminant Analysis." *Academy of Management Journal* 27: 687–705.

———. 1985. "Characteristics of Organizational Climate and Perceived Wrongdoing Associated with Whistle-Blowing Decisions." *Personnel Psychology* 38: 525–44.

Near, J.P., and Miceli, M.P. 1986. "Whistle-Blowers in Organizations: Dissidents or Reformers?" *Research in Organizational Behavior* 9: 321–68.

O'Day, R. 1974. "Intimidation Rituals: Reactions to Reform." *Journal of Applied Behavioral Science* 10: 373–86.

Pfeffer, J., and Salancik, G.R. 1978. *The External Control of Organizations: A Resource Dependence Perspective.* New York: Harper & Row.

Soeken, K.L., and Soeken, D.R. 1987. "A Survey of Whistleblowers: Their Stressors and Coping Strategies." Unpublished manuscript.

Staw, B.M. 1980. "Rationality and Justification in Organizational Life." *Research in Organizational Behavior* 2: 45–80.

Staw, B.M.; Sandelands, L.E.; and Dutton, J.E. 1981. "Threat-Rigidity Effects in Organizational Behavior: A Multilevel Analysis." *Administrative Science Quarterly* 26: 501–24.

Tetlock, P. 1985. "Accountability: The Neglected Social Context of Judgement and Choice. *Research in Organizational Behavior* 7: 297–332.

Weinstein, D. 1979. *Bureaucratic Opposition: Challenging Abuses at the Workplace.* New York: Pergamon.

Westin, A.F. 1981. *Whistleblowing! Loyalty and Dissent in the Corporation.* New York: McGraw-Hill.

Yin, R.K. 1981a. "The Case Study Crisis: Some Answers." *Administrative Science Quarterly* 26: 58–65.

———. 1981b. "The Case Study as a Serious Research Strategy." *Knowledge: Creation, Diffusion, Utilization* 3: 97–114.

Yin, R., and Heald, K. 1975. "Using the Case Survey Method to Analyze Policy Studies." *Administrative Science Quarterly,* 20: 371–81.

Zald, M.N., and Berger, M.A. 1978. "Social Movements in Organizations: Coup d'Etat, Insurgency, and Mass Movements." *American Journal of Sociology* 83: 823–61.

5

Federal Ethics Controls:
The Role of Inspectors General

Paul C. Light

However successful the Inspectors General (IGs) in the federal government had been in building their organizational independence over their first ten years in operation, nothing was more damaging to their reputation than the Department of Housing and Urban Development (HUD) scandal in 1989.[1] Washington seemed ready to believe the worst about the HUD IG, perhaps the entire IG community. In what was already a dismal year for the IGs—a year marked by an effort to constrain their scope of investigatory power, questions about their willingness to protect whistleblowers, continued confusion over their reappointment to office, and a lack of leadership at the Office of Management and Budget (OMB)—the HUD scandal brought the emerging backlash against the IGs to a full boil.

Congress eventually turned to the IG in search of answers to a scandal that involved even HUD secretary Samuel Pierce—a scandal that involved influence peddling, outright theft by local escrow agents (including one aptly named "Robin HUD"), as well as blatant political favoritism. As *Time* asked in its story "The Housing Hustle," "How could such a scandal remain uncovered for so long? The answer lies partly in the fact that no one was looking" (Traver 1989, 19). By implication, that "no one" included the HUD IG.

Indeed, as members of Congress and the media scurried for cover, the IG became a convenient target. "How could we have missed this one?" members asked. "We simply were not told," they answered. "And, if we were told, we were not told in the right way. Too much audit language. Not the right vehicle. Not loud enough." For Representative Christopher Shays (R-CT), a member of the House Government Operations Subcommittee on Employment and Housing that investigated the scandal, the IG was somehow part of what he saw as a "cover-up." The following exchange between Shays and HUD IG Paul Adams merely placed on the record what some in Washington were privately thinking:

> Mr. Shays: My impression of the IG's office was that you looked at wrong-doing, found it out, and then you made sure something was done about it. . . .
>
> Mr. Adams: First of all, Mr. Shays, the investigation was ongoing, so we didn't have the final report nor did we have the final audit. We did report it to Congress in our September 30, 1988, report, semiannual report to Congress, that we had problems and it was an ongoing effort.
>
> Mr. Shays: You are missing my point here. I am talking in general. See, I have a lot of faith, historically have had a lot of faith in the concept of an IG's office. My understanding is we have an IG's office so we wouldn't have the kind of problems we are uncovering, and I, frankly, this is—you know, I am not going to be shocked any more, I am simply not going to be because nothing is going to shock me. . . .
>
> My point, though, it is your job to make sure this doesn't happen, isn't it? That is the whole reason why we have the IG's office. And once you uncover it, to make sure it doesn't happen again. [U.S. House of Representatives 1989, 499]

This is not the place to review the HUD scandal; that challenge has been met by both congressional investigating committees. In this essay, the HUD case is of use as an illustration of the IG's role in looking for scandal in the agency.

An Introduction to the IG Concept

The autumn of 1978 was a busy time for government reformers. In just three weeks, Congress passed the Civil Service Reform Act, the Ethics in Government Act, and a government-wide Inspector General Act. These were some of the most important administrative reforms in decades.[2]

Of the three reform measures passed that fall, the Inspector General Act was certainly the least visible. The bill, which was designed to consolidate internal audit and investigation, was hardly the stuff of which major floor debates are made.

On the surface, the purpose of Public Law 95–452 seemed simple: (1) conduct and supervise audits and investigations of programs in the twelve departments and agencies covered; (2) promote economy and efficiency and prevent fraud and abuse; and (3) keep the "head of the establishment" and Congress fully and currently informed. The list of IG duties was similar, albeit much more detailed:

1. supervise, coordinate, and provide policy for auditing and investigations relating to programs and operations of the department or agency;
2. recommend policies for, and conduct, supervise, or coordinate other

activities carried out or financed by the department or agency for the purpose of promoting economy and efficiency and detecting fraud, waste, and abuse in its programs and operations;

3.   recommend policy for, and conduct, supervise, or coordinate relationships between the department or agency and other federal agencies, as well as state and local governments;

4.   review existing and proposed legislation and regulations concerning impact on the economy and efficiency in the administration of programs administered or financed by the department or agency or the prevention and detection of fraud, waste, and abuse; and

5.   keep the head of the establishment and Congress informed by means of reports and other communication.

In pursuit of these purposes and duties, every IG was to be appointed by the president "solely on the basis of integrity and demonstrated ability" and confirmed by the Senate. Every IG also was to appoint an assistant IG for audits and an assistant IG for investigations. The I.G. also had full authority to undertake whatever audits and investigations deemed necessary to ferret out fraud, waste, and abuse.

Furthermore, every IG was to have access to all "information, documents, reports, answers, records, accounts, papers, and other data and documentary evidence" needed for an audit or investigation; was to have the right to request assistance from within the agency and information from across government; was to be granted the authority to subpoena documents (but not witnesses or testimony); was to be given the right to hire and fire staff; and was to have "direct and prompt" access to the secretary or administration whenever necessary and for any purpose.

All Congress required from the IG in return was a semiannual report that would include the following: a description of every significant problem, abuse, and deficiency the IG encountered in the previous six months; a description of recommendations for action; an identification of each significant recommendation upon which action had not been taken; a summary of matters referred to "prosecutive authorities," meaning the Department of Justice and the FBI; a summary of each report made to the secretary or administrator and a listing of each report completed during the reporting period. In short, a summary of everything.

Under law, each semiannual report was to reach the head of the department or agency not later than April 30 and October 31 of each year. In turn, the secretary or administrator was to forward the report to Congress *without any changes* within thirty days. In addition, any IG who became aware of "particularly serious or flagrant problems, abuses, or deficiencies" was to report immediately to the department or agency head. That department or agency head was, in turn, to transmit the report, again *without any changes*, to Congress within seven days.

It was a simple statute, only ten pages long, hardly enough to matter. Yet of all the good government bills passed in the 1970s or 1980s, the IG Act may be most important as a metaphor for an increasingly visible philosophy of governance, a philosophy that focuses on monitoring and internal regulation—not employees, dollars, or agencies—as the primary devices for assuring program success.

As Table 5.1 suggests, the IG concept was clearly an idea whose time had come. Starting with Health, Education, and Welfare (HEW) in 1976, Congress expanded the concept *thirteen* times over the next fifteen years. Inspectors general were added to the newly created Department of Energy in 1977; they were added to Agriculture, Commerce, Housing and Urban Development, Interior, Labor, Transportation, the Community Services Administration, Environmental Protection Agency, General Services Administration, National Aeronautics and Space Administration, Small Business Administration, and the Veterans' Administration in 1978; to State in 1980; to Defense in 1982; and to Justice, Treasury, and a host of small agencies in 1988. With their expansion to the Central Intelligence Agency in 1989, IGs existed in virtually every corner of government.

By 1990, there were twenty-seven presidential advise and consent IGs—these were appointed by the president with Senate confirmation—and there were thirty-four smaller agency IGs—all appointed by an agency head without presidential sanction or Senate confirmation. Two of the early presidential IGs, at Community Services and Synfuels, went out of business when their agencies were abolished in the early days of President Ronald Reagan's administration.

Looking back over the legislative history of the IG Act, it is important to note that, notwithstanding Representative Shays, the IG was given no authority to *solve* problems—that is, to suspend programs, fire incompetent appointees, or reprogram funds. The IG's only duty under statute was to *inform* Congress and the secretary of the concerns, *offer* possible remedies, and *monitor* responses, if any. Indeed, Congress reserved the problem of high-level scandal for the independent counsels created at almost the same moment; this gave the IG no power whatsoever to mandate reform. Thus, as Pierce himself testified, he had refused to act on a March 1988 IG recommendation to suspend the Section 8 Moderate Rehabilitation (Mod Rehab) Program.[3] When he was asked how he could so "cavalierly disregard" the IG, Pierce said "I wanted to give the [other staff] a chance. After all, there were other people involved with this who were working on this thing and that was my General Counsel, the Under Secretary as well as the Assistant Secretary of House. These people know something too. *The IG is not God*" (U.S. House of Representatives 1989, 209).

Indeed so. The IG, only one of seven executive level IV appointees at HUD, reported to an executive level II deputy and was only one of many senior and not-so-senior appointees vying for the secretary's attention. By 1987, HUD had become the fourth most politicized agency in government, with thirty-one non-career senior executives and 100 schedule C personal and confidential assistants surrounding the secretary. One of these assistants just happened to be thirty-five-

Table 5.1

Expansion of the IG Concept, 1976–90

Date	Statute	Establishment
		Presidentially Appointed IGs
1976	P.L. 94–505	Health, Education, and Welfare
1977	P.L. 95–91	Energy
1978	P.L. 95–452	Agriculture, Commerce, Housing and Urban Development, Interior, Labor, Transportation, Community Services Administration, Environmental Protection Agency, General Services Administration, National Aeronautics and Space Administration, Small Business Administration, Veterans' Administration
1979	P.L. 96–88	Education
1980	P.L. 96–294	U.S. Synfuels Corporation
1980	P.L. 96–464	State
1981	P.L. 97–113	Agency for International Development
1982	P.L. 97–252	Defense
1983	P.L. 98–76	Railroad Retirement Board
1986	P.L. 99–399	U.S. Information Agency
1987	P.L. 100–213	Arms Control and Disarmament Agency
1988	P.L. 100–504	Justice, Treasury, Federal Emergency Management Administration, Nuclear Regulatory Commission, Office of Personnel Management
1989	P.L. 101–73	Resolution Trust Corporation
1989	P.L. 100–193	Central Intelligence Agency
		Agency Head Appointed IGs
1988	P.L. 100–504	ACTION, Amtrak, Appalachian Regional Commission, Board of Governors of the Federal Reserve System, Board for International Broadcasting, Commodity Futures Trading Commission, Consumer Product Safety Commission, Corporation for Public Broadcasting, Equal Employment Opportunity Commission, Farm Credit Administration, Federal Communications Commission, Federal Deposit Insurance Corporation, Federal Election Commission, Federal Home Loan Bank Board, Federal Labor Relations Authority, Federal Maritime Commission, Federal Trade Commission, Government Printing Office, Interstate Commerce Commission, Legal Service Corporation, National Archives and Records Administration, National Credit Union Administration, National Endowment for the Arts, National Endowment for the Humanities, National Labor Relations Board, National Science Foundation, Panama Canal Commission, Peace Corps, Pension Benefit Guaranty Corporation, Securities and Exchange Commission, Smithsonian Institution, Tennessee Valley Authority, United States International Trade Commission, United States Postal Service

Source: Kaiser, Fred. "Inspectors General: Establishing Statutes and Statistics." Washington, D.C.: Congressional Research Service, The Library of Congress, July 10, 1990.

year-old Deborah Gore Dean, who allegedly converted the Mod Rehab program into a political slush fund. Congress could hardly expect the IG, tasked as he was to be the strong right arm of the secretary, to suddenly turn lone wolf, particularly after six years of cuts in the number of his auditors and investigators. Nor could Congress expect a greatly weakened OIG to keep track of programs that, at the same time, had been converted to give the HUD secretary much greater discretion.

Finally, Congress could hardly expect the IG alone to prevent activities planned by individuals so clearly intent on defrauding the government. There is at least some evidence that the participants in the scandal designed their schemes anticipating potential IG investigations. In regard to misuse of the HUD Technical Assistance (TA) program, the HUD deputy assistant secretary for program policy development and evaluation testified that he deliberately shifted responsibility from headquarters to the field after he looked at the IG staffing:

> What I would do is, I began to move funds . . . to the field because in central headquarters he was very strongly staffed and had the capability and staff numbers set aside to review and do pre-audits on TA contracts. So what I would do is, I would kind of look at his organization pattern on where he had the fewest employees at, and I began to move money because I knew that they didn't have the time to do pre-audits . . . this allowed me the flexibility to move funds out of headquarters into the field, into area offices where his manpower and resources had to be categorized and prioritized, and therefore the TA Program would not be one of them they were prioritized for auditing purposes as far as pre-audits. [U.S. House of Representatives 1990, 67].

Even when the HUD IG did find a problem, there was often little cooperation from the top. The House Government Operations Employment and Housing Subcommittee that investigated the scandal went so far as to use an old audit term—"material weakness"—to describe what it saw as "the HUD inspector general's inability to force an issue at HUD with Secretary Pierce. This was exacerbated by a HUD management which was often not responsive to and in some instances antagonistic to the findings and recommendations by the Inspector General" (U.S. House of Representatives 1990, 6).

A Different Path

Congress could have taken a different path with the IGs, however, particularly if it had considered seriously the original concept introduced in 1975 as H.R. 5302 by Representative Benjamin Rosenthal (D-NY). That Rosenthal envisioned a very different IG cannot be in question. Consider, for example, the five basic tenets of Rosenthal's bill (U.S. House of Representatives, H.R. 5302).

First, like all future IGs, Rosenthal's IG was to be a presidential appointee subject to Senate confirmation. Unlike the future IGs, however, this IG was to "serve for a term of ten years; may be removed only by impeachment, and may not be reappointed upon the expiration of such term or removal from office." Rosenthal believed that lack of reappointment would ensure that the IG would have no incentives to take the edge off any recommendation or report.

Second, unlike any future IGs, Rosenthal's IG was to only be responsible for investigations. The word "audit" does not appear anywhere in the entire bill, nor does the list of duties and responsibilities mention anything about economy, efficiency, fraud, waste, or abuse. The IG's mandate was simple yet sweeping: "Investigate each program which is administered by the Department of Health, Education, and Welfare and which involves the application or disbursement of Federal funds."

Third, unlike any future IGs, Rosenthal's IG was to "appoint and fix the pay of such personnel as he deems advisable." What Rosenthal intended by the provision remains in doubt. Did he imagine the IG, who was to be paid at level IV of the executive pay schedule, paying staff more than that, or did he merely want to reserve for the IG the routine pay and classification decisions that go into the creation of a new government enterprise? Whatever the answer it was a highly unusual authority, and it clearly separated the IG from normal HEW procedures.

Fourth, Rosenthal's IG was to transmit an annual report summarizing the year's investigations to Congress and the secretary of HEW simultaneously under the following proviso: "Notwithstanding any other provision of law or regulation issues thereunder, the Inspector General shall directly transmit such report to Congress and may not be required by any person to submit such report to such person for approval prior to such transmission." In short, there were to be no clearance or changes from HEW.

Fifth, and quite relevant to the contemporary debate, Rosenthal's IG was to have testimonial subpoena power. Although all future IGs would have the authority to compel documents through subpoena, Rosenthal's IG was the only one that was ever granted such sweeping power to demand attendance of witnesses and the production of evidence "from any place in the United States at any designated place of hearing within the United States."

When it is compared to the IG bill that eventually emerged under Representative L.H. Fountain's (D-NC) sponsorship, Rosenthal's proposal can be seen as narrow yet extreme. On the one hand, the IG would operate within a relatively limited mandate and would investigate only programs involving federal funds, not the third-party providers, Social Security counterfeiters, generic drug manufacturers, steroid salesmen, or cigarette vendors selling to teenagers—all areas of inquiry for future Health and Human Services (HHS) IG Kusserow. Moreover, by denying a role for audit, the IG would lose an important source of day-to-day information.

On the other hand, Rosenthal's IG was unassailably independent, reporting to no one but Congress, protected against removal, insulated from personal ambition, and given a potent investigatory tool—the testimonial subpoena—that today's IGs desperately want. As Rosenthal explained his proposal before Fountain's subcommittee, to which the bill had been referred:

> Consider HEW, if you will, as a mammoth service-oriented corporation. With a budget of $188.4 billion, HEW has larger revenues than Exxon, General Motors, Ford, Texaco, Mobil Oil, and Standard Oil of California combined.
>
> Now imagine that each of these six largest industrial corporations in the United States was audited by an accounting firm whose head was hired by the chief executive of the corporation and whose financial report had to be reviewed as approved by the chief executive before being submitted, if ever, to the board of directors. That, obviously would be ludicrous. It not only does not make sense, but it would violate numerous Federal securities laws. [U.S. House of Representatives 1976, 10]

Ultimately, of course, Congress went a very different direction, and created an IG who would be more a part of the HEW management team. This IG would be subject to easier removal by the president, free from any term of office and therefore reappointable for roughly forever, stripped of testimonial subpoena authority, yet he would report simultaneously to Congress and the president and would be granted broader audit and investigative duties—in short, less power but more oversight territory.

On the appointment side of the measure, for example, the bill dropped Rosenthal's proposal for a fixed term of office and removal only through impeachment. It substituted the essentially hortatory requirement that the IG and deputy IG be appointed "solely on the basis of integrity and demonstrated ability and without regard to political affiliation" and adopted a modified version of language recommended by the General Accounting Office, which placed the IG under the general supervision of the secretary "*or, to the extent such authority is delegated,*" the undersecretary.

The fine print of the Fountain proposal is not so important, however, as the overall thrust. Congress had reached a crossroads on the IG concept and had elected to take the quieter path. As we shall see, the decision to make the IG both a strong right arm of the secretary and an independent conduit to Congress created an IG job description of great risk and potential.

It was inevitable that Rosenthal's "IG with chutzpah," as he once described it, would be lost, particularly given the later fights with the White House over the 1978 bill. As the Governmental Affairs Committee noted in its legislative report, which accompanied the final bill, the IG concept had to balance independence against the needs of management and take into account the lingering concerns that "the Inspector and Auditor General may become an adversary of the agency head and undermine his ability to run the agency." Although the committee recognized the need to protect the IG from undue pressure, it also stated its view that "an Inspector . . . General's efforts will be significantly impaired if he does not have a smooth working relationship with the department head." In the most significant statement of future expectations in the legislative record of the IG Act, the committee offered the following assessment:

> If the agency head is committed to running and managing the agency effectively and to rooting out fraud, abuse, and waste at all levels, the Inspector . . . General can be his strong right arm in doing so, while maintaining the independence needed to honor his reporting obligations to Congress. The committee does not doubt that some tension can result from this relationship, but the committee believes that the potential advantages far outweigh the risks. [U.S. Senate 1978, 9]

The IG and HUD

Even this brief review suggests that Congress could hardly expect the IG to be the last best hope against high-level scandal and certainly not scandal of the kind involved in the Pierce administration. Nevertheless, when one reads back through the sixteen reports covering the Reagan/Pierce administration in one sitting, the warnings now seem abundantly clear. These warnings always began on a the very first page, in the brief IG's forward.[4]

In fact, only in the very first report covering April–October 1981, did the first page *not* mention some significant department problem or problems. Even in this first report, which likely gave Pierce the benefit of the doubt as a new secretary, the IG pulled no punches with strong criticisms in sections titled "Serious Accounting Deficiencies," "Inadequate Monitoring of Program Participants," and "Corrective Actions Promised But Not Taken."

After 1981, the criticisms moved to the front page, as every report detailed yet another problem or repeated a request for congressional action. According to the following excerpts from the seven reports that covered Pierce's first term—the period in which Congress and the press would have the greatest cause to blame the IG for complacency—the problems were present long before Reagan was sworn in for his second term:

> *October 1981 to March 1982*   The Department has problems with (1) program management (including planning, executive and monitoring); and (2) resource and asset management. This report deals with a number of major weaknesses in program monitoring and accounting functions. Our prior semiannual reports contained specifics on other aspects of these two broad areas. The Department has had a long history of these problems.

> *April to September 1982*   As we stated in our last report, the Department has problems with (1) program management . . . and (2) resource and asset management. This report highlights a number of major weaknesses in controls over fund management by the Department and its program participants, as well as problems in program management by HUD staff. Also the report provides illustrations of significant abuses of various HUD programs by participants.

October 1982 to March 1983   One particularly frustrating item needs to be mentioned here. For almost two years our office has been working with program managers to obtain legislation that would enable the Department to collect and use data for computer matches of applicant eligibility. The proposals have not been brought to the Congress for a vote due to a variety of reasons. Our efforts and related problems have been reported in the last two semiannual reports and now in this current one. We urge the Congress to take note of this matter and assist in the passage of this sorely needed legislation.

April to September 1983   This report summarizes the significant problems noted and recommendations made during the period and emphasizes our audit focus on weaknesses in the operations of financially troubled Public Housing Agencies.

October 1983 to March 1984   Our office devoted significant resources to reviewing the public housing program. Within the Department, we examined HUD's operating policies and procedures. Externally, we focused on the overall management of financially troubled Public Housing Agencies (PHAs). While the majority of PHAs operate effectively, there are inherent weaknesses that need attention. The Department must improve its ability to detect problems and assist PHAs in meeting their goals and objectives. We believe there is a pressing need for cooperative efforts at the Federal, State, and local levels to address these weaknesses, thereby improving the public housing program.

April to September 1984   This report illustrates continued weaknesses in HUD's monitoring of program participants. Although the Department has repeatedly attempted to improve its performance, inadequate monitoring continues to be a persistent problem of significant concern to us.

October 1984 to March 1985   This report summarizes problems in such diverse HUD programs as Single Family insured loans, Section 8 Moderate Rehabilitation, and Section 312 Rehabilitation loans. As an example, the Single Family Program has had significant new initiatives during the past few years. However, management controls to ensure program integrity do not appear to have kept pace with these changes. [U.S. Department of Housing and Urban Development 1981–85]

Moreover, buried within the reports is warning after warning about accounting systems, financial controls, lack of internal oversight, and managerial weaknesses. "Scandals like HUD's make big news," GAO reported in 1990, "But what makes them possible is a situation less 'newsworthy' but more far-reaching than any particular case of wrongdoing or mismanagement. Weak internal controls and second-rate accounting systems allow these incidents to happen" (U.S. General Accounting Office 1990, 11). As GAO noted,

In 1987, for example, HUD reported in its annual Financial Integrity Act report that inadequate controls in the property disposition process provided the potential for closing agents to manipulate or otherwise take funds for their own use. In 1989, a closing agent nicknamed "Robin HUD" testified that she had done just that. [U.S. General Accounting Office 1990, 11]

Warnings about these weaknesses had been available from the beginning of the Pierce administration. The IG's April–September 1981 report specifically noted that audits "have consistently noted many problems such as the failure to reconcile accounts, erroneous financial reports, delays in processing financial data, incorrect entries, and incorrect and incomplete data supplies by program offices. As a result, HUD's finances cannot be determined with any degree of reliance." It does not take a Certified Public Accounting degree to understand the language. This was a system ready for manipulation.

Looking back, there can be little doubt that Congress, the president, the secretary, and the press had ample warning of the impending collapse, particularly if they read back through their stacks of semiannual reports in one sitting.

Alas, this is not how most IG reports are read. From my personal experience as a Senate staffer, I know that most IG reports get a quick skim and a toss, if they get read at all. Moreover, at the same time the HUD IG reports gave warning, they gave reassurance. As Senator William Roth (R-DE), chairman of the Senate Governmental Affairs Committee during the first six years of the Reagan administration, remarked, "Frankly, just reading through these, you know, you sort of think there really is not a problem, that it is being taken care of" (U.S. Senate 1990 A, Vol. 1, 10).

First, as with reports from other IGs, every HUD report started with the list of statistical accomplishments, a list that grows with each year. From April–September 1981—"Our office . . . was instrumental in achieving cash recoveries and savings to HUD from audits, accounting to nearly $24 million. Recoveries from investigations produced an addition $1.9 million. . . .We also opened 1,168 investigation cases and referred 457 cases for prosecutive considerations. A total of 111 persons or firms were indicated, while 68 persons or firms were convicted, including one HUD employee"—to the very end of the Pierce administration in the April–September 1988 report that celebrated the tenth anniversary of the IG Act—"During the 10 years as a statutory IG Office, our accomplishments have included: cash recoveries of over $542 million; cost efficiencies of over $307 million; convictions of 2,840 persons or firms; and the implementation of a fraud awareness program"—there was always evidence of progress, without congressional action to pass the computer matching legislation.

Second, and much more important, the IG's message almost always contained hope and even the occasional celebration of progress made. The messages began in the IG's forward in the first semiannual report covering Pierce, the one that contained nary a note of criticism, and continued throughout the first two terms. Except for the October 1984 to March 1985 reporting period, which contained nothing but warnings and a promise to keep working on the problem, the rest of the reports in the first four years held at least some excuse for Congress to breathe easily:

April to September 1981   As evidenced by the efforts described in this Semi-annual Report, the Secretary and his staff are fully committed to improving the integrity, efficiency, effectiveness, and responsiveness of HUD management and programs. The support and cooperation afforded our office has been excellent. We are looking forward to further cooperative efforts in the future.

October 1981 to March 1982   As a matter of perspective, we would like to comment on the unprecedented cooperation we have received from the current management team. We commend the attitudes and actions of those managers who are dedicated to addressing the problems in HUD.

April to September 1982   HUD managers and employees are cooperating and supporting our work. There has been an increased emphasis by managers on accountability of HUD staff and program participants. . . .We are encouraged by these signs of growing concern for improved management and program integrity.

October 1982 to March 1983   We are working with program managers to resolve and correct these problems.

April to September 1983   This effort is continuing and HUD management has been very receptive to our recommendations for improving Public Housing Agency operations.

October 1983 to March 1984   Departmental efforts to assess program vulnerabilities, increase employee awareness, and redirect monitoring to high-risk areas clearly demonstrate the Department's commitment to strengthen operations and to minimize fraud and abuse. We commend management for this commitment and strongly urge its continuation.

April to September 1984   The Secretary and Under Secretary have taken an active interest in correcting this situation. They have supported changes in monitoring policies and procedures. Their interest is demonstrated in the Department's effort to obtain legislative authority that would make computer matching more feasible and to initiate a quality control system for rental assistance payments.

October 1984 to March 1985   In the next 6 months, we will be doing additional work to determine the extent of these problems and how to help the Department solve them.

The positive signals were also evident in the only hearing Congress ever held on a HUD semiannual report, during which Adams blamed the media in part for inflating perceptions of the pervasiveness of HUD's problems.

Looking back, with perfect hindsight of course, Adams and his staff seem far too gentle. After all, this was not some isolated wrongdoing. As the House Government Operations Committee put it:

> During the 1980s, HUD was enveloped by influence peddling, favoritism, abuse, greed, fraud, embezzlement and theft. In many housing programs objective criteria gave way to political preference and cronyism, and favoritism supplanted fairness. "Discretionary" became a buzzword for "giveaway." [U.S. House of Representatives 1990, 3]

Looking Up

How could the IG have missed it? A first answer is that the IG did not miss "it" at all. In fact, it was a two-year audit of the public housing agencies that culminated in the damning allegations regarding almost $413 million in excess payments that led Representative Thomas Lantos (D-CA) to launch the primary HUD investigation. After that, Lantos and his subcommittee, using the full investigatory powers of Congress, quickly unraveled the massive fraud.

As for the influence-peddling scheme at the top of the agency, the IGs simply were not equipped to pursue such high-level wrongdoing. Their task was primarily to look down for scandal, not *up*. Indeed, one can easily argue that such a pursuit might violate fundamentally the nature of the strong right arm model. The IGs are not independent counsels nor are they given the special authority needed for high-level investigations. In short, had Congress wanted a lone wolf investigator it would have adopted the Rosenthal alternative.

Congress itself signaled the IGs that the investigation of high-level scandal was not to be their forte. It reserved that role for independent counsels. In passing the 1978 Ethics in Government Act, Congress created an entirely different mechanism for investigating scandal among executive level I and II appointees—that is, secretaries, administrators, and their deputies. The Ethics Act was not a slap at the IGs at all, but an explicit recognition of the need to limit conflicts of interest in investigations of high-level misconduct. As David Reicher (1983, 985–86) argues,

> When an Inspector General must audit or investigate the head of his own department or agency, however, the Inspector General's statutory responsibility to the head of the establishment will create at least the appearance of a personal conflict of interest. And where personal ties exist between the two officials—ties that have generally developed from the close working relationship contemplated by the statute—an actual conflict of interest is likely to arise. . . . Thus, when an Inspector General is called upon to investigate the head of his own agency, his is asked to investigate the one individual to whom the Act makes him responsible on a day-to-day basis and with whom the Act's drafters expected he would form a close working relationship [Reicher 1983, 985–86]

This is not to suggest that Adams had somehow been duped by Pierce. There is no doubt that both Adams and Charles Dempsey, his predecessor, pursued every lead they had. Rather, it should not be surprising that the IG's focus would be far below the secretary, since that is precisely where the IGs are best equipped to look. Only in the most egregious cases—where the scandal (a) is so odious that it cannot be missed, or (b) has been first uncovered by a congressional committee or the press—can an IG be fully expected to pursue leads to the top of the agency. In such cases, the IG's responsibility to the secretary or administration can be said to be discharged.

In the HUD scandal, this is exactly how the investigation played out. Once Lantos began to take action, the IG became an integral actor in the hunt for evidence, a fact noted by the committee in its final report.

More to the point of this chapter, the central question in the HUD scandal is not so much whether the IG reported clearly, but whether the IG can be held accountable for the failure to catch and highlight the problems earlier, the point raised by Representative Shay. Simply asked, to what extent can the IGs be expected to prevent HUD-like wrongdoing? The answer, as suggested above, is that the IGs offer but one line of defense against scandal, one that is only effective if Congress and the president listen.

In the HUD case, the roots of the scandal were much deeper than simply a problem in fund accounting. As the House Government Operations Committee concluded, the scandal reflected a decade-long politicization of HUD as dozens of new appointees were added at the top of the department, as high rates of turnover occurred among those appointees, as appointees failed to make a commitment to the basic programs they operated, and as there seemed to be an increased tolerance for the "revolving door" by which former appointees returned for favors from their political cronies. According to the report's summary of the Mod Rehab program,

> Projects pushed and lubricated by political well-connected consultants and a cadre of ex-HUD officials received the lion's share of these increasingly scarce and valuable mod rehab funds. Some people with little or no experience in housing made a lot of money for a very limited amount of work. Well-connected political consultants such as former Interior Secretary James Watt received hundreds of thousands of dollars for talking to the "right people" at HUD, including Secretary Pierce, to obtain mod rehab funds. The selection process then in place at HUD for awarding mod rehab funds had all the competitiveness of professional wrestling. [U.S. House of Representatives 1990, 4]

This misuse of discretion was the result of legislation waiving the geographic fair-share allocation process. Under that process, HUD had to spread its Mod Rehab money evenly by formula. With dollars dwindling rapidly under the Reagan budget cuts, Congress acted favorably upon HUD's request for greater freedom, even though Congress surely already knew the extent of petty scandal in the department, a recurring theme in the *Washington Post* and *New York Times* headlines of the early 1980s.[5] Having repealed the fair-share requirement, HUD quickly moved to a noncompetitive, influence-based approach, one about which Congress apparently never asked.

When one looks back with perfect hindsight, the HUD scandal provokes a number of musings about investments made or not made over the past two decades. One cannot help but wonder, for example, whether all the money eventually spent on IG audits, GAO reviews, and congressional investigations after the HUD scandal might have been unnecessary had some money been spent earlier on a financial management system that allowed clear and easy review of exactly where the HUD money was to go. Instead, by the end of the 1980s the HUD financial management system was so weak that the GAO had concluded that HUD was an unauditable agency (U.S. Senate 1990 A, Vol. 1, 470).

Nor can one ignore questions about the politicization of HUD. For example, of the 120 positions that could be said to compose the senior management team corps of HUD in 1984, forty were reserved for political appointees of one kind or another.[6] "With over a third of its top management positions going to noncareer appointments," the Senate HUD investigating committee reported, "political appointees were making in-roads at HUD. And, as an agency, HUD had a significantly higher number of political SES [Securities and Exchange Commission] appointments government-wide. In comparison to other Cabinet agencies for the last ten years, HUD ranked third in the percent of its SES members who were political appointees" (U.S. Senate 1990 B, 180).

The politicization of HUD worried the House as well, although for very different reasons. The House never argued that there was anything inherently wrong with large numbers of political appointees. Rather, the House worried about the *quality* of the appointments, calling the department a "dumping ground," the agency of last resort for political hacks who could not fit elsewhere (U.S. House of Representatives 1990, 68). As one of Pierce's own lieutenants later testified, "Samuel Pierce got loaded up on him a group of Young Turks who were very political and on [White House] must hire list, and we had no housing skills whatsoever" (U.S. House of Representatives 1990, 68).

No doubt it was the president's right to pack the department; no doubt the incentives favored politicization. Yet, surveying the HUD wreckage after the fact, one cannot help but ask whether there might be room for a normative judgment that going with the incentives is not always the best public policy.

If there is one lesson to be learned from the HUD scandal it is that IGs are singularly dependent on their secretaries and administrators for whatever results they achieve. Despite a decade of staff increases and organizational growth, including separate personnel offices and their own general counsels, the IGs still have no power to enforce their recommendations, nor authority to suspend programs *a la* the original State Department Inspector General Foreign Assistance.[7]

In the strong right arm system created under the 1978 IG Act, the IGs have the power to persuade and little more. What else can an IG do?

The IGs can always report to *Congress*, one might answer. Alas, rarely if ever will Congress react. When asked if Congress had ever expressed an interest in his semiannual reports, for example, former HUD IG Dempsey testified, "I never received as much as a phone call. And if I may say . . . at that time, between 1981 and 1984, we investigated the HUD Undersecretary, the Assistant Secretary, the Deputy Assistant Secretary, and three regional administrators. Action was taken against all. We received very heavy publicity in the *Washington Post* and other papers around the country. And I still didn't receive one call. It was reported to the Congress in the semiannual reports but it was also with heavy publicity. I never received one call from a congressional committee" (U.S. Senate 1990 A, Vol. 2, 479).

A second and more important point is that Congress appeared far more interested in "fire alarm" oversight than in the more systematic "police patrol" approach (McCubbins and Schwartz 1984). As the Senate's final HUD report concluded,

> For members of Congress, time is critical. Continuous, in-depth oversight takes significant amounts of time and attention. Increasing pressures on Congress to devote time to new problems leaves little to the analysis of ongoing programs. Congress also finds oversight unglamorous, unless it turns up something which can grab media attention. [U.S. Senate 1990 B, 223]

The failure to implement an IG recommendation is hardly front-page news, rarely the kind of story that yields the political rewards that members of Congress so often value.

Thus, as much as one might criticize the IGs for their reporting style—one congressional staffer remarked that "the IGs could obscure the Revolutionary War"—and as much as one can note that HUD IG Adams used his one congressional appearance in 1986 more to defend Secretary Pierce than to criticize him, there is no doubt that Congress has never taken ownership of the IGs in quite the way opponents once feared they would. The IGs are far less "moles" of Congress in the executive branch than they are orphans, often ignored by members and their staffs alike.

If Congress remains impervious to even the most urgent report, one might answer, the IGs can always report to the *Office of Management and Budget*, as they did on so many occasions in the 1980s. Here, too, interest is likely to be spotty. As noted earlier, the IG relationship with OMB is almost entirely dependent on stable leadership, something that is frequently lacking in the upper reaches of the president's budget office. Unlike Joe Wright, who was Reagan's deputy OMB director for six years before he advanced upward, Bush's first deputy director was gone within two years. He was replaced by the associate deputy director for management, whose main concerns seemed to be more "B" than "M," particularly given his part-time role as the budget officer for national security and defense.

In the HUD scandal, for example, OMB's primary watchdogs were not on the management side of the agency, where but one staffer was available to review the seventy yearly internal control reports required under the Federal Managers Financial Integrity Act; they were in the budget review division, where five budget examiners were responsible for housing, Treasury, and federal personnel. According to the Senate HUD investigation,

> Not surprisingly, these examiners spent almost all their time reviewing very general aggregate program data and addressing major budget policy issues. They claim they had no knowledge that HUD projects were being improperly awarded by officials in the Pierce administration—a fact which is not surprising given that the average examiner spends only two days per year in the field reviewing how the particular programs under his or her jurisdiction are administered. [U.S. Senate 1990, 194–95]

It is precisely this lack of sustained interest that has led some public administration scholars to call for the establishment of a separate Office of Federal Management (OFM) to be cleaved from the old OMB. According to its advocates, what this OFM might lose in budget influence—influence well-used by Wright to provide year after year of IG increases—it would gain in greater focus on government-wide improvement.

With Congress and OMB as unpredictable allies, the IGs have only one other place to turn to win implementation of their recommendations: their own *secretaries and administrators*. What other options do the IGs have? Given the prevailing structure incentives in Congress and OMB, an IG's impact usually starts and ends with a secretary or administrator who takes note. Not unlike U.S. vice presidents, the IGs can be only as influential as their secretaries and administrators want them to be (Light 1983). They may have guaranteed access, ample staff, and sophisticated organizations, but they have no authority to compel their bosses to respond.

Once again, however, the incentives to ignore appear to outweigh the incentives to embrace. As HUD secretary Jack Kemp noted, "HUD inspectors in the past had suffered at best from a kind of benign neglect, as IG report after IG report after IG report outlined the deficiency, mounted one upon the other, year after year, in program after program, and no one listened or took any action" (U.S. Senate 1990 A, Vol. 2, 588). Even when HUD reluctantly admitted a weakness, it often promised repairs that were never made and sometimes claimed progress when none was made.

The challenge of getting internal attention is twofold. First, contrary to the image Congress may have held when it enacted the strong right arm approach in 1978, most secretaries and administrators are not in office long enough to care about long-term management improvements. Appointees, who have an average *in-position* tenure of twenty months, barely have time to learn their jobs, let alone develop working relationships with IGs, or any other long-term institutional players for that matter.

Unfortunately, to many appointees the IGs are just another irritant in what is a long list of "do's and don'ts." "You can't hire who you want, you can't do this, they tell you that you can't fly first class, they tell you that you have to live on per diem, they tell you that you have to be careful not to accept meals," a Carter assistant secretary of labor told the National Academy of Public Administration, referring to no one in particular. "You have to do this, you have to do that, you can't do this, you can't do that. And all you are getting is grief (Mackenzie, 1987, 185–86).

Second, the longer a secretary/administrator stays in office, the more the IG may represent a threat to his or her tenure. The problem is unavoidable. "Anybody in the Executive Branch is going to be suspicious as heck if anybody in his employ reports directly to the Hill and there are honest concerns about that," Funk testified in 1988.

> Now, let's multiply those concerns. Suppose an IG gives bad news to the Hill, and someone up here slips it to a newspaper. The next thing, the bad news is blazed on page 1. It is no wonder that we often are regarded with great suspicion. The Hill is worried about the IG's being co-opted by management, and management is worried about our being a conduit to the Hill. We are stuck right in the middle. If we are seen talking to somebody from the Hill, "Ah-huh, the IG's leaking information or giving away stuff about his findings." If we get too cozy with management, we are being co-opted. This is what I call straddling the barbed wire fence. [U.S. Senate 1989, 55]

In this collision of interests, IGs are at best an annoyance; at worst they are an indictment of a secretary or administrator's own judgment.

Straddling the Barbed Wire Fence

Given the challenge of gaining either external or internal support for their recommendations, it is no surprise that IGs see their jobs as a fine balance between toughness and persuasion. Consider the following 1988 exchange between Jack Brooks and Brown, Kusserow, and Funk regarding what it takes to be an effective IG:

> Ms. Brown: One has to have integrity, exercise independence, and be ready to report candidly and completely on the results of the work, regardless of where the chips may fall. . . .
> Mr. Brooks: And for a diet, you recommend what, steak tartare three times a day?
> Ms. Brown: I think you should hire people that have steak tartare three times a day, sir.

Mr. Brooks: Mr. Kusserow, do you agree with Ms. Brown as to the key to being an effective IG?

Mr. Kusserow: Yes, Mr. Chairman. In fact, if you have integrity and maintain good credibility, you can be a good inspector general. If your integrity is in question or the credibility of the products that you produce is in question, you cannot be. . . .

Mr. Funk: I think the key is the exercising of will, the exercising of the courage needed to make your integrity known throughout the agency, and to make it known that you are doing your job. It also requires the ability to motivate your staff so that the staff is willing to exercise its own will and its own technical competence. Without either of those, I don't think the job can be done. [U.S. House 1988, 121].

The question, of course, is how to ensure that each IG has just those qualities—strength, yet flexibility; a strong right arm ready to pull for the good of the crew or batter the coxswain if necessary. The natural temptation, for example, is to make individual secretaries and administrators more responsive by giving them a much greater say over who becomes IG, just as the White House did in 1989.

Tempting as it may be to do so, making the IGs more responsive to a given secretary or administrator may actually render the concept less valuable to future successors. The more an individual IG becomes linked to an individual secretary or administrator, as at EPA in the early 1980s, the more vulnerable that IG becomes to the barbed wire fence, particularly since cabinet-level appointees have even higher turnover rates than their own subcabinet appointees. Instead of becoming an institutional resource across individual regimes or administration, the IG would become inextricably part of the same short-term thinking that drives his or her appointed supervisors.

Counterintuitive as it may seem, the greater the IG independence the greater their value to their secretaries and administrators. Granted, this independence may come at the expense of empathy for those the IGs must monitor. Granted, secretaries and administrators may still choose not to listen. Nevertheless, if one views the offices of inspector general as a reservoir for institutional memory, greater independence may be a worthwhile investment in protecting one of the few remaining sources of nonpoliticized advice and expertise in government. With political appointees now moving down to the deputy assistant secretary level of government—five steps down into the bureaucratic hierarchy—and with no prospect that Congress or the president will act to stem the tide, the IG concept may be the last best hope for a durable counterweight to the short-term thinking that often prevails among political appointees.

Even with additional protection against high-level manipulation—in the form, for example, of a fixed term of office—the IGs cannot be expected to become a front-line defense against high-level wrongdoing. That role is neither their responsibility nor their strength. No matter how much one patches the IG concept with additional sources of independence, the IG remains much more the strong right arm than the lone wolf, which is exactly what Congress intended.

Notes

1. This chapter is based on research conducted as part of a larger project titled *The New Monitors: The Rise of the Inspector General Concept in Government*, which was sponsored by the Governance Institute and the Administrative Conference of the United States, and will be published jointly by the Governance Institute and the Brookings Institution. The author gratefully acknowledges the support of Governance Institute president Robert Katzmann. The research in this paper is based, in part, on over 100 interviews with inspectors general, congressional staffers, OMB officers, assistant secretaries, and others familiar with the evolution of the IG concept, as well as a detailed survey of thirty-four of the thirty-eight individuals who served as presidentially appointed IGs between 1976 and 1989.

2. I have elected not to give the statutory location or public law numbers for every statute mentioned in this brief review.

3. The recommendation was made on the basis of what the IG called a "strong perception of impropriety," and was implemented immediately by Bush's new HUD secretary, Jack Kemp.

4. These forwards usually consist of four or five brief paragraphs summarizing the material to follow, hardly more than a few hundred words at most, a two or three minute's reading.

5. An analysis by James Cook, a research assistant on this project, suggests that the media focused almost exclusively during the first four to five years of the Reagan administration on petty scandals in the IG reports—an assistant secretary forced out for using his personal assistant to type a book manuscript, a regional administrator forced to resign for "lax" administration. Only in the later years did the media start to turn their focus to the more substantive problems in the agency. Even then, it was only after the IG released the 1989 Public Housing Agency report, with its allegations of $400 million in waste, that the media seized upon the scandal.

6. This number includes nine executive schedule appointees (secretary, deputy secretary, assistant secretaries), thirty-one noncareer members of the Senior Executive Service, and eighty-four career members of the Senior Executive Service.

7. Ironically, suspension of programs is exactly what the HUD IG recommended in 1988, a recommendation that new HUD secretary Jack Kemp adopted in 1989.

References

Light, Paul. 1983. *Vice Presidential Power: Advice and Influence in the White House.* Baltimore, MD: Johns Hopkins University Press.

McCubbins, Matthew, and Schwartz, Thomas. 1984. "Congressional Oversight Overlooked: Police Patrols and Firm Alarms." *American Journal of Political Science* 28, no. 1 (February).

Mackenzie, G. Calvin, ed. 1987. *The In-and-Outers: Presidential Appointees and Transient Government in Washington.* Baltimore, MD: Johns Hopkins University Press.

Reicher, David. 1983. "Conflicts of Interest in Inspector General, Justice Department, and Special Prosecutor Investigations of Agency Heads." *Stanford Law Review* 35, no. 2 (May).

Traver, Nancy. 1989. "The Housing Hustle." *Time*, June 26.

U.S. Department of Housing and Urban Development, Office of Inspector General. *Reports to the Congress*, 1981–1985. Washington, DC.

U.S. General Accounting Office. 1990. *Facing Facts*. 1989 Annual Report. Washington, DC: U.S. General Accounting Office.

U.S. House of Representatives. 1975. HR5302, Representative Benjamin Rosenthal. *An Act to Establish Inspectors General*. 94th Congress, 1st Sess. Washington, DC: U.S. Government Printing Office.

————. 1989. Committee on Government Operations, Subcommittee on Employment and Housing. *Abuses, Favoritism, and Mismanagement in HUD Programs*, Pt. 1. Hearings, 101st Congress, 1st Sess. Washington, DC: U.S. Government Printing Office.

U.S. House of Representatives, Committee on Government Operations. 1990. *Abuse and Mismanagement at HUD*. 101st Congress, 2d Sess. Washington, DC: U.S. Government Printing Office.

U.S. House of Representatives, Committee on Government Operations. 1976. *Establishment of an Inspector General in the Department of Health, Education, and Welfare*. 94th Congress, 2d Sess. Washington, DC: U.S. Government Printing Office.

U.S. House of Representatives, Committee on Government Operations. 1988. *Inspector General Act Amendments of 1988*. 100th Congress, 2d Sess. Washington, DC: U.S. Government Printing Office.

U.S. Senate, Committee on Banking, Housing, and Urban Affairs, HUD/Mod Rehab Investigation Subcommittee. 1990. *Final Report and Recommendations*, 101st Congress, 2d Sess. Washington, DC: U.S. Government Printing Office.

U.S. Senate, Committee on Banking, Housing, and Urban Affairs, HUD/Mod Rehab Investigation Subcommittee. 1990. *The Abuse and Mismanagement of HUD*. Vol. 1 & 2. 101st Congress, 2d Sess. Washington, DC: U.S. Government Printing Office.

U.S. Senate, Committee on Governmental Affairs. 1978. *Inspector General Act of 1976*. 95th Congress, 2d Sess. Washington, DC: U.S. Government Printing Office.

U.S. Senate, Committee on Governmental Affairs. 1989. *Serious Management Problems in the U.S. Government*. 101st Congress, 1st Sess. Washington, DC: U.S. Government Printing Office.

6

The Ethics of Physicians and Citizens: An Empirical Test of the "Separatist Thesis"

E. Sam Overman and Linda Foss

The role of expert or of professional judgment in public policy and decision making has long been an issue for public administration (Mosher and Stillman 1977; Jennings 1987; Tong 1986). The appropriate contribution of professional judgment in a democratic society is an especially acute problem when decisions are made not solely on scientific grounds, where professionals can claim some technical superiority, but on ethical grounds, where generally there is no moral consensus and ethical claims must compete (Camenisch 1983). In a democratic society with as much available professional and technical knowledge as has American society, it is especially important to know whether or not professional judgment represents the public interest, particularly on issues involving ethical choice (Burke and Pattenaude 1988).

When the role of professionals in ethical decision making is considered, the core research question is "Do professionals have different ethics than the general public?" The "separatist thesis" is one theoretically well developed proposition. It states that professionals, by virtue of their expert knowledge and social roles, have ethical positions that are unique and that may not only be different from but even contrary to ethical positions held by others not in their profession (Gewirth 1986, 282).[1] The purpose of the study reported here was to test empirically the separatist thesis that professional ethics differ from "ordinary citizen" ethics.

The role of professional judgment in ethical decision making is particularly visible in contemporary medical care. Medical care in the United States has traditionally been dominated by health-care professionals, especially physicians

(Califano 1986; Starr 1982). Whether by design or by default, physicians have often been placed in a position to "play God" and make serious ethical judgments on such matters as the quality of life and death. But as medical care increasingly has been confronted with serious ethical issues (euthanasia, the use of invasive technologies, equity, and the allocation of resources), the dominance of the health-care professional in ethical decision making has been seriously challenged. This challenge has been based largely on the assumption of the separatist thesis (Martin 1981; Goldman 1980).

Theories of medical ethics exist in order to separate the professional physician from the general public, particularly in regard to beneficence, autonomy, justice, access, equity, and other ethical issues faced in the delivery of medical care (Veatch 1981, 1989). Medical-ethics theories are based largely on a separatist thesis premise, namely that professionals' medical ethics significantly differ from, or are contrary to, the ordinary ethical positions of the clients they serve.

The study reported here tested this thesis in order to determine whether professional ethics differ from "ordinary citizen" ethics in critical-care medicine. Generally speaking, the analysis indicated that professionals do have different ethical attitudes than do citizens, but that these differences are more in degree than in kind. These differences are more acute on individual ethics, such as autonomy and beneficence, and less acute on social ethics, such as equity, access, and resource allocation. At least for this sample, the separatist thesis is descriptively true.

Professional Ethics

Professions developed as a peculiar social structure based on superior technical knowledge, though not necessarily superior social status or higher moral character (Parsons 1954); professions created social differentiation based on technical specialization (Weber 1958). In contemporary society, professionals occupy positions of importance. Many modern professions have institutionalized their roles into associations and epistemic communities by extending their technical knowledge to superior social status, economic advantage, and in some cases claims of improved moral knowledge (Holzner and Marx 1979). Today, the technical and moral authority and responsibility that professions receive from society can be viewed as a form of social contract (Page 1975). In exchange for their economic and social advantages, professionals have been entrusted by society to define and administer their own ethical practice and personal conduct, albeit with mixed effectiveness (Bayles 1982). Professionals are increasingly called upon to render ethical judgments on issues that may include, but are broader than, their traditional areas of expertise. As a result, serious questions have been raised about the appropriate contribution of professionals to ethical decision making.

There are three theses regarding the contribution of professionals to ethical decision making (Burke and Pattenaude 1988, 229–33). The first thesis, "ordinary ethics," maintains that nothing distinguishes professional ethics from ordinary public morality (Goldman 1980). This thesis has been criticized for its assumption that there is one unique set of ordinary ethics and for its tendency to state complex ethical positions in simplistic and often absolutist ways. The second thesis, dubbed the "political approach," posits a plurality of ethical positions with no single moral authority, professionals included. This approach is often criticized as leading to an inescapable moral relativism and succumbing to politically defined criteria for ethical choice.

Third, and most controversial, is the "separatist thesis," which assumes that professionals have separate, identifiable ethical positions that are different from the ethical positions held by "ordinary citizens," that is, people not in their profession. According to the separatist thesis, professionals—by virtue of their training, expertise, and social and occupational roles—have moral rights and duties unique to members of their profession, even to the point where infringement on another's moral rights can be justified (Freedman 1981; Gewirth 1986). The separatist thesis does not place professional ethics above more general principles of morality in society at large; rather, professional ethics are strictly limited to the professional practice (Gewirth 1986).

> The essence of professional morality involves the idea that professionals are more constrained by their professional values. . . . this leads professionals to decisions in resolving value conflicts which conflict with the decisions which could be recommended by ordinary morality. [Freedman 1978, 10]

The issue here is not how one develops professional ethics, but if and how professional ethics differ from ordinary-citizen ethics.[2] Arguably, "One thing that happens to a young person who comes into a profession is that she or he encounters the professional as a moral teacher: The profession itself claims teaching authority" (Shaffer 1987, 111). For professional ethics even to exist, the separatist thesis must be descriptively accurate to some degree; it has not, however, been empirically tested among any set of professionals.[3] The general theoretical questions are: Is the separatist thesis accurate? On ethical issues that are relevant to their expertise, do professionals have different ethics from the rest of society?

Medical Ethics

Medicine is one area that has both a high degree of professionalism and a relatively well defined set of ethical principles (Jacob 1988). Medicine is a profession in the sense that, in addition to its having a body of specialized knowledge, it is also committed to a special ethic that binds its members to special norms, duties, and virtues (Smith and Churchill 1986; Veatch 1989). Medical ethics recognizes the separatist thesis in order "to provide a moral basis for relations between parties who are unequal in skill and resources" (Veatch 1981, 12).

The study of medical ethics is the analysis of ethical choices in medicine. Any theory of medical ethics "deals with promise keeping, autonomy, truth telling, avoiding killing, and just distribution of benefits and burdens" (Veatch 1981, 11). Medical ethics is an interrelated set of individual and social principles designed to influence substantive actions by physicians.

For the purpose of this study, seven different medical-ethical dimensions on three levels were identified:

- two individual ethics regarding (1) professional *autonomy* and (2) *beneficence*
- three social ethics pertaining to the (3) *access*, (4) *equity*, and (5) *resource allocation* of medical care[4]
- two substantive ethics pertaining to the specific medical practices of (6) *organ transplants* and (7) the critical care of *handicapped newborns*.

These seven dimensions sparked research questions, which were fashioned into the hypotheses tested in this research; an eighth, overall hypothesis related to *ethical commitment* was also tested.

Autonomy is the determination of one's own actions and behavior. Professional-role autonomy is an important component of the separatist thesis (Gewirth 1986, 284–85). In medicine, professional autonomy is the right to determine treatment and make choices for the patient without being constrained by others. Professional autonomy governs the physician-patient relationship and is also referred to as the ethic of paternalism since it places the physician's view of patient benefit above the wishes or desires of the patient (Brody 1981, 1989). *Physician autonomy* has been challenged recently by the claim that patients have the right both to be fully informed about their care and to make decisions regarding their own care. The *patient's right* to truth and decision versus professional autonomy is particularly ethically problematic when the patient is not individually capable of understanding and choosing (for example, newborns, comatose patients, and the elderly). Are physicians more committed to professional autonomy than they are to the patient's right to be informed and to make decisions? *Hypothesis 1:* Physicians more strongly support professional autonomy in ethical decisions than do other citizens.

Beneficence is the act of doing good. It is certainly the most well known part of the Hippocratic Oath, expanded well beyond its original intent to comprehensive application to all medical treatment and heroic measures in medicine. Beneficence is commonly understood as the professional obligation of the physician to help others in need. Beneficence is often contrasted with the principle of doing no further harm. Medical ethics must deal with cases that balance *beneficence* and the act of doing good (such as giving medical treatment), on the one hand, with preventing further harm of an action (for example, prolonging of suffering) on the other. This ethical debate between doing good and doing no further harm is frequently framed as the *sanctity of life* versus the *quality of life* (Beauchamp and Childress, 1983; Brody 1981; Jonsen et al. 1981). Do physicians have a greater concern for beneficence and the sanctity of life than have citizens? *Hypothesis 2:* Physicians more strongly support beneficence and the sanctity of life in ethical decision making than do other citizens.

Access is the ability to make use of some good or service. One ethical position considers medical care a *right* and therefore open to public access. Another ethical position considers the *need* for individual medical care as usually determined by society or government, which is ultimately more restrictive to access. Access is inextricably tied to the ability to pay, whether on the part of the patient or the society.[5] Are physicians, bound in part by the principle of beneficence, more likely to favor an individual's right to open access regardless of ability to pay? *Hypothesis 3:* Physicians more strongly support open access and the right to medical care than do other citizens.

Equity is the right of individuals not to have their access to health care blocked by bias or favoritism. Like access, equity is at this point in the health industry primarily an economic issue, although there are clear indications that being uninsured or underinsured is closely related to one's sociodemographic condition. *Full equality* would not discriminate between patients seeking access to medical care, while a less than fully equitable system of medical care would introduce some *selection bias*, such as the ability to pay.[6] Are physicians more likely to favor full equity regardless of ability to pay? *Hypothesis 4:* Physicians more strongly support full equity in medical care than do other citizens.

Resource allocation is the manner in which resources, in this case medical care, are distributed. Decisions that were once made between physician and patient can now be perceived to allocate the scarce resources of society (Beauchamp and Childress 1983, 20). While medical care was once perceived to be *unlimited*, there are now arguments that favor *limits* on the allocation of medical care (Buchanan 1989). The ability-to-pay criterion traditionally has been used when there was need to allocate costly medical care resources, but other criteria such as diagnostic groups are now also being used. Do physicians more strongly support unlimited allocation of resources than other citizens? *Hypothesis 5:* Physicians more strongly support unlimited allocation of medical care resources than do other citizens.

Organ transplant is a contemporary issue that involves high medical cost and scarce resources (available organs) and raises the question of the role of society and government in medical decision making. Given this situation, some would argue for a *comprehensive* program of organ transplantation, including public laws designed to increase and regulate the supply of donor organs, while others would view transplants as *contingent* on a host of circumstances such as age, ability to pay, or general need. Do physicians more strongly support a comprehensive approach to organ transplants than other citizens? *Hypothesis 6:* Physicians more strongly support a comprehensive program of organ transplants than do other citizens.

Handicapped newborn medical care is certainly one of the most emotion-evoking issues in medical ethics today. It involves not only medical questions but issues of cost, quality of life, and family and societal burden for care. Medical decisions about newborns are always based on incomplete knowledge of the future, as well as the inescapable fact that another person or group must make the decisions about the newborn's life (Macklin 1987). One approach to the care for handicapped newborns—based on the principle of beneficence—is *unconditional* in prescribing and administering medical care to maintain the best possible life; another approach—based more on the principle of doing no further harm—is *conditional* and depends on a number of circumstances regarding the newborn's expected quality of life and family situation and beliefs. Do physicians more strongly support unconditional medical care for the handicapped newborn than other citizens? *Hypothesis 7:* Physicians more strongly support unconditional medical care for handicapped newborns than do other citizens.

Ethical commitment is the degree of consistency or agreement that a group holds for its ethical positions. In other words, there is not only a question of ethical differences between the two groups, but also a question of central tendency or commitment to ethical positions. While physicians and other citizens may or may not be different in their ethical positions, there is an independent question of how consistently they hold their respective ethical positions. A test for ethical commitment is based on the theoretical assumption that professionals are more homogeneous and thus hold their ethical positions with greater consistency and commitment as a group than do members of the general public. Are physicians more committed to their ethical positions than other citizens, regardless of differences, on each of the ethical dimensions? *Hypothesis 8:* Physicians have greater ethical commitment than other citizens have.

In summary, in order for professional ethics to exist in medicine and the separatist thesis to be accurate, one would expect to find empirical support for some or all of these eight hypotheses. Physicians are expected to differ significantly from the public in their support for the ethical positions outlined above and in the degree of commitment to their ethical positions.

Method

Survey data were collected from two samples.[7] The first, the public sample, consists of the responses of 5,855 citizens of Colorado who identified themselves as not health-care professionals; the respondents were from among 7,413 choosing to participate in the survey. Comparison of the demographics of the public sample to those of the general Colorado population (using 1980 census data) suggests that it is a fairly representative sample. Women (63.9 percent), however, are overrepresented; there are proportionally more citizens over age sixty-five (20.6 percent) and fewer minority representatives (13 percent) in the sample than in Colorado as a whole (50.4, 8.5, and 16.7 percent, respectively). On other demographic dimensions—education, religion, income, and occupation—the sample does not differ significantly from the general Colorado population in 1980.

The second sample consists of the responses of the 2,218 physicians of a total of 7,095 licensed in the state of Colorado who chose to participate in the survey; this is a response rate of 31.2 percent. The demographics of the physician sample closely resemble demographic data found in similar surveys, except for clinical specialty; most physicians in this sample listed family practice (21.7 percent) or internal medicine (16.9). These differences in both groups between sample and population, though minimal, should be considered when interpreting the results.

The two groups were surveyed concerning positions on the seven key ethical dimensions. Multiple survey items using five-point Likert scales ("strongly agree" to "strongly disagree") measured opinions on each dimension. The respondents were all asked the same questions, except for wording changes on several items to account for citizen or physician identity. Data were analyzed using SPSS analysis of variance and tests for homogeneity-of-variance.

Findings

The analysis suggests that there is enough evidence to support separate professional ethics for five of the seven hypotheses: Autonomy, Beneficence, Equity, Resource Allocation, and Organ Transplants. (Table 6.1 presents the statistically significant differences between physicians and (other citizens) responses that were found on these five medical ethics dimensions; $\alpha = 0.05$.) The separatist thesis, on first examination, appears to be descriptively true; however, there are more subtle findings to be explored.

The most significant differences between physicians and citizens are on the individual ethics of *autonomy* and *beneficence*. Physicians more strongly supported professional autonomy when asked about telling the truth to patients, following patient wishes, and acknowledging patients' rights to refuse medical treatment than did other citizens, who were more likely to support patients' rights on these same questions. This expected finding has the greatest degree of empirical support among all the hypotheses in this study. Most of the difference between the two groups occurred when physicians and 'other citizens' were asked whether the physician has the duty to follow the patient's wishes.

The two groups also differed significantly in the responses on *beneficence*, but less strongly than in the case of *autonomy*. Physicians more strongly supported the sanctity of life—though certainly not unreservedly—when asked about using heroic measures, employing critical-care technology, and maintaining the expected quality of life than did other citizens, who were more likely to support maintaining the expected quality of life. This expected finding shows

Table 6.1

ANOVA Results of Comparing Citizen and Physician Ethics

	df	F	p
Individual Ethics			
Autonomy	7392	7.05	0.0001
Beneficence	7392	2.39	0.0001
Social Ethics			
Access	7392	3.28	0.0702*
Equity	7392	4.44	0.0001
Resource Allocation	7392	6.78	0.0001
Substantive Ethics			
Organ Transplants	7392	2.98	0.0001
Handicapped Newborns	7392	1.68	0.6818*

*Not statistically significant

that physicians do demonstrate a separate professional ethic, at least in terms of individual ethics of autonomy and beneficence.

On social ethics of *access, equity,* and *resource allocation,* there was not as much support for a distinctly separate ethics, but there was some support for differences of opinion regarding *equity* and *resource allocation.* On questions of *access* and the ability to pay, physicians and citizens showed no statistically significant differences; both groups indicated that both patients' needs and their ability to pay should be considered when deciding upon medical care. On *equity* and *resource allocation,* there were statistically significant differences between physicians and citizens in the degree of their responses, but not in the overall direction. While both groups indicated that there are constraints on full equity and that there should be limits on resource allocation, citizens more strongly agreed with these positions regarding social justice than did physicians.

One possible reason for the small degree of difference on social ethics is that questions of access and allocation have only recently been directed to the medical community, and the professions—particularly physicians—have simply not had the time to develop and incorporate a coherent professional ethic in this area. Another plausible explanation is that once the ethical issue moves from a personal and individual level to a more abstract and social level, the separatist thesis is less likely to be true as professional groups rely on other social identities and ideologies to formulate their ethical positions.

On the substantive ethical issue of *organ transplants,* physicians more strongly supported organ transplants when asked if these were a worthwhile investment of health-care dollars, if the physicians supported legislation to increase the supply of organs, or if the physicians were willing to disregard age as a discriminating factor for receiving transplants. Citizens tended to place greater constraints on organ transplants when asked the same questions. Physicians, however, did not completely support comprehensive organ transplants.

On the substantive ethical issue of the care of *handicapped newborns*, there was no statistical difference whatsoever. Both groups split right down the middle when asked questions regarding saving and preserving the lives of severely handicapped newborns.

Two explanations of these results come to mind. First, there is a logical difference between the ethical issues represented by *organ transplants* and *handicapped newborns*. In the latter case, both physicians and citizens were clearly being asked to make a judgment about a third person, the baby. When making a medical decision that is clearly about someone else in a helpless position, both groups—citizens in particular—were more cautious and conservative in balancing sanctity of life with quality of life. Also, questions on substantive ethical issues elicit a more emotive response precisely because respondents can understand or sympathize with the substance or context of the issue.

There is an apparent paradox in that there was neither difference nor agreement by either group on the care for handicapped newborns, yet there was both difference and agreement by physicians and citizens regarding the principle of beneficence. This apparent contradiction possibly is explained by the way in which people respond to a particular substantive case, such as a handicapped newborn, that always has special circumstances and always influences one's ability to isolate and apply any general principle, ethical, or otherwise.

The ANOVA results presented in Table 6.1 show the differences between group means, but there are times when it is also interesting to compare variances in order to know differences in the homogeneity-of-variance in the groups (see Table 6.2). Specifically, is the homogeneity-of-variance on medical ethics among physicians greater than among other citizens? To determine this, we used the variance within each group to test the null hypothesis: σ^2 physicians = σ^2 citizens. The assumption is that physicians are collectively more similar in their responses (that is, have less variance) than other citizens are because the professionalization process results not only in ethical positions that are different but also in a greater consistency or agreement among professionals on those ethical positions.

Few of the tests for homogeneity-of-variance revealed strong significant differences, and moreover, the prediction of the *ethical commitment* hypothesis that physicians will have greater homogeneity-of-variance than other citizens was not always true and was often reversed. On individual ethics of *autonomy* and *beneficence*, both were statistically significant, but only on *autonomy* did physicians show greater homogeneity; on *beneficence*, citizens indicated greater homogeneity. Also of interest, on social ethics of *access*, *equity*, and *resource allocation*, only the latter two were significant, but both were the opposite of what was

Table 6.2

Homogeneity-of-Variance Results Using Bartlett-Box F

Dependent Measures	df	F	p
Individual Ethics			
Autonomy	7392	4.265	0.038
Beneficence	7392	9.444	0.002
Social Ethics			
Access	7392	2.309	0.129
Equity	7392	5.146	0.023
Resource Allocation	7392	21.246	0.001
Substantive Ethics			
Organ Transplants	7392	31.391	0.001
Handicapped Newborns	7392	7.429	0.006

hypothesized: citizens showed a *greater* homogeneity-of-variance than did physicians. On substantive ethical issues, there was again some statistical significance, but physicians displayed greater homogeneity regarding *handicapped newborns*, while other citizens displayed greater homogeneity on *organ transplants*.

These findings about the *ethical commitment* hypothesis are confounding, to say the least. The hypothesis is not supported; neither physicians nor citizens have greater ethical commitment in any consistently predictable direction.[8] In the absence of both strong differences between variances and a consistent direction of the existing differences, it has to be concluded that these professionals have no greater ethical commitment than do other citizens.

Conclusions

The findings indicate that, for the most part, physicians do have different ethics than other citizens have, but that these differences are more in degree than in kind. The separatist thesis is descriptively true, at least for physicians in this sample, and professional ethics differ in significant ways from citizen morality. These differences, however, are mostly in the direction of individual ethics such as autonomy and beneficence and much less in the direction of social ethics such as access, equity, and resource allocation. There are no differences in ethical commitment between physicians and citizens.

These findings are important for further development of ethical theory concerning the separatist thesis and ordinary morality. First, the separatist thesis should make the distinction between levels of ethical choice such that the more personal and directly relevant an ethical choice is to a professional, the more likely the thesis will hold. Conversely, the more social and abstract an ethical choice is to professionals, the more likely their ethics will correspond to ordinary morality, or at least will depend on other social roles and ideologies.

Second, there needs to be a distinction made between abstract ethical principles and ethical choices applied to substantive decisions. The findings in this study suggest that applying ethics to concrete, substantive ethical decision making is much more complex than asking questions about a general ethical principle, such as beneficence. As was found with the questions concerning handicapped newborns, it is difficult to identify distinctly any separate ethical principles among either professionals or citizens when respondents are divorced from the specific context of a given ethical decision. Both of these refinements in the separatist thesis require further study.

To study professional ethics is to study the role of reason in society (Churchman 1971; Diesing 1962, 1982; Simon 1983). Classically, the theoretical debate on the role of reason in society has meant choosing either the singular rationality of a professional and scientific elite or the more ambiguous pluralistic considerations of the public interest and all that that entails. The great fear of the pluralist approach is that "pluralism is the seedbed of reductionism that is not far removed from [a]nihilism," in which professional participants politically bargain for resources using an ethics of civility (Gawthrop 1984, 141). On the other hand, pluralists fear the undemocratic consequences of an empowered professional elite and the moral order they may impose.

To the extent that the findings in this study are generalizable to other populations and professions, the debate over the role of reason in society becomes a more normative exercise. If the separatist thesis is more generally true, then the concomitant rise in professions and ethical issues in American society seems inevitably to lead down the pluralist path to reason in society. Yet if we take the pluralist path we need not get lost in the woods of moral relativism, as many fear. Rather, theoretical strategies of reasoned ethical discourse (MacRae 1976) or debate among competing rational ideologies (Paris and Reynolds 1983) can provide resolutions to ethical problems in policy analysis. Similarly, dialogical communities for scientific and ethical decision making are necessary if the separatist claim is to be reduced (Bernstein 1983). Practical strategies of ethical review committees are important, regardless of profession and regardless of how slow and frustrating their work may be. It is, after all, a meta-ethic in American society that democratic norms supersede ethical efficiency.

There are several additional avenues for future research on professional ethics. Obviously, generalizability to other professional groups and geographic areas would increase the theoretical validity of the separatist thesis. For example, are professional ethics also evident among engineers making environmental decisions, lawyers representing public interests, or teachers making choices about the education of children? These are all research questions for professional ethics and public administration, but there is also a need for future research on specific theories of administrative ethics.

Implications for Research and Theory

There are many implications for research and theory in public administration. First, the rise of the professional class is well documented in public administration (Mosher 1968). More recently, theories of ethics in public administration have been articulated. While there is a strong body of theory on professional ethics—and while many of these theories have received substantial interpretive treatment—there has been little empirical effort to test their validity. It is not so much that the intellectual status of ethical theory in public administration is wrong as that it is incomplete. This lack of empirical inquiry on administrative ethics in public administration is an important oversight.

The research reported here demonstrates one pattern for examining theories of professional ethics in public administration. Further questions would revolve around whether there is a separate professional ethic in public administration. If so, what is its descriptive character? What factors may determine its formation and maintenance? And, if there is such an ethic, what are the consequences for government? A further test of the separatist thesis in public administration might compare groups within the public service, including elected officials, or compare the public-service professional with citizens and outside groups, such as private managers. The research constructs could easily be drawn from available theory, such as the ethics of civility and systems ethics (Gawthrop 1984), the ethics of structure and neutrality (Thompson 1985), the bureaucratic and Protestant work ethic (Jackall 1988), the application of regime values (Rohr 1988), or the pathology of professional impersonality (Harmon 1990). There are many such concepts in the literature on ethics in public administration that require multiple operational and empirical attention.

Empirical studies of ethical attitudes and behavior of public servants would yield new insights into the relationship between bureaucracy and democracy in American society. One hypothesis is that differences in ethical positions may be even more subtle than those found here. If bureaucracy is truly representative, then professional ethics should differ little from ordinary morality. It may be that pluralism pervades public bureaucracies to the extent that a separate ethic is not now distinguishable, or that pluralism itself has become a public-administrative ethic.

A rival hypothesis would maintain that public bureaucrats might develop a greater ethic of civility (Gawthrop 1984) or a more accentuated ethic of structure and neutrality (Thompson 1985), especially when accounting for such variables as years of service, organizational culture, or isolation from clients. The findings of this study also suggest that it is important to examine the constraints on administrative ethics at the social, organizational, and individual levels (Denhardt 1988, 100).

Finally, in addition to testing the separatist thesis, the successes and failures of the "political approach" (Burke and Pattenaude 1988) are also in need of more empirical investigation. What are the influences of political, social, and managerial ideologies, rational or otherwise, on public-administrative ethics, and how are these "mediated" in public policy debate?

The research reported here raises more questions than it answers, but in doing so it accomplishes its purpose of setting an agenda for the empirical study of ethics in public administration. It is time—to paraphrase William James—for the tough-minded empiricist and the tender-minded rationalist to engage each other more directly in the development of ethics in public administration.

Notes

1. There are many nuances of the separatist thesis, not all of which can be covered in this chapter. For example, we interpret the separatist thesis to be both a descriptive/empirical claim and a normative/ethical claim but we address only the former. The separatist thesis is the object of a rich and complex dialogue conducted primarily in the journal *Ethics.* Generally, the separatist thesis is upheld by Freedman (1978, 1981) and in a more qualified form by Gewirth (1986); it is opposed by Martin (1981) and Goldman (1980). We found the single best review and discussion to be Gewirth (1986).

2. There are a substantial number of studies of how one develops a professional ethic in medical education under the more general topic of the socialization of the professions. Some, such as Becker's *Boys in White* (1961), are classic. An interesting first-hand account by medical student Wendy Carlton has the telling title *"In Our Professional Opinion . . ." The Primacy of Clinical Judgment over Moral Choice* (1978). In her accounts, both clinical and legal judgment should supersede moral judgment for practicing physicians. We wonder how her moral development has changed this opinion.

3. It is not too surprising that doctors and lawyers are the two most-studied professional groups in terms of their ethics. There are numerous qualitative studies and discussions in ethics and law (e.g., Hazzard 1978; Shaffer 1987) and in medical ethics (e.g., Frohock 1986; Shaffer 1987).

4. These three aspects of social ethics are often discussed singly as issues of social justice in the medical ethics literature (Veatch and Branson 1976; Veatch 1981), in which the fundamental dichotomy reflects the societal needs versus individual rights paradigms, and utilitarian versus libertarian approaches. Although the constructs of *access, equity,* and *resource allocation* are disaggregated from the social justice concept and scaled separately in this study, they are obviously interrelated.

5. The questions used in the survey depend heavily on the ability-to-pay criterion to provide constraints on access and equity in medical care. It seems justified to use ability to pay, given that it still dominates other more politically or socially defined selection criteria used in the provision of medical care.

6. A more conservative economic argument separates the ability-to-pay issue from the issue of equal access to health care by claiming that opportunity to access, not actual access, is the more important. The questions in this survey were designed to measure opinion on equity as related to the ability to pay. For example, "If a hospital becomes overwhelmed with patients who cannot pay, public funds from taxes should be made available to cover the cost of care."

7. The collection of data was funded in part by the Robert Wood Johnson Foundation as the Colorado Speaks Out on Health project and conducted by the Center for Ethics and Health Policy at the Graduate School of Public Affairs, University of Colorado at Denver. The survey data were collected in 1987–88.

8. A methodological problem with this test is that the large sample size for both groups would minimize any within-group variance and cause even small differences in variance to appear significant.

References

Bayles, Michael D. 1982. *Professional Ethics*. Belmont, MA: Wadsworth.

Beauchamp, Thomas L., and Childress, James F. 1983. *Principles of Biomedical Ethics*. New York: Oxford University Press.

Becker, Howard S. 1961. *Boys in White: Student Culture in Medical School*. Chicago: University of Chicago Press.

Bernstein, Richard J. 1983. *Beyond Objectivism and Relativism: Science, Hermeneutics and Praxis*. Philadelphia: University of Pennsylvania Press.

Bowman, James S., and Elliston, Frederick A., eds. 1988. *Ethics, Government, and Public Policy: A Reference Guide*. New York: Greenwood.

Brody, Howard. 1981. *Ethical Decisions in Medicine*. 2nd ed. Boston: Little, Brown.

————. 1989. "The Physician/Patient Relationship." In *Medical Ethics: An Introduction*, edited by Robert M. Veatch, 67–91. Boston: Jones and Bartlett.

Buchanan, Allen. 1989. "Health-Care Delivery and Resource Allocation." In *Medical Ethics: An Introduction*, edited by Robert M. Veatch, 291–327. Boston: Jones and Bartlett.

Burke, John P., and Pattenaude, Richard L. 1988. "Professional Expertise in Politics and Administration." In *Ethics, Government, and Public Policy: A Reference Guide*, edited by James S. Bowman and Frederick A. Elliston, 225–45. New York: Greenwood.

Cahill, Anthony, and E. Sam Overman. 1988. "Contemporary Perspectives on Ethics and Values in Public Affairs." In *Ethics, Government, and Public Policy: A Reference Guide*, edited by James S. Bowman and Frederick A. Elliston, 11–27. New York: Greenwood.

Califano, Joseph A. 1986. *America's Health Care Revolution*. New York: Random House.

Camenisch, Paul F. 1983. *Grounding Professional Ethics in a Pluralist Society*. New York: Haven Publications.

Carlton, Wendy. 1978. *"In Our Professional Judgment . . .": The Primacy of Clinical Judgment Over Moral Choice*. Notre Dame, IN: University of Notre Dame Press.

Churchman, C. West. 1971. *The Design of Inquiring Systems*. New York: Basic Books.

Denhardt, Kathryn G. 1988. *The Ethics of Public Service*. New York: Greenwood.

Diesing, Paul. 1962. *Reason in Society*. Urbana: University of Illinois Press.

————. 1982. *Science and Ideology in the Policy Sciences*. New York: Aldine.

Freedman, Benjamin. 1978. "A Meta-Ethics for Professional Morality." *Ethics* 89:1–19.

————. 1981. "What Really Makes Professional Morality Different: Response to Martin." *Ethics* 91: 626–30.

Frohock, Fred M. 1986. *Special Care: Medical Decisions at the Beginning of Life*. Chicago: University of Chicago Press.

Gawthrop, Louis C. 1984. *Public Sector Management, Systems, and Ethics*. Bloomington: Indiana University Press.

Gewirth, Alan. 1986. "Professional Ethics: The Separatist Thesis." *Ethics* 96 (January): 282–300.

Goldman, Alan H. 1980. *The Moral Foundations of Professional Ethics*. Totowa, NJ: Rowman and Littlefield.

Harmon, Michael M. 1990. "The Responsible Actor as 'Tortured Soul': The Case of Horatio Hornblower." In *Images and Identities in Public Administration*, ed. by Henry D. Kass and Bayard L. Catron, 151–80. Newbury Park, CA: Sage.

Hazzard, Geoffrey C. 1978. *Ethics in the Practice of Law*. New Haven, CT: Yale University Press.

Holzner, Burkart, and Marx, John H. 1979. *Knowledge Application: The Knowledge System in Society*. Boston: Allyn and Bacon.

Jackall, Robert. 1988. *Moral Mazes*. New York: Oxford University Press.

Jacob, Joseph M. 1988. *Doctors and Rules: A Sociology of Professional Values*. New York: Routledge.

Jennings, Bruce. 1987. "Public Administration: In Search of Democratic Professionalism." *Hastings Center Report*. Special supplement on "The Public Duties of the Professions." (February): 18–20.

Jonsen, A.; Seigler, M.; and Winslade, W. 1981. *Clinical Ethics*. New York: Macmillan.

Macklin, Ruth. 1987. *Mortal Choices*. New York: Pantheon Books.

MacRae, Duncan. 1976. *The Social Function of Social Science*. New Haven, CT: Yale University Press.

Martin, Mike W. 1981. "Rights and the Meta-Ethics of Professional Morality." *Ethics* 91: 619–25.

Mosher, Frederick C. 1968. *Democracy and the Public Service*. New York: Oxford University Press.

Mosher, Frederick C., and Stillman, Richard, Jr. 1977. "Symposium on the Professions in Government: Introduction." *Public Administration Review* 37 (November/December): 631–33.

Page, B. B. 1975. "Who Owns the Professions." *Hastings Center Report*. October.

Paris, David C., and Reynolds, James F. 1983. *The Logic of Policy Inquiry*. New York: Longman.

Parsons, Talcott. 1954. *Essays in Sociological Theory: Pure and Applied*. New York: Free Press.

Rohr, John A. 1988. *Ethics for Bureaucrats: An Essay on Law and Values*. 2d ed. New York: Marcel Dekker.

Shaffer, Thomas L. 1987. *Faith and the Professions*. Provo, UT: Brigham Young University.

Simon, Herbert. 1983. *Reason in Human Affairs*. Stanford, CA: Stanford University Press.

Smith, Harmon, and Churchill, Larry. 1986. *Professional Ethics and Primary Care Medicine*. Durham, NC: Duke University Press.

Starr, Paul. 1982. *The Socialization of American Medicine*. New York: Basic Books.

Thompson, Dennis. 1985. "The Possibility of Administrative Ethic." *Public Administration Review* 45: 5 (September/October): 555–61.

Tong, Rosemarie. 1986. *Ethics in Policy Analysis*. Englewood Cliffs, NJ: Prentice Hall.

Veatch, Robert M., ed. 1981. *A Theory of Medical Ethics*. New York: Basic Books.

———, ed. 1989. *Medical Ethics: An Introduction*. Boston: Jones and Bartlett.

Veatch, Robert, and Branson, Roy. 1976. *Ethics and Health Policy*. Cambridge, MA: Ballinger.

Weber, Max. 1958. *The Protestant Ethic and the Spirit of Capitalism*. Talcott Parsons, trans. New York: Charles Scribner's Sons.

7

Ethics Codes and Ethics Agencies: Current Practices and Emerging Trends

Carol W. Lewis

Since Hammurabi, Moses, and Hippocrates, codifiers and executors have operated on the theory that it is easier to do the right thing when one knows what that is. As a result, codified standards of conduct have become a popular vehicle for clarifying minimum expectations about acceptable behavior. Codes are now being adopted, refined, or strengthened in jurisdictions throughout the United States.

All the dialogue over the years has produced prototypical arguments for and against codes. Implemented codes are coercive and spawn more red tape; they reduce managers' maneuverability and restrict practical options. An unenforced code's symbolism is a weak message, just a piece of paper scribbled over with platitudes. Codes alter the course from aspiration to asphyxiation, from ethics to obedience, and they substitute rules for reasoning. But must one rely on mysteries, which guide behavior by unspoken, axiomatic norms? "Managers need to know what is regarded as acceptable and what is not. . . . Can an organization afford to have its members trying to guess what its standards are?" (Bowman 1981, 61).

Those sections of this article drawn from the author's *Ethics Challenge in Public Service: A Problem-Solving Guide* (San Francisco: Jossey-Bass, 1991) are reprinted by permission of Jossey-Bass. Appreciation is extended to The University of Connecticut's Graduate Research Foundation for funding research travel and attendance at the Conference on the Study of Government Ethics, Park City, Utah, June 12–15, 1991.

Proposing the first codification of federal conflict-of-interest statutes, President John F. Kennedy outlined the pros and cons of ethics codes in his message to Congress on April 27, 1961.

> The ultimate answer to ethical problems in government is honest people in a good ethical environment. No web of statute or regulation, however intricately conceived, can hope to deal with the myriad possible challenges to a man's integrity or his devotion to the public interest.
>
> Nevertheless formal regulation is required—regulation which can lay down clear guidelines of policy, punish venality and double-dealing, and set a general ethical tone for the conduct of public business.
>
> Criminal statutes and presidential orders, no matter how carefully conceived or meticulously drafted, cannot hope to deal effectively with every problem of ethical behavior or conflict of interest. Problems arise in infinite variation. They often involve subtle and difficult judgements. . . . And even the best of statutes or regulations will fail of their purpose if they are not vigorously and wisely administered.

Only through a systematic comparison of federal, state, and local experience can Kennedy's propositions be disconfirmed and the ongoing controversy be informed by empirical data.

A comparative analysis is useful from an applied perspective as well. Customarily, a first step codifiers take is to scan other jurisdictions. Alaska did so in 1990, Los Angeles in 1989. National public interest organizations propose model statutes, while professional associations, research institutes, and national consulting groups also contribute to the interjurisdictional and interinstitutional give-and-take. In light of the variation and flux described in this paper, a systematic comparison provides a benchmark against which to gauge future direction; permutations among jurisdictions offer potentially adaptable innovations in a domestic version of technology transfer. By way of scanning, we turn now to a comparison of ethics provisions and practices among the states, federal agencies, selected cities, and influential model statutes.

Current State Practices

Most states now bar use of public position for personal gain (see Table 7.1) and have antibribery statutes on the books (Common Cause 1989b, 16). However, only about a dozen states have "something comprehensive enough to be called a state code of ethics" (Weimer 1990, 2). Diversity best describes the overall pattern of state ethics laws and practices. Competence, jurisdiction, organization, and specific prohibitions vary from state to state. Practices typical among the states are shown in Table 7.1.

Data from the Council on Governmental Ethics Laws' Blue Books and a study by Alaska's legislative staff (Weimer 1990) reveal only a few standard

Table 7.1

Typical State Practices

	As of January 1, 1990 Minimum No. of States
Designated board, commission, or office with legal authority in the area of ethics	36
Jurisdiction over appointed officials and state employees	30
Own investigatory authority	33
At least one ethics body authorized to issue advisory opinions or interpretations	36
Opinions rendered are always public	33
Some type of personal disclosure by senior state appointees+	29

	As of January 1,	
Restrained Activities++	1986	1990
Using public position for personal benefit	41	35
Providing benefits to influence official actions	41	34
Using confidential government information	35	28
Receiving gifts by officials or employees	39	33
Representing private clients before public bodies	31	27
Outside employment/business activities	27	27
Nepotism*	29	23
Competitive bidding*	36	25
Receiving fees/honoraria*	26	28
Postemployment restrictions*	22	23

+At least thirteen states require personal disclosure from all state employees earning over a specified income, and twenty-two states require personal disclosure from volunteer members of state boards and commissions. When elected officials are included, thirty-six states require disclosure.

++Modes of restraint include state constitution, case law, statute, executive order, administrative action, or union contract.

*Nepotism and competitive bidding are included as typical practices because of the likelihood that the actual count is higher. Despite the likely undercount, honoraria and postemployment restrictions evidenced an increase.

Source: Compiled from data in the Council on Governmental Ethics Laws' Blue Book (1990, 1986–87). Because of response failures, the 1990 figures represent minimum counts; the 1986 figures in some cases may more accurately reflect current standards. Ethics, elections, campaign finance, and lobbying oversight authorities are included.

practices. A majority of states (thirty-six) do have a designated board, commission, or office with legal authority in the area of ethics.[1] Of these, thirty have jurisdiction over appointed officials and state employees. Although the Council on Governmental Ethics Laws (COGEL), the National Municipal League, and Common Cause call for a commission's jurisdiction to extend to elected or appointed officials and employees in all government branches, actual practices vary among the states. States also differ markedly in enforcement mechanisms and procedural protections. West Virginia's 1989 act, a comprehensive statewide ethics law, is the first state statute to provide for a special prosecutor (Hall 1989).

The scandal trigger is apparent from initiation dates. While only four state codes predate 1973, nineteen states adopted codes in response to Watergate between 1973 and 1979, and five between 1980 and 1988. That the pace of activity picked up more recently is hardly surprising given headlines across the country. Moreover, the ethics arena in state governments appears unsettled. According to a study by R. Roth Judd, executive director of Wisconsin's ethics board, in 1989 alone codes were adopted in Arkansas, New York, and West Virginia, proposed in Idaho and Vermont, and died in Georgia's Senate Judiciary Committee. All told, there were more than five dozen legislative and judicial actions involving thirty-one states in 1989 (compiled from Judd 1989, 36).

At least thirty-three of the thirty-six state ethics commissions are empowered to conduct investigations on their own volition (see Table 7.1). In thirty-six states at least one body is authorized to issue advisory opinions, declaratory rulings, or interpretive statements. In practice, the advisory function supports the code's conflict-of-interest rules. Most requests to Connecticut's commission for advisory opinions between 1978 and 1983 involved possible conflict of interest by state employees (Lewis 1986, 26).[2] During the ethics commission's first decade of operation in Massachusetts, the number of formal opinions issued declined substantially, to be replaced by informal staff letters and reviews of town counsels' opinions. The Massachusetts State Ethics Commission's report (Commonwealth of Massachusetts 1988, 1) explains, "This shift reflects the fact that as precedents set by the formal opinions established more of the law's general guidelines, the ability to address individual situations through informal correspondence, often restating opinions previously addressed by the commission, increased."

Conflict of Interest

Designed to assure that the public interest is pursued by creating barriers to personal interest, the standard pertaining to conflict of interest is logically fundamental to codes at every level of government. Beyond this, little uniformity appears across jurisdictions (see Table 7.1).

The COGEL and the National Municipal League restrict conflict to the financial or economic. The League explains in the introduction to its 1979 model state law that "conflict of interest laws are concerned with financial conflicts which set apart an individual officeholder from most of the general public." California's 1974 Political Reform Act similarly narrows conflict to economic matters (Cowan Commission 1989a, 147):

A public official has a conflict of interest when all of the following occur: (1) the official makes, participates in, or uses his or her official position to influence a governmental decision; (2) it is foreseeable that the decision will affect the official's economic interest; (3) the effect of the decision on the official's economic interest will be material; [and] (4) the effect of the decision on the official's economic interest will be distinguishable from its effect on the public generally.

More expansive formulations extend conflict to "financial, social, and political relationships and transactions which may compromise or give the appearance of compromising their [public servants'] objectivity, independence or honesty" (Josephson Institute 1991, vii).

Financial Disclosure

A conventional way to encourage compliance with conflict-of-interest prohibitions is financial disclosure, "the 'linchpin' of government ethics laws" (Weimer 1991, 2). Common Cause (1989b, 40) argues, "To be effective, financial disclosure must be public."

With thirty-six states requiring some type of financial disclosure and federal service featuring two types, the many variations on the specifics come as no surprise. Laws in nineteen states require certain local officials to file, but executive orders issued on ethics in at least eighteen states over the years sometimes included a disclosure directive (Common Cause 1989b, 16–17). Different administrative positions may have different disclosure requirements, keyed to salary and/or discretionary authority. Thirteen states require disclosure from all state employees who earn over a specified income (see Table 7.1).

In Pennsylvania, state, county, and local elected and appointed officials and public employees must file a disclosure with the state, while senior appointees in Philadelphia must file an additional disclosure to comply with a mayoral executive order. The Massachusetts State Ethics Commission reports that it reviewed approximately 45,000 disclosures between 1979 and 1988 and achieved a 95 percent compliance rate. "What began as one of the commission's major activities has become a routine matter within the agency, and a basically accepted requirement of public life for those officials and employees who must file" (Commonwealth of Massachusetts 1988, 2). New York State's Ethics in Government Act of 1987 requires employees who earn less than about $53,000 or hold nonpolicy-making positions to submit a limited disclosure form.

Information subject to disclosure varies from specific dollar amounts to narrow or broad categories (Common Cause's recommendation). Coverage may extend to assets, income, financial transactions, liabilities such as personal and bank loans, gifts from nonfamily sources, and reimbursements for travel and other activities. Disclosure is usually limited to immediate family and dependents, and no state requires reporting beyond this traditional circle of personal relationships (Weimer 1990, 10). Some jurisdictions such as Philadelphia allow nonreporting even for immediate family members. Definitions in model statutes from the National Municipal League, Common Cause, and COGEL are broader; to some extent they allow for mixed, blended, and unorthodox domestic arrangements.

Avoiding the Appearance of Impropriety

Appearance is not a universally adopted and legally enforceable standard, despite its centrality to federal standards. The COGEL's draft model statute adopts it, as do many professional codes, including the American Bar Association's well-known Canon 9. Common Cause and the National Institute of Municipal Law Officers' codes do not. Among the cities in the municipal study described below, Philadelphia, Chicago, and Buffalo expressly require avoiding the appearance of impropriety. Definitional lapses make a legally enforceable appearance standard problematic at best. Given the variations in legal provisions, state practices, and public interest organizations' stands, the most definitive conclusion is that the jury is still out on appearance as an enforceable standard suitable for public service codes.

Revolving Door

The number of states with postemployment restrictions climbed to twenty-three by 1990 (see Table 7.1). What may soon become another standard practice among the states usually prohibits the lobbying of former agencies on matters in which the official or employee was personally and substantially involved. Other common provisions place permanent bans on disclosure of privileged information.

Coming Attractions

Table 7.2 shows selected constrained or regulated activities compiled from current practices across jurisdictions throughout the country. Modes of restraint include state constitution, case law, statute, executive order, administrative action, or union contract. This inventory may appear to be an already daunting menu of behavioral classifications. But discriminating, specialized, and even creative invention marks the ethics arena as much if not more than does developing consensus. In the evolutionary, adaptive system described herein, today's innovation may foreshadow tomorrow's standard practice.

The ethics business is booming, and training adds a new element.[3] With education pinpointed as "a key element to an effective ethics code," most states require commissions to publish reports or handbooks (Weimer 1990, 6). Ethics training became mandatory for selected federal employees in 1989[4] and in California and in Los Angeles in 1990; it was proposed for Alaska in 1990. The 1989 report of the code-drafting commission for Los Angeles posited that

Table 7.2

Selected Constrained or Regulated Activities

General Conflict of Interest
• Use of position for personal (self, other, any) gain or interest
• Interest or gain defined as pecuniary (other), actual (potential), or direct (indirect)
• Unauthorized use of jurisdiction's resources (property, personnel)
• Bribery, nepotism
• Use (or disclosure) of confidential and/or privileged information, ex parte
   communication
• Recusal, whistleblowing, procedural protections
• Avoiding the appearance of impropriety
• Gifts, gratuities, and travel
• Represent interests against jurisdiction's interests (legal counsel, expert)

Outside Employment and Income
• Prior authorization (paid, unpaid) for employment
• Consulting, publishing, teaching, volunteer work
• Representing (or aiding) private interests/clients before jurisdiction
• Honoraria and fees
• Loans to jurisdiction's employees or officials
• Direct (indirect) business interest in jurisdiction's business
• Business relationships with superiors and/or subordinates
• Restricted income sources, investment limits in jurisdiction
• Divestiture (actual, blind trusts) of ownership (or participation) for concerns doing
   business with jurisdiction or regulated by jurisdiction (or directly by employee)
• Contract negotiation with former employers/co-workers
• Contract inducements, contingent fees, gratuities, kickbacks
• Liability for unauthorized contracts

Postemployment (Revolving Door)
• Negotiation for future employment
• Appearance before former agency
• Disclose former employment with jurisdiction in dealings with jurisdiction
• Appearance before jurisdiction's regulatory agencies (purchasing units)
• Lobbying (permanent, contingent) officials (former employees/co-workers) (if
   substantive or other relationship in official capacity)

Personal Disclosure
• Scope (financial, personal, other)
• Coverage (officials, candidates, nominees, employees, appointees, volunteers,
   government branch) related to salary levels, policy-making positions, and/or
   regulatory functions
• Scrutiny (public, private, mixture)
• Interests of family (spouse, children, parents, dependents, other)
• Reporting outside income (by dollar amounts or source, in narrow or broad
   categories)
• Sources (investments, interest income, deposits in financial
   institutions, pension, other benefits)
• Real estate (including or excluding primary residence)
• Level of ownership (partner, shareholder, other)
• Professional and occupational licenses, consulting (fees, relationships)
• Inheritances, trusts and beneficiaries

"the central function of an ethics code is to prevent—rather than punish—unethical conduct. To achieve that goal, the commission believes an educational and training program must accompany the new code" and recommended mandatory training and ongoing education (Cowan Commission 1989b, 11–12). The same argument was made in Senate testimony in 1988, when former director of the federal Office of Government Ethics, Judge Frank Q. Nebeker, said, "Ethics education programs are an essential key to a vibrant government ethics program of prevention" (quoted in Gilman 1991, 16).

A second development is the use of forward, multi-year, or protected funding in several jurisdictions to insulate the ethics commission from political pressure, executive or legislative retaliation, and budgetary vagaries. A third emerging practice is that of seeking and sometimes getting direct subpoena powers for ethics commissions. A fourth is inclusive coverage of all jurisdictions and all branches of government statewide. Fifth, postemployment restrictions and treatment of part-time, contractual, and volunteer government officials and employees are volatile issues in which developments only hint at an emerging consensus. Today, at least twenty-two states require financial disclosure from volunteer members of state boards and commissions (see Table 7.1).

Other issues may strike some as even more controversial. Consider shaping financial disclosure to contemporary life-styles and responsibilities associated with, for example, dual-career couples, blended families, adult guardianships, adult children in household, and life partners. The increase in number, status, and influence of legislative staff members in state governments suggests that extending or adopting code provisions may mark a future phase. In states such as Connecticut and Minnesota, the state code is a term and condition of employment by virtue of its incorporation into union contracts. Some privacy concerns, including polygraph and integrity tests and medical and insurance records, are still in their embryonic stage but are sure to emerge on state agendas.

Model statutes are visions of the future to the extent that they are influential. Common Cause recently was a key player in California, West Virginia, and Massachusetts. Core elements in its model statute for state government include prohibitions on abuse of office for personal gain and on conflicts of interest; standards of conduct to prevent and avoid abuse; personal financial disclosure for candidates and high-level officials; and a strong, independent commission with investigatory and civil enforcement powers. Its *Model Ethics Law for State Government* (Common Cause 1989a) covers detailed disclosure, prohibitions against conflicts and procedures to avoid and prevent them, postemployment restrictions, a strong ethics commission, and investigatory procedures to assure due process.

Federal Offices and Standards

Conflict-of-interest prohibitions are central to federal standards of conduct. These standards range from affirmative ideals to unequivocal restrictions and on to the criminal code. The standards include the more positive, prescriptive Code of Ethics for Government Service (P.L. 96–303, enacted in 1980), detailed proscriptions administratively adopted by executive orders plus regulations from the U.S. Office of Government Ethics and individual agencies, and criminal conflict-of-interest statutes in 18 U.S.C. 201–09.

Federal conflict-of-interest statutes date to the Civil War, but the principle can be traced formally to 1789, when the Act to Establish the Treasury Department (1 Stat. 12, 1789) created the first domestic federal agency and prohibited conflict of interest (and promised a financial reward for whistleblowers). Section 8 states that "no person appointed to any office instituted by this act shall directly or indirectly be concerned or interested in carrying on the business of trade or commerce." The many federal statutes were first codified in 1962 and, except for postemployment provisions, have not been amended "substantially" since then (U.S. Office of Government Ethics 1990b, 814). The general conflict-of-interest law is in 18 U.S.C. Section 208. The Ethics Reform Act of November 30, 1989, revised this section by adding civil prosecution and injunctions to criminal prosecution.

Broader and more stringent standards have been adopted administratively. The first of three executive orders (E.O.) dates to President Lyndon Johnson's E.O. 11222 of 1965. President George Bush issued E.O. 12674 in 1989 and, in October of the next year, E.O. 12731; the latter puts limits on outside earned income. The U.S. Office of Government Ethics (OGE) promulgates regulations to implement the standards. Agencies issue supplementary rules and procedures jointly with the OGE. These account for agency particularities, which include organic act limitations, statutory gift acceptance authority, and procurement, human subject research, or other functional specialities. E.O. 12731, Section 301(a), directs agency heads to augment the OGE regulations with "regulations of special applicability to the particular functions and activities of that agency."

According to a memorandum from the OGE (1990b, 814) on the difference between criminal and noncriminal rules,

> There is a significant difference in the range of conduct covered by these two sets of standards. Conduct covered by the criminal statutes is what Congress has determined is punitively inappropriate in public service. The regulatory standards of conduct for executive branch officials, which cover a larger range of conduct, reflect a Presidential determination. . . . Such conduct does not rise to a level requiring use of criminal process.

U.S. Office of Government Ethics

The OGE was initially created in the federal Office of Personnel Management by the Ethics in Government Act of 1978, and it was given separate agency status when the act was amended a decade later. The 1988 reauthorization act defines the OGE's mission as "overall direction of executive branch policies relating to preventing conflicts of interest on the part of officers and employees of any executive agency." The OGE, which is a small agency with a small budget, is vulnerable as one of the relatively few discretionary components of the federal budget.

Since 1989, the executive order in force has required the OGE to promulgate regulations establishing a "single, comprehensive and clear set of executive branch standards of conduct" (E.O. 12674 specifies they be "objective, reasonable, and enforceable."). On January 18, 1990, the agency published interim regulations in the Federal Register in order to standardize rules and correct deficiencies in agency ethics programs.[5] While the OGE's tasks extend beyond regulatory authority to include financial disclosure, education and training, guidance and interpretation, enforcement, and evaluation of conflict-of-interest laws, its regulatory reach touches every executive employee in federal service and every agency.

Compliance and the Ethics Industry

Although ethics may appear to be a growth industry in the federal government, the evidence is contradictory. Agency budgets belie a growth pattern and the OGE's surveys show only one agency with a separate line item for ethics in both 1989 and 1990 (U.S. Office of Government Ethics 1991, 1990a, 22). Although E.O. 12674 states that agencies should have separate budget line items when "practical," and the 1990 order repeats the directive, not one respondent to the OGE's first survey of executive agencies indicated that greater budget independence would increase the program's effectiveness; increased staff (and "other") dominated responses about program effectiveness (U.S. Office of Government Ethics 1990a, 23). Staffing is another indicator that is sending out conflicting signals. There were only 178 full-time equivalent employees working in ethics in 1990, but more than 7,000 were involved part-time (see Table 7.3).

Whether ethics is in a growth phase or a holding pattern, its accent on legal compliance and enforcement dominates the overall enterprise in the executive branch. With administrative and criminal standards and numerous agencies and offices involved in oversight, reporting, investigation, prosecution, and other activities, the overlap and complexity is impressive. The roster includes the OGE itself, the Merit System Protections Board, U.S. attorney offices, Office of the Special Counsel, inspectors general offices,[6] general counsels, agency heads, designated agency ethics officers (see below), and the departments of Justice's and Treasury's public integrity units. To the list add special units, committees, and procedures in different agencies such as the Department of Defense, presidential commissions and the President's Council on Integrity and Efficiency,[7] and congressional hearings and investigations.

The compliance focus of federal ethics programs is reinforced by the desig-

Table 7.3

Ethics Practices in the Federal Executive Branch

	1989	1990
Reporting executive agencies	109	115
Designated agency ethics officer		
in legal office	81	88
in personnel office	4	4
in ethics office	NA	1
other	NA	22
Employees working in ethics program		
total full-time	126	178
total part-time	6167	7109
average part-time	57	62
Restrictions based on agency-specific legislation	25	34
Public financial disclosure (permanent, full-time employees)		
compliance rate (ratio of required:filed)	97%	98%
reports inspected	591	1105
by news media	48%	4%
Confidential financial disclosure (permanent, full-time employees)		
compliance rate (required:filed)+	93%	97%
actions*	6330	8946
as percent of filed reports	3%	4%
disqualifications as percent of actions	60%	71%
Other practices		
agency standards provided to new employees	96	100
new employee briefings	84	89
written explanation (e.g., handbook)	82	93
employee never certifies reading	63	58
DAEO (or alternate/deputy) responsible for training	101	104
agency regulations used in training	93	100
Regulations require written prior approval or notification for outside employment	67	78

	1990
Counseling on ethics issues provided by	
legal office	96
ethics office	37
personnel office	24
other	33
Disciplinary actions for restrained activities++	2957
misuse of government resources**	731
misuse of position**	274
misuse of information	101
gifts from outside sources	86
compensation from nonfederal sources	76
conflicting outside activities	65
conflicting personal interests	63
conflicting financial interests	50
gambling, betting, and lotteries	30

(continued)

Table 7.3 (continued)

	1990
Disciplinary actions for restrained activities *(continued)*	
gifts between employees	11
seeking other employment	10
other	1460
Criminal referrals from agency	122

+The military's compliance rate for 1989 was higher than the civilian rate but in 1990 it fell to below 92 percent, presumably because of Operation Desert Storm.

*Actions include divestiture, resignation from outside position, written disqualification, waiver, reassignment, and other. Note that there was a 60 percent increase in written disqualifications between 1989 and 1990.

++Time and attendance violations are excluded. Disciplinary actions include removal, demotion, suspension, and written reprimand or its equivalent.

**The most frequent categories, misuse of government resources and of position, respectively account for 25 percent and 9 percent of disciplinary actions. The two categories of gifts together account for 3 percent of actions; of the advice provided in 1989 by the OGE to ethics officials, 13 percent involved the issue of gifts.

Source: Compiled from the U.S. Office of Government Ethics, *First Biennial Report to Congress* (1990), and Preliminary results: Agency Ethics Program 1990 Survey Report (1991).

nated agency ethics officers (DAEO), the overwhelming majority of whom are in legal offices where most of the counseling on ethical issues occurs (see Table 7.3). A DAEO "serves as a technical resource to the IG [Inspector General], but the DAEO's primary duties are to provide training and counseling to agency employees on conflict of interest matters and to review financial disclosure statements" (U.S. Congress, General Accounting Office 1987, 7). The compliance focus of ethics officers is apparent in the vacancy notice issued by the U.S. Department of Housing and Urban Development in April 1990. The notice for vacancy number 00-MSD–90–0057 states,

> The incumbent, serving as Director of the Office of Ethics and the Deputy Agency Ethics Officer, is responsible for directing a staff charged with developing, coordinating, and managing the department's programs regarding ethics and standards of conduct. The incumbent will develop policies and procedures, assure proper review of disclosure reports, provide advice and assistance to HUD executives on ethics-related issues, and assure that remedies are effected to correct violations or potential violations of HUD standards of conduct.

Program goals reinforce the compliance commitment. The OGE's surveys (1990a, 1991) use questionnaires that constitute agencies' annual report required under P.L. 100–598, the 1988 reauthorization legislation for the OGE. The survey on 1990 practices asked respondents to rank program goals from most important (first rank) through least important (ninth rank). The responses clustered, with "employee awareness of ethics" ranked foremost in importance by 68 percent of respondents. A majority (52 percent) of responses awarded "understanding standards of conduct" second rank, although this was the dominant goal in the survey of 1989 practices. Attributed importance then declined to a middle ranking, but none of the five major goals fell below middle range. While "oversight of financial disclosure" was ranked "3" by 39 percent of respondents, 65 percent of responses fell in the combined "3" and "4" categories. "Advising departing employees on post-employment issues" elicited a "4" from 48 percent of responses whereas ranks "4" and "5" combined accounted for 81 percent of all responses. "Developing improved standards" was ranked lowest among the five major goals (as in the earlier survey) at "5" by 60 percent of respondents; nonetheless, it was still accorded a middle-range ranking.

Enforcement and Administrative Actions

Disciplinary actions for violations of noncriminal standards include termination, suspension, restitution, reassignment, reprimand, admonishment, recusal, and divestiture. The taking of administrative action does not preclude criminal sanctions. Inspectors general (IGs) review the action and "commonly refer cases that are declined by Justice to the employee's bureau-level supervisor for administrative action" (U.S. Congress, General Accounting Office 1987, 12). In 1989, about one-quarter of the over 2,000 adverse actions on standards violations dealt with misuse of government vehicles and other property, while less than 2 percent related to conflicting financial interest and less than 3 percent to conflicting outside action (U.S. Office of Government Ethics 1990a, 27). The pattern for disciplinary actions for 1990 (based largely on noncomparable survey questions) is shown in Table 7.3. The most frequently cited categories, misuse of government resources and of position, respectively account for 25 percent and 9 percent of disciplinary actions. The two categories of gifts together account for 3 percent of actions taken in 1990; apparently an enduring problem area despite specific federal regulation, gifts accounted for 13 percent of the advice provided in 1989 by the OGE to ethics officials (U.S. Office of Government Ethics 1990a, 7).

Financial Disclosure

The Monitoring and Compliance Division of the OGE collects and reviews the public Executive Personnel Financial Disclosure Report, the SF 278. Senate-confirmed presidential appointees (excluding federal judicial offices) file disclosures annually and when they leave federal service. This drives an impressive transition-period workload for the unit, which reviewed and certified 474 disclosures to the Senate in one fourteen-month period (U.S. Office of Government Ethics 1990a, 11).

Those who file annual public disclosures include the president, vice president, and officers and employees at senior grades 16 and above on the General Schedule. Thus, high-level managerial, supervisory, and policy positions and the entire career Senior Executive Service (SES) file disclosures that are available for public review. Others who file are those with military ranks at pay grade 0–7 or above, administrative law judges, employees determined by the OGE, selected senior postal service officers and employees, the OGE's director, and agency DAEOs.

In 1989, incumbents filed more than 14,000 annual public reports, and the career SES achieved a 99 percent compliance rate (calculated from U.S. Office of Government Ethics 1990a, 27). In the entire executive branch in 1989, only one case of filing a false public disclosure was referred to the Department of Justice and there were no referrals for failing to file (U.S. Office of Government Ethics, 1990a, 24). One can gain some sense of the magnitude of the public disclosure enterprise by adding the reports from more than 2,700 new entrants and the 1,700 terminations. Inspections, almost one-half of which emanate from the news media, increased 187 percent from 1989 to 1990 (see Table 7.3). Actions such as divestiture, disqualification, reassignment, letters, waivers, and warnings taken on the basis of public disclosure reports totaled fewer than 1,500, or just shy of 11 percent of all SF 278s filed in 1989, and the career SES accounted for fewer than 700 of all actions (U.S. Office of Government Ethics 1990a, 28–29).

Initiated by executive order in 1965, confidential disclosure is required from more than 200,000 employees each year (compared to the cumulative 45,000 during a decade of operation in Massachusetts). The overall compliance rate reached 93 percent in 1989 and 97 percent in 1990 (see Table 7.3), a climb all the more impressive given the decline in military compliance presumably related to field activities. Dollar amounts are not required, and nonbusiness ventures are excluded. (The directive for reporting household interests reflects a traditional view of the American household.) While confidential reports have led to numerous actions, actions represent only 3–4 percent of all filed confidential reports (see Table 7.3).

The President's Commission on Federal Ethics Law Reform (1989, 81) concluded that financial disclosure is valuable and allows review and employee counseling, but it warned against excessive detail:

> [T]he use of unduly narrow categories for specifying asset value and income seems to the commission to result in a needless burden on filers without providing particularly useful information to the public and also increases the risk that filers will make inadvertent mistakes.

Local Patterns

Standardization is no more characteristic of municipal practices than of state practices, and patterns at both these levels of government stand very much in contrast to the federal thrust toward standardization. A 1990 study by Paul

Potamianos of fifteen large municipalities uncovered few common features, as did the survey of ethics legislation in seventy-five cities conducted in 1990 by Harriet McCullough, first executive of the City of Chicago's Board of Ethics.[8]

The Potamianos study shows that the authority behind formal standards varies: two municipalities rely on state-promulgated municipal codes, one combines state statute and municipal provisions, another has no ethics legislation from state or municipal government, yet another uses a general council policy only, and four jurisdictions, the largest in the survey, have detailed, extensive municipal codes. McCullough (1990b, 1–2) discloses ethics legislation in forty of the sixty-eight reporting cities. Only eighteen cities have a board or commission. (It is noted below that fourteen states' ethics laws cover municipal jurisdictions.)

Code provisions also vary, and the surveyed jurisdictions have relatively few standards in common. McCullough's (1990b, 3–6) survey shows twenty-five cities with gifts restrictions, twenty-two with travel restrictions, seventeen with postemployment restrictions, and fourteen with a prohibition on nepotism. However, the count for all categories falls short of a majority of the sixty-eight responding cities. Of the many possible permutations for conflict-of-interest restrictions (see Table 7.2), only six emerged in a majority of the cities studied by Potamianos. Direct and indirect interest in business dealing with the city is forbidden or restricted; representing private interests before the city is forbidden; disclosure and use of confidential information is barred; use of position for personal pecuniary gain is banned; limits on honoraria, travel, and gifts are imposed; and disclosure of interest is required (Potamianos 1990).

As a result of variations in official standards among local jurisdictions, legalistic responses to ethical questions also alter as one moves from locality to locality. Nonetheless, some standardization may yet emanate from the activities of national professional associations. For example, in its treatment of conflict of interest, the National Institute of Municipal Law Officers' draft code (intended for use by municipal attorneys when drafting municipal codes) limits interests to "direct or indirect pecuniary or material benefit." However, the draft code would require disclosure of financial or personal interest in proposed municipal legislation and forbids "special consideration, treatment or advantage to any citizen beyond that which is available to every other citizen" (National Institute of Municipal Law Officers 1990, 3, 5–6).

McCullough (1990b, 3) shows twenty-six of the sixty-eight reporting cities with some type of financial disclosure. Only two of many possible provisions affecting personal disclosure (see Table 7.2) are identified as majority practices among the fifteen cities in the Potamianos study. These are financial or economic disclosure from city officials and employees and disclosure of nonhomestead real estate. Three procedural majority practices that are identified in this study are having a commission or board of ethics, giving it investigatory authority, and giving it authority to issue or request subpoenas. No majority practices emerged in the areas of abuse of office, procedural protections, or whistleblowing (Potamianos 1990).

Change constitutes a second pattern that is identifiable in local jurisdictions. Several major municipalities have instituted or revised ethics codes within the last half-decade. For example, Mayor Harold Washington issued Chicago's ethics code by executive order in 1986, and it was passed by the city council in 1987 (in a vote of 49–0 that concealed earlier political disputes).

In June 1990, voters in Los Angeles approved by referendum a full-blown code that was developed largely by the drafting commission but that accommodated some city council amendments. Under the leadership of Geoffrey Cowan (former chairman of California's Common Cause), the commission made itself independent of city government and city financing. It took a relatively strict approach to conflict issues by incorporating financial and noneconomic ties that potentially induce partiality or give that appearance. The commission's options report on resolving conflicts of interest summarized the state's 1974 act and then went further, noting that Los Angeles had imposed by virtue of its city charter a stricter test for recusal. The city attorney's office decided matters on the basis of "whether the public could reasonably conclude that there is an appearance of a conflict of interest" and used a not-in-the-public-interest standard (Cowan Commission 1989a, 147–48). As a result of the June referendum, Los Angeles has the most comprehensive ethics package of any city in the country. A strong ethics commission can call for a special prosecutor if the city attorney has a conflict of interest and revolving-door restrictions limit postemployment and government employees' involvement with former employers' contracts.

Blanket Coverage

Although most states' ethics laws do not extend to local officials and employees, at least fourteen states have coverage that blankets officials and employees in state, county, and municipal governments (Council on Governmental Ethics Laws 1990, 10–17). The obvious trade-off between statewide uniformity and local adaptability is complicated by differences in size and complexity and other dimensions (such as strong implicit or distinctive moral codes, the size of the talent pool, readily observable and widely known behavior, and unavoidable personal interests involving local contracting). As a classic administrative taboo, duplication of effort warrants some consideration and in this regard Harriet McCullough (1990a, 1) notes, "The passage of ethics legislation in large cities can be a huge task. It takes time, commitment, compromise, political posturing, citizen involvement, media attention, and lots and lots of debate." A statewide approach avoids repetition of the task, but the debate itself may be deemed useful.

Localities are treated differently in different states and in different model statutes. Common Cause endorsed uniform standards years ago while the National Municipal League did not include local jurisdictions in its 1979 model statute. More than two decades ago, New York's state legislature defined conflicts of interest and required each jurisdiction, from counties to school districts, to adopt its own code. According to the New York State Commission on Government Integrity (1988, 2), the state's 1987 Ethics in Government Act "had little application to local government," and 95 percent of all municipalities in the state are "totally unaffected" by its provisions. The commission (p. 1) noted "a confusing patchwork of contradictory, inadequate and sometimes overly restrictive ethics codes, some of which are unenforceable and some of which are simply not enforced" and recommended a statewide municipal ethics act.

By contrast, selected state, county, and city officials as well as state and local employees designated in the conflict-of-interest code are required to file annual statements of economic interest in California. City officers include mayors, council members, city managers, chief administrative officers, planning commissioners, and city attorneys. The state ethics commission in Massachusetts ("the primary civil enforcement agency") reports that the state's conflict-of-interest law

> has regulated the conduct of public officials and employees in the Bay State since 1963. The law limits what public employees may do on the job, what they may do after hours or "on the side," and what they may do after they leave public service and return to the private sector. It also sets the standards of conduct required of all state, county, and municipal employees in Massachusetts, articulating the premise that public employees owe undivided loyalty to the government they serve, and must act in the public interest rather than for private gain. [Commonwealth of Massachusetts 1989, 2]

Municipal employees saw a perverse kind of progress over one decade. While the fifty complaints to the Massachusetts commission in 1979 involved no municipal employees, they were the subjects of about four-fifths of the more than 750 allegations in each of fiscal years 1988 and 1989.

Limits to the Regulatory Approach

Empirical evidence undercuts the plausibility of error-free regulation. A few recent samples illustrate the potential, complexity, loopholes, and even perverse outcomes from writing and implementing standards of conduct. They also illustrate the variations in standards operating in the more than 80,000 government units in the United States.

• Although an investigation into advance knowledge was inconclusive, a police chief in Buffalo, New York, was found in violation of ethics standards when he purchased a house in an urban renewal district two days after the renewal plan was announced. His daughter had worked on the city's renewal plan (Potamianos 1990).
• Private interest in official action reared its head in Ohio in 1989. A bill was introduced into Ohio's state legislature to provide that "the relationship of a

public official or employee, or of his family members, to a church or other religious organization solely as a member, participant, worshiper, or volunteer shall not be considered as manifesting a substantial and improper influence on him with respect to his duties or as otherwise constituting a conflict of interest." This bill was a response to an ethics commission's opinion advising four city officials including the mayor that the ethics law prohibited them from participating in decisions about property held by a church of which they were members (Judd 1989, 25–26).

• California's Fair Political Practices Commission's summary of enforcement decisions and its bulletin (FPPC) cites individuals by name, affiliation, violation, and sanction. Some other commissions summarize and sanitize reports of rendered opinions.

• Chicago's Board of Ethics (City of Chicago 1988, 60, 99) limited spousal interest by taking the view that "[a] city employee who negotiates an agreement for the city with a corporation represented by the law firm where the employee's wife is a lawyer [but not directly participating] does not by virtue of his wife's employment have an economic or financial interest in the negotiations." Another finding: sisters-in-law are not covered by the nepotism restrictions in the ethics ordinance.

• A 1986 letter to a federal employee from the U.S. Office of Government Ethics (1990b, 643–646) advises, "To avoid adverse appearances, we think you should consider imposing limitations on the use of the [agency's] gift acceptance authority. Under [statutory] gift acceptance authority, the agency, rather than the employee, accepts the payment. As a result, the adverse appearances . . . are not necessarily present . . . Even so, we generally suggest that agencies avoid accepting reimbursements from organizations that do business with or are regulated by the agency." The letter goes on to distinguish appearance by nonprofit versus for-profit status of the gift-giving entity. For nonprofits, "the appearance problem is not substantial since the entity is not in a position to profit as a result."

The President's Commission on Federal Ethics Law Reform recognized the limits to the regulatory approach in its report, *To Serve with Honor* (1989, 1):

> Laws and rules can never be fully descriptive of what an ethical person should do. They can simply establish minimal standards of conduct. Possible variations in conduct are infinite, virtually impossible to describe and proscribe by statute. Compulsion by law is the most expensive way to make people behave.

Even a highly regulatory approach cannot improve the moral climate in the true meaning of the phrase. One state–local report states that the code, disclosure, commission, and penalties "will improve the moral climate and contribute to the prevention of corruption in government in the future" (quoted in Common Cause 1989b, 6). This is unfortunate because it is unrealistic, and reality is bound to fall short. Realistically, no code will turn deliberate scoundrels into law-abiding public servants. With respect to overhauling the Senate's code, Senator Adlai Stevenson of Illinois remarked, "If there are culprits in our midst, they are unlikely to be deterred by ethics codes" (U.S. Senate 1980, 137). At the municipal level, S. Stanley Kruetzer (who drafted a code for New York City and was chief counsel of a New York State legislative ethics commission) "recounts how, when he wrote to 100 mayors about ethics codes, they responded along the lines of 'we know in our hearts what right and wrong is and no code will prevent someone from the wrong' " (Lewis 1986, 14).

Conclusion

There is no empirical evidence to support an ethics deterrence theory; down that road lies futility. Even the best code will not substitute for good government or good people. In this vein, Sissela Bok (1978, 250) cautions that "codes must be but the starting point for a broad inquiry into the ethical quandaries at work."

The ongoing controversy over the advisability of codification spawns three generic choices. Jurisdictions can adopt intricate rules with interpretations, advisory opinions, and complex enforcement mechanisms and protections. Alternatively, governments can elect blanket prohibitions that are simple to understand and apply but inflexible and difficult to live with. Finally, explicit rules, categorical prohibitions, and articulated standards can be rejected altogether. Many governments today increasingly choose the first option and seem to respond to the questions, "If not cure-alls, then what good are codes? What can they do?" with simple answers. Ethics codes do less than everything and more than nothing.

This study offers evidence of rapid and significant change in the governmental jurisdiction approach to formal standards of conduct. The direction of change overall favors a more regulated administrative environment marked by increasingly stringent, specific standards and demarcated procedures. The federal executive is moving obviously and vigorously in the direction of increased regulation and standardization. Tables 7.1 and 7.2 indicate a regulatory bearing at state and local levels as well, but standardization is another matter. Despite some identifiable areas of consensus such as conflict-of-interest prohibitions, there remain substantial variations (for example, the appearance standard). In sum, formal standards, legal sanctions, and constrained administrative behavior vary significantly across state and local jurisdictions.

Notes

1. Common Cause (1989b, 18) identified thirty-two independent state ethics commissions in 1989.
2. Similarly, much of the federal advisory assistance—7,000 telephone calls for ad-

vice in 1989—involves interpreting and applying conflict-of-interest statutes (U.S. Office of Government Ethics 1990a, 7).

3. With respect to graduate education in public administration, the National Association of Schools of Public Affairs and Administration (NASPAA) in 1987 incorporated ethics education into its official curriculum standards ("the common curriculum components shall enhance the student's values, knowledge, and skills to act ethically and effectively"). Many graduate programs offer ethics courses, although they differ fundamentally (Hejka-Ekins, 1988) and their efficacy is debated (Lilla 1981; Mainzer 1991).

4. Training was identified as one of the steps or resources by which to enhance agency ability to meet the ethics program goals by a majority of agencies responding to a survey of practices in the executive branch (U.S. Office of Government Ethics 1991). According to Stuart Gilman (1991, 16), chief of the Education Division, U.S. Office of Government Ethics, the issuing of final training regulations in the summer of 1991 "present[s] an added emphasis on ethics education in the executive branch."

5. Agency ethics programs are reviewed by the OGE's Program Review Branch "about once every five years" (Gilman 1991, 15).

6. The Inspector General Act of 1978 provided for independent inspectors general (IGs) "to conduct and supervise audits and investigations and recommend policies to promote economy, efficiency, and effectiveness as well as the prevention and detection of fraud and abuse in programs and operations of their agencies" (General Accounting Office 1990, 1). The 1988 amendments (P.L. 100–504) increased to twenty-four the number of presidentially appointed IGs, now including all cabinet-level departments; IGs in more than thirty smaller agencies are appointed by agency heads.

7. Created in March 1981, the council was charged by the president to "be mean as 'junkyard dogs' in pursuing fraud and waste of taxpayers money" (President's Council on Integrity and Efficiency, 1987, foreword by President Ronald W. Reagan). Chaired by the deputy director of the Office of Management and Budget, its members are statutory IGs, the Office of Government Ethics' director, and senior representatives of the Federal Bureau of Investigations, Office of Personnel Management, Merit Systems Protection Board, Treasury, and others. In fiscal year 1988 alone, IGs were credited with over 4,000 "successful" prosecutions and $10.8 billion in savings, expenditure avoidance, and recoveries and restitutions (President's Council on Integrity and Efficiency for fiscal year 1988).

9. The Potamianos study includes Los Angeles, San Diego, Jacksonville, Miami, Atlanta, Chicago, Minneapolis, Buffalo, New York City, Oklahoma City, Philadelphia, Austin, Dallas, San Antonio, and Washington, D.C. Each has a population in excess of 300,000 and six exceed one million; together, they account for more than 21 million residents and represent every region of the country and both mayor–council and city manager forms of government. McCullough surveyed the largest city in each state and the twenty-five largest in the country and, with sixty-eight cities responding, reports a response rate of more than 80 percent (McCullough 1990b, 1).

References

Bok, S. 1978. *Lying: Moral Choice in Public and Private Life.* New York: Random House.

Bowman, J.S. 1981. "The Management of Ethics: Codes of Conduct in Organizations." *Public Personnel Management Journal,* 10: 59–66.

City of Chicago. *Annual Report of the Board of Ethics.* Chicago: Board of Ethics, fiscal years 1987, 1988.

Common Cause. 1989a. *A Model Ethics Law for State Government.* Washington, D.C.: Common Cause, January.

Common Cause. 1989b. *Conflict of Interest Legislation in the States*. Washington, D.C.: Common Cause, September.

Commonwealth of Massachusetts. *Annual Report of the State Ethics Commission*. Boston: State Ethics Commission, fiscal years 1988, 1989.

Council on Governmental Ethics Laws. 1986–87, 1990. Blue Book, *Campaign Finance, Ethics and Lobby Law*. Lexington, KY: Council of State Governments.

Cowan Commission. 1989a. Option Reports Prepared for the Commission to Draft a Code of Ethics for Los Angeles City Government. Los Angeles: Cowan Commission staff, October.

Cowan Commission. 1989b. *Ethics and Excellence in Government*. Final Report and Recommendations of the Commission to Draft an Ethics Code for Los Angeles City Government. Los Angeles: Cowan Commission, November.

Gilman, S.C. 1991. "The U.S. Office of Government Ethics." *The Bureaucrat* 20: 13–16.

Hall, R.T. 1989. *The West Virginia Governmental Ethics Act: Text and Commentary*. Foreword by G. Caperton and introduction by R. "Chuck" Chambers. Charleston, WV: Mountain State Press.

Hejka-Ekins, A. 1988. "Teaching Ethics in Public Administration." *Public Administration Review*, 48: 885–91.

Josephson Institute. 1991. *Preserving the Public Trust: Principles of Public Service Ethics, Standards of Conduct and Guidelines for Government Decision Making*. Marina del Rey, CA: Josephson Institute for the Advancement of Ethics, Government Ethics Center.

Judd, R.R. 1989. "Ethics Codes and Commissions: Legislation and Litigation in 1989." Paper prepared for the annual meeting of the Council on Governmental Ethics Law, New Orleans, December 6.

Lewis, C.W. 1986. *Scruples and Scandals, A Handbook on Public Service Ethics for State and Local Government Officials and Employees in Connecticut*. Storrs: University of Connecticut, Institutes of Public Service and Urban Research.

Lilla, M.T. 1981. "Ethos, 'Ethics,' and Public Service." *Public Interest* 63: 3–17.

McCullough, H. M. 1990a. "Ethics in the City of Angels." *COGEL Guardian* (April 30): 1, 6.

———. 1990b. "Municipal Ethics Legislation: The State of the Cities." Chicago: Harriet McCullough, December.

Mainzer, L.C. 1991. "Vulgar Ethics for Public Administration." *Administration and Society* 23: 3–28.

National Institute of Municipal Law Officers, 1990. *NIMLO Model Ordinance on Code of Ethics*, Draft by J.C. Pinson. Washington, DC: National Institute of Municipal Law Officers.

National Municipal League. 1979. *Model State Conflict of Interest and Financial Disclosure Law*. New York: National Municipal League.

New York State Commission on Government Integrity. 1988. *Municipal Ethical Standards: The Need for a New Approach*. New York: New York State Commission on Government Integrity.

Potamianos, P. 1990. "Codes of Ethics in Municipal Government: A Survey of Major Cities." Paper submitted to author's seminar on administrative ethics at University of Connecticut, Storrs.

President's Commission on Federal Ethics Law Reform. 1989. *To Serve with Honor, Report and Recommendations to the President*. Washington: Government Printing Office.

President's Council on Integrity and Efficiency. 1987. *Major Impacts of the Federal Offices of Inspector General, 1981–86: The First 5 Years*. Washington, DC: President's Council on Integrity and Efficiency.

————. n.d. *A Progress Report to the President.* Washington, DC: President's Council on Integrity and Efficiency, fiscal year 1988.

U.S. Congress, General Accounting Office. 1987. "Ethics Enforcement, Process by which Conflict of Interest Allegations Are Investigated and Resolved," GAO/GGD–87–83BR. Washington, DC: General Accounting Office, June.

————. 1990. Inspectors General, Progress in Establishing OIGs at Designated Federal Entities," GAO/AFMD–90–46. Washington, DC: General Accounting Office, April.

U.S. Office of Government Ethics. 1990a. *First Biennial Report to Congress.* Washington, DC: U.S. Office of Government Ethics, March.

————. 1990b. *The Informal Advisory Letters and Memoranda and Formal Opinions of the United States Office of Government Ethics, 1979–1988.* Washington, DC: Government Printing Office.

————. 1991. *Preliminary Results: Agency Ethics Program 1990 Survey Report.* Washington, DC: U.S. Office of Government Ethics, March 18.

U.S. Senate, Select Committee on Ethics. 1980. "Revising the Senate Code of Official Conduct Pursuant to Senate Resolution 109." 96th Congress, 2d sess., November.

Weimer, L. 1990. *Memorandum on Ethics Codes.* Legislative staff, State of Alaska, May 2.

8

The Realpolitik of Ethics Codes: An Implementation Approach to Public Ethics

J. Patrick Dobel

One of the results of widespread cynicism and distrust of American government is the proliferation of ethics codes. They are supposed to increase confidence in government by reassuring citizens that private power and interest do not subvert government decisions. Thirty-six states have passed ethics codes and established commissions or agencies to oversee ethics issues (Burke and Benson 1989; COGEL 1991). Countless cities and counties have also established ethics codes and boards (McCullough 1990). Eighty percent of major American corporations have adopted Codes of Ethics (Burke and Benson 1989). The American political system, however, is not necessarily self-correcting. Governments often try to correct problems with flawed programs that become institutionalized (Ingraham 1987). Ethics codes may now verge on becoming a panacea for problems that they cannot solve. This could contribute to the cynicism and distrust they are supposed to address (Robin, Giallourakis, and Moritz 1989).

Despite their proliferation, very little is known about how ethics codes are implemented or how they function. No fine-grained case studies exist, and there are only a few aggregate studies that collate the nature of the codes (Bowman 1981). One major study of codes in private industry could find no discernable difference in the behaviors of corporations with codes and those without codes (Matthews 1988). The rhetoric that surrounds the passage of ethics codes often emphasizes that they will function above politics and solve the problems that undermine the legitimacy of government (COGEL 1991; Chandler 1983). But ethics codes face a peculiar set of problems in their development and implementation. They are deeply enmeshed in political and bureaucratic life and should not be considered as a separate and idealistic undertaking set apart from the realities of politics. The self-conscious injection of ethics into political life invites its own pathologies and abuses, which must be addressed in developing and implementing codes.

This chapter will discuss the development and implementation of the ethics code in King County, Washington, as an illustrative case study of problems inherent in adopting an ethics code in a local setting.[1] The first section examines the politics of ethics and the paradoxical consequences of injecting "ethics" and institutionalized codes into political life.[2] The second section discusses the implementation and reform of the ethics code in King County, Washington. The third section uses the King County case to suggest a managerial approach to implementing an ethics code.

The Politics of Ethics

A well-crafted and well-staffed ethics code can accomplish a number of vital public purposes. Broadly, the code can help restore and support public trust and the legitimacy of government. It accomplishes this purpose by limiting the ability of private power and interest to subvert fair access to government or the independent judgment of public officials. The codes and agencies also can provide forums of judgment where citizens can question practices which they believe violate the public trust and where concerned public officials can get guidance on complex issues.

As a corollary to these broad purposes, the codes must affect the daily lives of public officials. A good code and agency can buttress and support the independence of government officials and provide direction and advice on complicated issues. The board and the code increase the resources available to managers and public officials to aid them with identification and clarification of issues and to help them resist blandishments and efforts to influence them from the outside. Codes can also remove a number of temptations that might undermine good judgment or fair access. They can also regularize and professionalize relations with clients, vendors, and lobbyists.

A principled code can become a source of professional identity and a reference for individuals, rather than an imposition. A code succeeds best if it affects the agency culture and its standards become imbedded in bureaucratic practice. Government officials can use the clear standards or prohibitions to protect themselves and professionalize relations with political actors and vendors, as well as to deflect attempts to influence them unduly.

If boards are understood by officials as a support for good management practice, managers and employees can use these boards for advisory opinions and to anticipate problems before they occur. Boards become the equivalent of the "ethics counselors" that some corporations have put in place to implement codes

(Dryvesteyn 1989). They give managers a way to get advice and support and they can remove the strains imposed on relations by the informal methods of lobbyists and vendors.

A well-designed code and a working board must be supported by ethics education and employee orientation, a good brochure and good literature, a visible staffing for the advisory function, and an investigative arm. Without these and without strong sanctions, they will be seen as paper tigers and will largely be ignored (Dryvesteyn 1989; COGEL 1991). In addition, if the code and board are seen primarily as investigative and punitive and only sporadically active in response to crises or charges, they will lose the possibility of being seen as a neutral advisor on ethics issues. This will undercut the major strategy to internalize the code in bureaucratic behavior.

As codes take effect, they change the way business is done, and can provide fairer access for vendors and stakeholders. Codes help professionalize interpersonal relations and eliminate many incentives for informal inducements. New vendors who seek to sell to the government do not feel as much pressure to engage in corrupt or questionable practices at added cost to themselves. To the extent that postemployment practices are viable, vendors feel less pressure to hire for political reasons and can focus on competence and needs when they assess prospective employees.

But in the real world of politics, the codes will be used in ways not envisioned by their writers. They will encounter resistance and abuse as well as play an unanticipated role in shaping political rhetoric and debate. The structure of politics and codes all but guarantees that this will occur. The politics of ethics places significant constraints upon implementing and reforming a code.

In politics, multiple groups with disparate goals and resources pursue their goals within vague and sometimes legally defined rules of the game. These rules themselves are bound by procedures and are always changing on the basis of precedent or agreement. In government, agencies will pursue their own missions as well as attempt to protect their budgets and core technologies by forming alliances with other agencies and outside groups. These agencies will respond to the demands of their own leaders, the courts, the legislators, the media, and interested groups. At any point, most individuals and agencies are playing several "games" at different levels of politics with many different actors (Bardach 1977; Lynn 1987; Long 1968).

Ethics codes and boards become one more set of constraints, but also one more set of rhetorical, legal, and institutional resources to use in political conflict. In addition, ethics codes sit astride several major nexus points of "games," which guarantee controversy. First, they break down barriers between private and public life, thus making personal aspects such as friendships, family, job seeking, and business interests subject to public scrutiny and judgment. Second, they profoundly affect the borderline between agency and political life, especially at the point where agency officials build alliances they need to support budgets and to gain outside support for initiatives. In this borderland, agencies contract for service, collect information, and find talent. Conversely, many vendors and contractors use informal communications, meals, benefits, and hiring patterns to solidify relations with agencies. They also see agencies as good training grounds for potential talent. Finally, an ethics board that has staff and resources as well as an independent mandate to investigate will be viewed with alarm by both managers and employees. Both will fear the charges from the other side and see this forum of judgment and investigation as a threat to their autonomy and authority.

The genesis and structure of most codes aggravate these political tensions. The vast majority of codes are created in response to scandal (COGEL 1991). The codes are written hastily and with punitive intent, and they usually embody laundry lists of prohibitions to eliminate the most recent scandalous actions. Over time, more scandals demand amendments to the codes, as well as glaring exceptions, which are usually demanded by the legislature and hurt their credibility. Codes seldom possess a positive cast and almost never are designed in consultation with the managers who must run agencies. They traditionally focus on conflict-of-interest definitions and the attempt to insulate public officials from the influence of money, family, or business. They try to demarcate public and private life by limiting the giving and receiving of gifts and the use of government property for gain or for personal use. More recently, they have attempted to solve revolving-door policies that tempt good judgment and create iron triangles. Generally, the tone conveys a clear lack of trust and respect for public officials. The codes reduce "ethics" to a negative prohibition on monetary and personal gain from private service, and enumerate long lists of minutia that now become ethics violations (Hays and Gleissner 1981). Most codes also are built around reporting and disclosure requirements, which make it possible for auditors or the media to identify hidden conflicts of interest by linking actions to revealed private interests. The failure to disclose properly or fully also becomes a violation of the code, and the disclosure forms become important information for the media.

Ethics codes exemplify what Murray Edelman labels "symbolic reassurance." As laws, they reassure the public that the ethics problem has been solved because a law stands on the books. Usually, the code and its attendant offices remain underfunded because they have no real allies to defend their interests and many enemies. Even if it is irrelevant to practice, understaffed, and moribund, the code reassures the public. Consequently, codes often lapse due to budgetary or staff insufficiency, at least until the next ethics scandal (Edelman 1967).

Ethics legislation creates a matrix of rhetoric to define problems and goals. Legislation becomes the legal, bureaucratic, political, and judicial resource of which political actors avail themselves. Once ethics becomes a resource and a subject for rhetoric it affects politics in profound ways. It now defines a set of new problems and issues that warrant government intervention and media scrutiny. Claims of impropriety and corruption are nothing new in the political order; neither are character assassination and charges based on character issues. But the formalization of the rhetoric and codes adds a level of detail and breadth to rhetoric and charges. This rhetoric provides a convenient and relatively low-cost way to attack an adversary, either in electoral or policy debate. Politics and integrity are narrowed to issues of conflict of interest and disclosure while finessing discussion of issues by subverting the credibility of the participants. The elevation of ethics at this level increases the temptations to what Alexander Bickel calls the politics of "moral assault." This pattern of political assault ignores issues and focuses on personal attributes or a detail of an ethics code that delegitimizes the character and judgment of those involved. This form of politics often bypasses elections to achieve political purposes (Ginsberg and Schefter 1991). As codes acquire great detail or minutia that might be violated inadvertently, they increase their usefulness in moral assault.

Issues of character and conflict of interest always invite media scrutiny. Because of their nonideological but sometimes lurid content, ethics charges make good news and enable the media to perform a watchdog function without investing in discussion of issues. Disclosure forms are a mother lode for investigative reporting. Given the information in disclosure forms and the way ethics codes extend culpability to family members or to friendship patterns, the opportunity to uncover wrongdoing or verify patterns suggestive of wrongdoing invites media intervention. In addition, the simple failure to report information adequately and in great detail now becomes a publicized "violation" in the press. Since much ethics legislation derives its urgency from a concern to maintain legitimacy of government, appearances matter profoundly. Consequently, investigations revealing patterns, not just realities of conflict of interest, are legitimized.

This opening to scrutiny of friendship, financial matters, and family relations, as well as patterns of giftgiving and social life, is resented by many public officials and considered to be a form of harassment. Disclosure can discourage participation in public life and can generate tremendous resistance among government employees and officials. They do not see codes as an obligation due to their special status, but merely as a constraint and a harassment that private-sector employees do not face.

People's resistance and fear will solidify around these issues. Managers will ignore the provisions and signal subordinates not to take them seriously; unions will reinforce this hostility. This resentment will be doubled with the addition of postemployment limitations. Such rules are very difficult to enforce and can undermine legitimate career moves, especially at points of financial need. This becomes especially burdensome if the former employee possesses technical expertise in a special field and wants to stay in the same geographic area. It also hurts employees if they must report a job search to their superior in order to protect themselves and the agency from conflict-of-interest charges.

For these reasons, many public managers view codes as problematic and set against effectiveness. These codes are not similar to professional codes of conduct. They do not presume special expertise and trust or internalized education or apprenticeship, and they have no self-enforcing mechanisms (Gortner 1991). Rather, the codes are thrust upon the manager by legislators with little consultation or concern for management. The codes make dealing with vendors more awkward and difficult by stilting relationships and undercutting the informal dimensions necessary to make vendor relationships work. They make hiring and recruiting more difficult by specifying postemployment limits and by limiting the use of newly hired experts from companies in the area. The codes end some perquisites and such extras as gift giving, meals, and travel. Funds from vendors augmented limited government budgets and often helped education or morale efforts, for when training budgets were cut vendors could pick up the slack. Codes add a layer of complexity in dealing with subordinates. And finally, the codes often seem intrusive and denigrating to public officials by their announced lack of trust and stringent regulation of private dealings.

This political world makes the implementing of a code very difficult. Successful implementation and reform require a number of characteristics. Programs need experience and knowledge gained from other programs as well as trained cadres of leaders and committed individuals to implement them (Williams 1989; Levin and Ferman 1985). This enables competence in execution. In order to initiate change and reform, the programs also need either strong executive or legislative support, or strong outside support. Any one will give the agency support during budget time and will ground some independence for the agency (Heymann 1987; Lynn 1987; Doig and Hargrove 1987).

The typical ethics code and agency possess none of the above characteristics. Little is known about ethics codes, and few administrators pursue careers in ethics. Born in scandal with little long-term support, ethics agencies are perceived as monitors of other agencies, and participation in them can cause problems on career paths (Downs 1976). Codes invite their pathologies while facing significant opposition. The story of the King County Ethics Code illustrates an approach to implementation of codes in this environment.

The Ethics Code of King County, Washington

The King County Code of Ethics had passed in the late sixties as part of a massive reform movement in King County.[3] A series of major scandals and kickbacks had generated a new charter for the county and a general assault on the old-style corruption that had permeated the county. The code was seen as one aspect of this general reform and was aimed very narrowly at issues of conflict of interest.

The code was five single-space pages long; it began abruptly with a prohibition on the use of city-owned vehicles and property for one's personal use. The code then enumerated a long list of prohibited actions, all of which constituted a conflict of interest. Almost all prohibitions dealt with having personal beneficial interests in firms doing business with the city in one's area of responsibility. A second section put limits on former commission members engaging in business with their old commissions. A third section required extensive financial disclosure forms from all commission members, council members, and most senior county employees. The last section cited penalties for "negligent violation" and gave the ethics board power to investigate charges, hold hearings, and issue findings. Interestingly, the code did not specify to whom the findings were to be sent nor did it empower anyone to enforce the findings of the board.

The ethics board consisted of three members, each serving a three-year term. One member was appointed by the executive, one by the council, and the chair was nominated by the other two members. All members had to be approved by the county council. The functions of the board and code were housed in the King County Records and Elections Office, since the code required the collection of the disclosure forms.

Soon after the code's creation, it fell into disuse. In its seventeen-year history, the board held only one major public hearing. Very few county employees knew of the code's existence. No line item existed in the budget for the code or the board, and all staffing was done on an ad hoc basis by the office of records and elections. The board met irregularly, usually once every three or four months, and held informal meetings in the office of the manager of records and elections. No minutes were kept of meetings and staffing was intermittent. The board had processed an average of two advisory opinions a year for the last decade. The disclosure forms were regularly collected and filed, but they had never been internally audited. Once every three years, a state agency audited the disclosure forms to see if they were all accounted for.[4]

In 1985, the board held its only major public hearing on an ethics violation and generated considerable media attention. As a result, in early 1986 a steady trickle of requests for advisory opinions began. At the same time, a new member joined the board. It now consisted of a senior attorney at a major Seattle law firm, an elected council member from a city in King County, and a recently appointed professor at the University of Washington. At the first meeting of the newly constituted board, the members asked the staff if any prior decisions existed which might set precedents to help them deal with new requests. They discovered that six short letters that announced opinions constituted the entire record for seventeen years of existence.

The board continued to meet once in every several months to address the new requests. Almost one-third of the cases were dismissed when they were investigated. They were found to be motivated by personal animus or political attempts to discredit the accused person. However, given the lack of staff, investigations took months; it took two months to get board decisions written and promulgated.

In mid-1986, the board received a complaint about an individual who sat on the county Human Services Commission and also served on the board of an agency that received funds from the commission. This commission decided on the location of centers for handicapped individuals. The same commission member had tried to change the site of one center to make it more convenient for his child, who would live at the center. He was also a member of the organization that would run that particular center.

The board discovered that it had no procedures with which either to conduct an investigation or hold a formal hearing. It quickly invented ad hoc procedures to protect confidentiality, met with the director of records and elections, demanded that the staff attorney review all decisions, and asked for independent staff. Records and elections assigned a six-month temporary employee to staff the board and conduct the investigation.

The board assigned the temporary staff person to the investigation, but also asked her to begin collecting other codes of ethics since the board had reached the conclusion that its own code and status needed a radical change. The temporary staffer fell behind in writing and she mislaid affidavits from the investigation. The board members took over the writing of decisions and pressed the manager of records and elections for better staffing.

Next, the board received a request alleging a conflict of interest involving a citizen who had served on a citizen's advisory committee about open space. The letter alleged that this citizen had influenced the selection process and then bought the land and sold the development rights to the city. The board asked its staff attorney, a member of the prosecutor's office, to investigate this issue and discovered that a developer made the complaint. The complaint was being used to harass a citizen who was opposed to a development project. The board found no conflict of interest and became very sensitive to the abusive possibilities of the code.

In late 1986, the temporary employee left with all her records. The board could not find the affidavits for the investigation, nor could they find any of the collected files on other ethics codes. At the same time, an investigative reporter from a local newspaper approached the board to get disclosure forms of two staff members of the King County Council. None of the disclosure forms for the previous two years could be found; other forms were in disarray and were filed in nonsecured places.

A very experienced political operative with wide contacts in the executive office was employed by the board. She immediately centralized all the disclosure forms, reorganized them, and got work-study money to hire help to keep records up to date. Access to the files was restricted, and procedures for release were developed and passed by the board. The board and staff also developed procedures to handles calls, complaints, and advisory requests. A new effort was initiated to collect and research other codes.

In December 1986, the board held a full hearing for the second time in its history. Since there was not enough money to hire a court recorder, the board taped the proceedings. Their lawyer devised an ad hoc set of rules, and the board decided that a conflict of interest did exist in the matter of the person who had tried to influence the choice of site for a center for the handicapped. The ethics board advised the chair of the commission to require the commission member to excuse himself on all deliberations concerning his organization and his daughter. The board issued the opinion but discovered it carried no weight. The chair of the commission, nonetheless, chose to act on the decision. This again convinced the board of the insufficiency of the existing code.

In early 1987, the chair of the board met with the manager of records and elections to ask her help with a budget for the board. The board believed there should be an educational program in its behalf and that a brochure would be sent to all city employees. They wanted a hotline and regular staffing to get decisions out faster and ensure a better turnaround time.

The board concluded that the code required an infrastructure of staff and education which neither King County nor most cities could support. In addition, upper-level staff needed ethics training. All new employees should have a brochure and orientation. Employees and managers needed to be aware of the code and to be willing to come to the board for advising. Ideally, each division would write and implement, in consultation with the board, its own ethics guidelines. The board had seen the abuses and the trauma of investigations, and they wanted to minimize punitive aspects and focus on being seen as a provider of services to managers and employees, rather than as an inquisitor.

The manager of records and elections agreed that they should seek to design a code and a board that would serve as a consultant and that this could be implemented within the budgetary and political resources of the county. She pledged to increase staff and financial support but demanded that the board have regular meetings, ensure fast turnaround time, focus upon service instead of investigations, and write formal procedures. The board agreed and by the end of 1987 it had formalized procedures and reduced turnaround time to six weeks. In 1987, the staff and board consolidated and reorganized all the ethics board files and reconstructed lost opinions, and computerized the disclosure files.

During the last half of 1986 and the first three months of 1987, four major ethics scandals hit the local media. In the worst case, an employee of the county assessor's office bought a house from a seventy-five-year-old man he had met in his official capacity. Two months later the employee sold the house for 120 percent profit. None of the cases came before the ethics board, and the board, in deference to its own traditions, did not initiate investigations. However, the assessor was publicly attacked and ethics became a major issue in her election campaign. Later, a member of the county executive branch who planned to run for assessor pressured the board to intervene in the scandal in order to put the assessor on the defensive. The official threatened to undercut the board's budget request if it did not agree. The entire board refused to get involved until the issue was brought before it.

In early 1989, a new ethics code was proposed in the King County Council.

The code had been drafted by the outgoing city attorney in anger at what he regarded as the increasing arrogance of lobbyists in the city. It contained stringent limitations on lobbying and it tightened the existing code in a number of areas. The new code had been written without consulting any other officials in the government, including the ethics board.

After a flurry of publicity in which the newspapers mentioned the recent problems, the code was referred to staff for review. It quietly lay there for several months. Although the proposed code had serious flaws, the board decided to exploit the opportunity the code and the scandals afforded. The board committed itself to pursue five revisions: First, the new code should have a strong preamble and a policy section that would enunciate a positive vision of public service and embody several principles that could guide decisions. Second, the code should cover all employees equally and not segregate council and executive or higher and lower levels. Third, the code should be reasonable and livable and should have a strong managerial and proscriptive component that would require county employees to identify potential conflict-of-interest issues and report them to their managers. Fourth, the code should cover some vital areas that were missed in the old code, such as the use of privileged information and tight limits on gifts, travel, and food from people seeking to do business with the county, as well as employment limits. Finally, the code should direct the board to make public findings that were reported to superiors and that became a cause for disciplinary action.

The board formed a working group with representatives of the prosecutor's office and the executive office. The group worked for two months to revise the new code. The board also incorporated the recommendations of the ombudsman into its revisions.

In its revisions, it sought a tough code, but one with limits the executive branch believed were compatible with good practice. This led to revisions of postemployment practices and an agreement to focus upon anticipating conflicts of interest and pushing supervisors to seek guidance. The board also recommended that limits on outside employment apply only to top officials and focused the rest of the revisions on the issue of employment incompatible with official duties. In its discussions, the board realized that the lobbying provisions of the bill probably made it unpassable and pushed to have this aspect severed from the code proper. It submitted all its recommendations to the chair of the King County Council.

At the same time, the board secured a promise from the executive office and the manager of records and elections to support a full staff position for the board and a regular budget to support records and education. In a meeting with the chair of the board, the chair of the King County Council fully committed herself to the code and made it a top legislative priority for herself and the council's attorney. Throughout the process, her support kept the code on the agenda and made its passage likely.

The summer rush of legislation and budget slowed the code's track. In late August, the chair of the council, at the board's request, prodded the legislation. Given political realities, the code was severed from the lobbying provisions, and the first draft was rather hastily written. It revised the old code rather than starting *de novo*. The draft incorporated many of the board's recommendations as well as ideas from the ombudsman and the county attorney's office, including the requirement that all county employees sign a receipt that they had received a summary of the code and that all were obligated to report violations.

This hybrid draft of the code went before the council in September. Several members opposed the "ratting" provision, which required employees to report violations. People were worried about the effect on morale and resistance from employees, given a requirement to inform on each other. One council member complained about the two-year ban on lobbying for ex–council members.

The code was assigned to committee for refinement. At this point, the prosecutor's office entered the fray. The head of the civil division had read the council draft and became extremely agitated. He believed that giving the ethics board simultaneous investigative and judicial powers violated the separation of powers in the state constitution and had violated the advice given to the board by the prosecutor's office.

The revised draft separated the investigatory and judging functions. But the council refused to create a separate executive office of ethics that could investigate the council itself; instead, they vested power with the ombudsman's office, which reported to the council. The council also added an extra investigator to give credibility to sanctions. Members believed strong sanctions were absolutely necessary to get managers and employees to seek advisory opinions.

The council subcommittee relaxed limits on gifts, travel, and food; in particular they exempted from such limits elected officials at ceremonial or informational meetings with constituents. The council believed that a different set of obligations was incurred by elected officials with their constituents. The "ratting" provision was eliminated, but the code included an obligation to report potential conflicts of interest to supervisors. The council also relaxed the ban on going before old commissions and councils to a one-year wait, and added a provision that encouraged political participation by county employees.

At this point, a number of department directors reacted against the code. They objected to hiring limitations and to the restriction on food and travel paid for by vendors, and they feared the power of the ombudsman to harass them. Although they had known about the code for months and had seen drafts of it, no managers had contacted the board or the executive representative in the working group during deliberations. The directors wanted to rewrite the entire code but found themselves trapped by the momentum behind the process. It became clear that the council saw the code as all one piece where the limits on gifts and on employment leveled the playing fields and undercut practices that united government and vendors. The directors realized that they would be portrayed in the press as individuals who were trying to protect their own perquisites. The executive finally asked for two weeks for "clarifying" amendments. In particular, the director negotiated a process to get an exception to the limitations on people who had recently been hired, and they permitted all officials appointed by and reporting to an elected official to attend meetings and receive travel or food.

In November 1990, the council unanimously passed the amendments and the code. Two weeks later, the council approved an extra investigator for the ombudsman and a staff person for the board. This staff person would also help administer the county's new election-financing law.

Upon the passage of the law, the board received a flurry of often worried or angry requests that anticipated the new code and were brought on by the press coverage. Most of them sought advice on provisions that had been in the old code but which no one knew existed. One in particular came from a major developer who charged an employee reviewing his environmental impact statement with a conflict of interest. The developer claimed her outside political activities and positions in support of controlled growth compromised her independent judgment.

Many county employees viewed this as intimidation by developers and feared that other ethics charges would be brought against them for reasons of moral or political belief. In a divided vote, the board concluded that a decision to find a conflict would make all employees' personal political beliefs subject to public scrutiny and judgment. A narrowly defined judgment found no conflict and announced in clear terms that the code encouraged political participation.

The board began the task of hiring a new staffer, and the chair met with a number of management groups to explain the new code and to encourage managers to come to the board for advisory opinions. The board also worked to professionalize its operations and it developed a computerized system to track and file each request for an advisory opinion, created a consistent format for all decisions, and distributed its decisions to top managers. The board initiated planning for a video presentation as part of orientation, and in cooperation with the personnel division it included an ethics presentation with each new orientation. A summary of the new code was mailed to all county employees with their last paycheck in February 1991, and they all had to sign a receipt for it. At the next stage, the board envisioned convincing the executive office to have each agency develop its own implementing standards for the ethics code. Meanwhile, the county unions balked at signing the receipt and many individuals returned the receipt unsigned on the advice of union leaders, who saw the code as a management plot to increase control over workers. A number of other managers continued to oppose the code and worked on plans for a midcourse correction package of amendments.

On March 31st, 1991, when the new code went into effect, the board was in place issuing decisions with staff and budget support.

Implementing a Code

The King County case illustrates the predictable problems of implementing codes of ethics. No organized constituencies consistently support the code and boards. Public support for ethics issues is thin and largely latent and reactive. Ethics seldom determines an election except as the result of a scandal. The changes were abetted by local scandals, and the need to reassure the public led to a short-term focus. At budget time, the board remains largely orphaned and its education program and staff are vulnerable. Few agencies or individuals find their own interests linked to the board; most agencies, officials, unions, and legislators have deep ambivalence if not outright hostility about boards and codes. Lobbyists and vendors who feel constricted by the code resent its limits on contact and on hiring practice. Consequently, the board remains powerless with little visibility, staffing, or influence. More troubling, individuals and officials are tempted to use the code for political gain, and organized groups, like developers, quickly realize that the provisions of the code can be used to harass public officials or citizens with whom they disagree.

The durable implementation of an ethics code, as with any program, requires strong and continuous support, either from the executive or the legislative branch. In reality, any successful ethics program requires the continuous support of the top executive (Dryvesteyn 1989; Matthews 1988). Most political executives, however, worry about ethics only after a scandal or if they succeed to office as a result of scandal and have made ethics an issue. Such support is uneven and seldom lasts through an administration, let alone across administrations.

Often ethics codes and agencies supported by legislatures are institutionalized as an extension of the monitoring and accountability functions of government. Ethics agencies complement ombudsmen or inspectors general. The relatively large federal program owes much of its success to Congress' seeing it as a method to control and monitor accountability. Unfortunately, the transfer of money to ethics and inspectors general represents a movement away from functional capacity in favor of monitoring (Light 1991). This approach is possible at the federal level and in wealthier states, but most states and localities do not have the resources or incentives to pursue it.

The King County case represents a different approach built around the board's philosophy that ethics agencies and codes can be supportive of good management practice. This envisions ethics as inculcated into the agency cultures in a manner that can endure political vicissitudes. It begins with executive support but must migrate to agencies to succeed. The agency and board would be seen as a resource to be used by managers, not as a control mechanism to be avoided. This becomes important because the forces needed to get an issue on the agenda and to get it passed often militate against its successful implementation (Pressman and Wildavsky 1973). In King County, presenting the code and board as a consultancy to support management has the added advantage of matching the realistic resources, and it addresses the major sources of opposition. These ideas are not about design of the code but are rather an approach to implementation with four components: a positive vision and consultation, independence, visibility and relevance, and service.

I. Positive Vision and Consultation

The code was built upon a positive vision of public service and it emphasizes its role in building legitimacy and respect for government as well as its support for independent judgment and public trust. It was written in consultation with public managers and enforcement officials and it tries to bridge the tensions between legislative and executive expectations over stringency. Informal consultation continued after its passage to help managers anticipate issues. The board worked to avoid the perception of the code's being forced upon people in a punitive manner, thus it emphasized the advisory opinion approach undergirded by a complaint process and strong enforcement.

II. Independence

The board was extremely sensitive to the abusive possibilities of the code and fought to preserve its independence and nonpartisan status. No manager will trust the code or process if this is not protected. All implementation needs a constant focus upon fixing problems (Bardach 1977). Given the politics of ethics, the board and staff devoted great energy to fixing threats to independence. In two major decisions, the board sent a clear message that it would not permit itself to be used for political purposes, and in other actions it risked budgetary support to prevent being used for political ends. In crafting the code, constant reference was made to what other jurisdictions had done, with emphasis on the code as an extension of standards of good practice. Every effort was made to build a consensus across the executive, the ombudsman's office, the prosecuting attorney, and the legislature.

III. Visibility and Relevance

Media focus on scandals gave the code a stark and threatening visibility and relevance that would soon fade. The board made provisions to regularly send code summaries to all employees as well as to write a brochure also to be sent to employees on a regular basis. It publishes synopses of its decisions and sends them to all senior managers to keep on file. New employee orientation now has an ethics component with a video from the county executive to highlight ethics. In the long run, all agencies should develop their own implementation standards, which will educate those in lower levels of the bureaucracy and sustain visibility and relevancy.

The emphasis upon service and nonpunitive dimensions runs some risk that the code will be ignored if no scandals loom or if executive support seems weak. This approach relies upon persuasion and on the offer to protect officials and support judgment. But indirectly, it builds on the incentive to avoid the costs of an uncovered media violation. Paradoxically, the strength of the new code's provisions and the presence of a respected investigator in the ombudsman's office give an element of credibility to enforcement that will make many employees and managers take the code more seriously than they would otherwise. The possibility of sanctions motivates managers to take the advisory function more seriously as an alternative to complaints (Weller 1988).

IV. Service

The board and its staff emphasize that they provide a service performed discreetly and efficiently for agencies and officials. A key provision of the code asks all employees to anticipate conflicts of interest and disclose them to superiors. The board supports this anticipation and works to create a culture where norms are internalized. The agency administers the disclosure forms but staffing is designed so as not to let the technical details of administration overwhelm the more subtle and important roles of advice and support. They also work closely with one attorney who provides a consistent voice in the prosecutor's office. The focus on the advisory process also works to keep issues out of the courts, where ethics codes have mixed success (Rohr 1991). The board emphasizes professional staff, computerized operations, and reasonable turnover time in getting advisory opinions out. They have developed clear formats, have tried to maintain reasonable turnaround despite the increase in requests, and have devised records to track and notify all the individuals who approached the board. The service orientation dovetails with independence as the means to gain the trust of agencies.

Any successful implementation means a constant focus on fixing problems as they arise (Ingraham 1987; Bardach 1977). The board is intent on matching its role with its resources, otherwise it would quickly be discredited or become primarily a tool for political or personal ends. This means anticipating and addressing problems involved in preserving independence as well as modifying service provisions when they fail and listening carefully to the feedback on service and decisions from agencies.

*   *   *

These approaches provide an ethics program with strategies to compensate for the predictable weaknesses it will confront in implementation. They also provide an orientation to address the politics that will surround the operation of the program. The King County story illustrates this, and even in place, the ethics program faces considerable resistance by top management and unions. Unpopular decisions that change the existing bureaucratic culture will amplify this hostility. As the story illustrates and the politics of ethics predicts, this is to be expected. Ethics codes and legislation are enmeshed in politics. They are usually born in scandal and passed as much to reassure the public as to accomplish any good. They have little positive support, will be feared by many, and may be seen as a rhetorical and institutional resource by self-interested political actors. A working code and board need to be attuned to their political limits and realities. To think otherwise risks having the codes and boards either fall into desuetude or abuse.

Notes

1. I would like to thank George Frederickson, Bayard Catron, Morton Kroll, Lisa Foster, Edward Guthmann, Cynthia Romero, and Sonia Soelter for their comments on the paper that became this chapter. It benefited immensely from their help.
2. This chapter will focus upon a "modern" code, which usually covers the following: definitions of conflict of interest; limitations upon gift giving and receiving from people doing business or seeking to do business with the government; limitations upon postemployment practices and lobbying one's old agency after employment; requirements of public disclosure of wealth and income for top appointed decision makers and members of boards and commissions; limitations upon economic interests in businesses doing business with government; creation of an independent board to judge violations and issue advisory opinions; creation of a mechanism to investigate complaints; provisions for penalties to be assessed for violations. I do not discuss the issue of campaign finance although many see it as related to an "ethics package" (McCullough 1990).
3. This case is based upon my own experience as a member of the King County Board of Ethics.
4. This is not an unusual fate for codes from 1960s and 1970s (Hays and Gleissner 1981; Bowman 1981).

References

Bardach, Eugene. 1977. *The Implementation Game: What Happens after a Bill Becomes a Law.* Cambridge, MA: MIT Press.
Bowman, James. 1981. "The Management of Ethics: Codes of Conduct in Organizations." *Public Personnel Management*, 10, no. 1: 59–66.
Burke, Fran, and Benson, George. 1989. "State Ethics Codes, Commissions and Conflicts." *The Council of State Governments* (September/October): 195–98.
Chandler, Ralph Clark. 1983. "The Problem of Moral Reasoning in American Public Administration: The Case for a Code of Ethics." *Public Administration Review*, (January/February): 32–39.
Council on Government Ethics Law (COGEL). 1991. *Ethics and Lobbying 1990: Legislation and Litigation.* Lexington, KY.
Doig, Jameson W., and Hargrove, Erwin C. 1987. *Leadership and Innovation: A Biographical Perspective on Entrepreneurs in Government.* Baltimore: Johns Hopkins University Press.

Downs, Anthony. 1976. *Inside Bureaucracy*. Boston: Little, Brown.
Dryvesteyn, Kent. Vice President for Ethics, General Dynamics Corporation. 1989. Interview with author. November.
Edelman, Murray. 1967. *The Politics of Symbols*. Bloomington: Indiana University Press.
Ginsberg, Benjamin, and Schefter, Martin. 1991. *Politics by Other Means*. New York: Basic Books.
Gortner, Harold F. 1991. *Ethics for Public Managers*. Westview, CT: Praeger.
Hays, Steven W., and Gleissner, Richard R. 1981. "Codes of Ethics in State Government: A National Survey." *Public Personnel Management*, 10, no. 1: 48–58.
Heymann, Philip B. 1987. *The Politics of Public Management*. New Haven: Yale University Press.
Hyman, Michael R.; Skippex, Robert; Tansey, Richard. 1990. "Ethical Codes Are Not Enough." *Business Horizons* (March/April): 15–22.
Ingraham, Patricia W. 1987. "Policy Implementation and the Public Service." In *The Revitalization of Public Service*, edited by Robert Denhardt and E. Jennings, 145–55. Columbia: University of Missouri Press.
Levin, Martin A., and Ferman, B. 1985. *The Political Hand: Policy Implementation and Youth Employment Programs*. New York: Pergamon.
Light, Paul. 1991. "High Level Wrongdoing and the Inspector Generalship." Paper read at conference on Research Issues in Public Ethics. Park City, Utah, June 13.
Long, Norton. 1968. "The Local Community as an Ecology of Games." *American Sociological Review* (November): 251–61.
Lynn, Laurence, Jr. 1987. *Managing Public Policy*. Boston: Little, Brown.
McCullough, Harriet. 1990. *Municipal Ethics Legislation: The State of the Cities*. Privately printed, Chicago.
Matthews, M. Cash. 1988. *Strategic Intervention: Resolving Ethical Dilemmas*. Newbury Park, CA: Sage.
Molander, Earl A. 1987. "A Paradigm for Design, Promulgation and Enforcement of Ethical Codes." *Journal of Business Ethics*, no. 6: 619–31.
Oliverio, Mary Ellen. 1989. "The Implementation of a Code of Ethics: The Early Efforts of an Entrepreneur." *Journal of Business Ethics*, no. 8: 367–74.
Pressman, Jeffrey L., and Wildavsky, Aaron. 1973. *Implementation: How Great Expectations in Washington Are Dashed in Oakland*. Berkeley: University of California Press.
Raiborn, Cecily A., and Payne, Dinah. 1990. "Corporate Codes of Conduct: A Collective Conscience and Continuum." *Journal of Business Ethics*, no. 9: 879–89.
Robin, Donald; Giallourakis, Michael; Moritz, Thomas. 1989. "A Different Look at Ethics Codes." *Business Horizons* (January/February): 66–73.
Rohr, John. 1991. "Ethical Issues in French Public Administration: A Comparative Study." *Public Administration Review* (July/August): 283–98.
Weller, Steven. 1988. "The Effectiveness of Codes of Ethics." *Journal of Business Ethics*, no. 7: 389–95.
Williams, Walter W. 1989. "Implementing Public Programs." *Handbook of Public Administration*, edited by James L. Perry, 248–57. San Francisco: Jossey-Bass.

Part Three

Ethics as Administration and Policy

9

The American Odyssey of the Career Public Service: The Ethical Crisis of Role Reversal

Douglas F. Morgan and Henry D. Kass

The extended wanderings of Odysseus, Gulliver, Tom Sawyer, and Alice in Wonderland are graphic reminders of the differences between an odyssey and a commonplace trip. An odyssey is characterized by unexpected occurrences. At any given moment the traveler is unsure of arrival at a predetermined destination. Even with the best of intentions and the most exquisite planning one may be thrust upon strange and even hostile shores. Clear channels become backwaters and backwaters open into clear channels. One drifts even as one is morally certain he or she is steering a plotted course, and, at length, the voyager may forget his or her presumed destination entirely and exchange it for a very different one. In sum, those on an odyssey seem constantly to pit their own will and intentions against forces that seem destined to alter and reshape those intentions in ways entirely unexpected. The only certainty about an odyssey is that one can never turn back. The trip, no matter the outcome, has changed one's life course forever.

In the sense just described, American public administration has been on an odyssey for the last century, an odyssey that has had profound impact on its ethical practice. Public administration embarked on its voyage with the clear intention of bringing the advantages of modern bureaucratic management—neutral competence, technical rationality, and efficiency—to our democratic system. The purpose of this voyage was to set modern American public administration on a course designed to achieve the great instrumental potential of bureaucracy without risking the control by technocrats over our democratic system.

The voyage has taken its travelers on some unexpected twists and turns. Administrators have found themselves taking on roles and moral obligations quite different than those charted by the progressive reformers who shaped the ideology of public administration at the turn of the century. In addition to being the moral protectors of neutral technical competence, administrators have at times been called on successfully to balance competing interests, but to do so in ways that promote the public interest. There are increasing instances when administrators, especially at the local levels of government, are expected to be the locus of political leadership in the community. When they are called on to play this leadership role, the public administrators find that their odyssey has taken them full circle on the trip that was launched at the end of the last century. Career administrators frequently may find themselves standing at the wheel instead of remaining in the hold or on the deck.

In this essay we are interested in exploring how career administrators confront the multiple moral obligations they have inherited from the odyssey of American public administration over the past century. How do they view the ethical obligations of their role? How do they reconcile competing moral claims, such as conflicts between neutral technical competence and balancing competing political interests, or protecting the long-term interests of the community against what is currently popular?

Research Methodology

We have chosen to focus on experienced career administrators as our primary source of information to answer these questions for two reasons. First, we believe with Schon and others that practitioners possess a "theory in action" that can inform and guide our academic understanding of the way the administrative world can and should work (Argyris and Schon 1974; Schon 1983). Second, the judgments made by practitioners in the crucible of action are obviously an important source of information in helping us to better understand the way in which career administrators confront multiple and frequently conflicting ethical obligations.

For purposes of this study, we assembled a focus group of six experienced senior-level local administrators.[1] The group consisted of the chief administrative officers of three city and county jurisdictions and three senior-level local government department heads. They all have a reputation among professionals within the field for being outstanding public servants with high ethical standards. They all have had distinguished careers and many advanced rapidly at a young age to positions with high levels of discretionary authority. Under the pledge of confidentiality, panel members were asked to take turns presenting ethical problems they have encountered to the group for discussion and decision.Our assumption was that these discussions would provide us with an opportunity to observe how career administrators view their current roles, how these roles have changed over time, and how they resolve the ethical conflicts that most commonly arise from these roles.

The Argument of This Essay

In the sections that follow we will use the information obtained from our focus group of career administrators to document a strange ethical odyssey that begins with the subordination of administration to politics and ends with considerable administrative control over the political process. In many ways there is nothing new about this odyssey. Based on our knowledge of the rise of the American administrative state, it is not news that career administrators increasingly "run the show," from policy development to policy implementation. But there is much that we do not know about the process that transforms the administrative function of government from being "on tap" to being "on top." First, how do career administrators experience this transformation process? Second, how do they resolve the ethical role conflicts that arise when they assume responsibilities that are not accepted as part of the legitimating ideology of the career public servant? When, how, and why do they assume political leadership while they remain servants of the people? These questions will be the focus of examination in the odyssey that follows.

In stage I we examine the first stage of this odyssey, in which our panel's commitment to the prevailing management ideology of efficient control gives way to the realities of uncertainty, ambiguity, and complexity that undergird much of the administrative landscape. In stage II we see how our panel embraces the need to engage in the tug and pull of pluralist politics, not simply as an inconvenient necessity, but as a legitimate moral claim that competes on equal grounds with administrative efficiency. Finally, in stage III we describe our panel's drift toward the language of the public interest to help resolve moral dilemmas that cannot be accommodated successfully by a commitment either to efficient management or to pluralist politics.

There are several characteristics of our panel's odyssey through each of these three stages of moral discourse. First, the odyssey resembles more of a drift from one stage to another than consciously chosen stops along a preplanned trip. Like the drift of oceanic currents, fine grains of sand, or meteorological formations, our panel's drift from one stage to another is precipitously slow, inexorable, and patterned.

A second characteristic is that each of the stages represents a universe of moral discourse, a separate set of moral claims that possess a coherent pattern of values our panel members feel compelled to respect. To borrow a term from Bellah and his associates (1985), our administrators seem to invoke three separate languages of moral discourse.[2]

Third, like most traveling experiences, the stages of the odyssey we describe leave our travelers with far more baggage than they started with! Rather than abandon moral claims they have acquired at previous stages of their careers, our panelists simply add one set of values to the other and do not spend much time constructing a framework to order or to reconcile their potential incompatibilities.

Finally, the portrait we draw is intended to capture the intellectual odyssey of our panel as a whole. It is not intended to be an accurate representation of the twists and turns each panelist has taken individually to arrive at her/his current public philosophy. In short, the odyssey of role reversal we describe below is the odyssey our panel believes has been traveled by the *administrative function* of American government. The odyssey is also an account of the kinds of moral dilemmas our administrators have encountered along the way and the manner in which these dilemmas have been engaged.

The Drift from Twentieth Century Management Ideology to Taking Charge of the Political Process

Stage I: The Drift from Conventional Management Ideology to the Ambiguities of Administrative Practice

Members of our panel are strongly committed to the leading principles of Wilsonian management ideology, which has dominated the intellectual landscape of American public administration since the turn of the century (Ostrom 1974, 197; Scott and Hart 1979). Equally important, they accept this commitment as a moral obligation.

The Wilsonian ideology means two things to our panel members. In the first instance, it means a strong commitment to the possibility of controlling and structuring the activities of others in an organizational setting. As one of our panelists described himself, "I am an expert in managing systems. This is what I was especially trained to do." By systems he means the conventional instruments of organizational control such as budgeting, finance, personnel, purchasing, organizational structures, and other similar internal administrative processes.

In the second instance, the Wilsonian ideology means that our panelists are committed to getting things done as efficiently and effectively as possible. In fact, there is considerable evidence that our panel's commitment to these values represents the first, if not the dominant, language of moral discourse. It is reflected in a variety of ways, but especially in our panel's lament about the growing forces that have eroded their collective capacity to promote effective and efficient administration of policy. It is also reflected in their willingness to opt for the appearance of efficiency and effectiveness even when these values are unachievable.

Our panelists uniformly lament the increased number of impediments that limit a manager's ability to promote efficient and effective administration of governmental services. They cite the rapid proliferation of state and federal regulations, the emergence of more participative management styles, court-mandated due process requirements, various forms of citizen participation, laborious bidding and procurement procedures, the making of decisions based on what "the lawyers will say," just to mention some of the more obvious barriers to efficient management. With all of these impediments, one member of our panel observes that it is a matter of "seeing how much efficiency you can get away with."

Despite so many barriers to the efficient administration of government, our panelists cling to the appearance of efficiency and effectiveness. We encounter several instances in which the dominant management ideology of control and efficient allocation of the public's scarce resources is invoked by our administrators to help them rationalize a very messy situation in which they must act. The "messiness" results from a variety of conditions that are increasingly more the rule than the exception.

Our panelists define "messiness" as a situation in which they are expected to act and they do not know what is wanted or even what the issue is. In such cases, conflicts among competing interest groups, the vagaries of technological change, or the ephemeral quality of modern public opinion all conspire to make the situation both ambiguous and equivocal.

In such a setting the Wilsonian management ideology provides both a rationale to act and a set of techniques for doing so. At the level of rationale, Wilsonianism creates a moral obligation for the administrator "to make things work." At the level of technique, Wilsonianism allows administrators legitimately to insert themselves (or be inserted by political superiors) into the decision making process in the name of technical rationality. But once in the "loop," the administrator's commitment "to make things work" makes it difficult to confine his/her intervention to merely technical issues. "Making things work" may require mediating conflict, tempering public passions, or modifying ill-conceived or precipitous action. While such intervention can sometimes be justified on technical grounds, frequently it cannot. In such instances, an interesting transformation begins to occur with members of our administrative panel as they find themselves drifting into a management setting with a moral framework that is ill-suited to the task at hand.

Instead of abandoning or calling into question the underlying premises of the management ideology of control and efficiency, they begin to use the ideology as a *rhetorical strategy*. The commitment to control and efficiency becomes tactically important in jockeying for position and buying time. The consequence of this "move" by our administrators is a growing gap between their theory *of* action and their theory *in* action (Argyris and Schon 1974). They enter public service with a legitimating moral framework that justifies what they do, but they find themselves using this framework as a mere tactical tool. This divergence between what our administrators are morally supposed to do and what they in fact do is greatly exacerbated by their necessity to engage in the tug and pull of local politics.

Stage II: The Drift from Efficient Management to Pluralist Politics

Our administrators are very much aware that they cannot find a safe haven from interest group pressures that constantly surface in the formulation, execution, or evaluation of public policy. These issues preoccupy them at every turn, starting with their political superiors who depend heavily on fragile, shifting coalitions of local interests for their election. In addition, the laws and ordinances they administer are often self-contradictory or amorphous products of pluralist legislative politics. Most decision making, particularly in the area of land use, is characterized by multiple opportunities for interests to participate and to appeal policy decisions. The end result of such pressures is that our panel of career executives and their staffs spend considerable time and energy in what they term "process management."

Perhaps most troubling to our panel is the increased role of single-issue interest groups, characteristically referred to by the epithet "the crazies." The "crazies" play the political game in ways that disturb our panelists. They refuse to engage in compromise and accommodation, viewing such action as a "pact with the devil." They tend to make all differences into what Rittel and Mill (1973) have called "wicked problems," matters of fundamental value conflict. When this occurs it is much more difficult for administrators to dub certain areas of policy making "technical." It is not surprising, then, that much of our panelists' time is spent anticipating what the "crazies" will do next.

In the kind of political world just described, "making things work" requires that administrators involve themselves in the mediation of conflicting communal values. This is difficult to do without ascribing an ethical value to their involvement in the pluralist political process that makes this mediation possible. Gradually and subtly our administrators thus obligate themselves to a second ethical language, that of pluralism.

The force of this obligation can be seen both in the process of defining administrative situations for action and in the way in which these actions are justified. At the problem-defining stage an appreciation of pluralism frequently shapes how a problem is administratively defined. This is well illustrated by one of the cases presented for discussion by a member of our panel. In the face of a sex discrimination charge made by a group of employees against one of his departmental deputies, the administrator established a labyrinthine investigative process that would have met the strictest court-like presumption of innocence. However, in this case appearances would have been deceiving. When called on to explain why such strict prophylactic processes had been used, the administrator emphasized the importance of accommodating a variety of competing interests that included the consequences on future relationships with the employee union, the desire to protect competent managers, the needs of the accused, and the impact of the process on the overall morale and capacity of the organization.

Members of our administrative panel not only rely on the pluralist ethic to shape how they approach the policy process, more important, they *use* the language of interest-group accommodation to *justify* policy outcomes. In a case presented for discussion, one of our panel participants succeeded in persuading a member of his elected board to refrain from pushing more restrictive reading access standards on the local public library because of the conflict this would foster at the board level. Even though the protection of first amendment issues was at stake for the administrator, he relied on the value of conflict avoidance at the elected board level when he persuaded the official to refrain from pushing for adoption of more restrictive standards.

These cases are typical of how the pluralist ethic affects both the process and substance of ethical decision making by members of our panel. The ethic encourages administrators to perform two roles that are critical to successful functioning of the political process. At times they are required to be "balancers of interests" and at other times to be "facilitators of consensus."

Both roles require administrators to keep the processes of government open and accessible to those who wish to participate. As indicated earlier, one of our panelists observed, "we have become more and more simply process managers." By that he meant that the appearance of efficiency and effectiveness frequently is more important than the reality. This has become the case, he explained, because the legitimacy of what government does today has become so tenuous that a career administrator has to spend a good deal of his/her time "stroking the process and the participants" so that all emerge feeling they have been treated fairly, have been heard, and will have continued access in the future to express their views. In order to accomplish this, administrators are encouraged to invoke the values of efficiency and effectiveness as a mere rhetorical device to obfuscate political and legal agendas.

At the end of the second stage of the administrative odyssey toward role reversal, our practitioners are quite confounded. On the one hand, they see themselves as stewards of efficient and effective allocation of the public's scarce resources. On the other hand, the conditions of administrative practice call this stewardship into question. It is first called into question as a *possibility* by the ambiguities, uncertainties, and complexities of political life. The stewardship's desirability also is called into question by our political commitment to citizen involvement in shaping communal life. At the end of the second stage of our administrative odyssey toward role reversal, career administrators are left to ponder how much of the language of efficiency and effectiveness should be invoked to help tame wicked problems by banning politics from the administrator's world, and how much they should accept these wicked problems as a sign of the healthy functioning of our democratic processes.

Stage III: The Drift from Pluralist Politics to the Public Interest

There are times when "making things work" requires that members of our panel go beyond technical rationality, neutral competence, or the mediation of conflict among competing group interests to justify their administrative actions. On such occasions, they freely invoke the language of the public or communal interest, thus they incur yet another set of moral obligations to complement the Wilsonian and pluralist languages of administrative discourse.

The public interest, while vaguely defined, is used in at least three ways. First, it is sometimes used to affirm the underlying values of the community. As one panelist observes: "This profession [public administration] is founded on preserving the fabric of the nation. That's serious business. The jurisdiction I serve is 150 years old and I know it will be around a hundred and fifty years from now. That's a sobering responsibility. I owe something to that history and to the future in the way I do my job."

Second, the language of the public interest is sometimes used to recognize collective interests over the partial group interests within the community. For example, the language provides a way for our administrators to protect the rights and interests of individuals who are unknown to them or who may be unrepresented as concrete interest groups. These "abstract others" are usually known by collective nouns such as the poor, the elderly, youth, taxpayers and, most of all, the public.

Finally, the public interest sometimes is used to express an obligation by administrators to future generations, to transmit the most cherished values of the past, without allowing that past to become a dead and lifeless hand holding the future hostage.

In short, the language of the public interest permits our panel of career administrators to shape the present in a manner informed by the past but with an eye to the future. This interpretive and expressive function becomes especially significant when viewed against the role our panelists believe elected officials and their professional/technical staffs can play in this process. Most elected officials are assumed to have a short-term perspective, driven by their desire to appease whatever interest presses them the hardest, regardless of the community-wide, long-term repercussions. Similarly, the professional/technical staffs who work for our panelists are characterized as narrow in focus and frequently unwilling to accommodate their technological/instrumental commitment to practical political realities and legitimate popular concerns. Surrounded by these kinds of perspectives, our panelists tend to view themselves as the lonely guardians of the larger public interest.

The Crisis of Role Reversal

The odyssey of the American administrative experience has left our panel of practitioners with a crisis of legitimacy. Without abandoning the moral obligation they were given at the start of the Wilsonian voyage, they have acquired additional obligations along the way.[3] The first of these is the obligation both to embrace, and in turn, reject aspects of pluralist politics (Truman 1955; Dahl 1956; Lowi 1979; Davis 1969; Morrow 1987). On one hand, we have urged public administrators to play extremely active roles in pluralist politics in terms of interest advocacy (Frederickson 1971) and aggregation (Truman 1955). On the other, we have often placed on them the moral obligation to ameliorate the worst excesses that attend the pursuit of pluralist self-interest, narrowly conceived. To accomplish this mediating role, we have cast our career administrators as protectors of a broad public interest or a set of communal, constitutional values (Rohr 1978, 1986; Morgan 1990; Morgan and Kass 1991).

Our career administrators are left at the end of this odyssey with a set of multiple and conflicting moral obligations without any kind of ordering framework. The problem is compounded by an increasingly balkanized political environment that creates considerable pressure in some cases to assume full responsibility for political leadership. Chief among these pressures is the decline in the quality of local elected leadership.

Members of our panel uniformly lament the conditions under which local elected officials must operate: they occupy poorly paid positions, they are placed under intense interest group pressures, and they operate under close scrutiny by a cynical and occasionally hostile public. Local elected bodies look less and less attractive to the traditional pool of professional and commercial leaders who once filled them. Their places have often been filled by single-interest politicians, marginal business people, neighborhood activists, and an occasional demagogue.

This new political leadership has two serious deficits from our panel's viewpoint. Many of the leaders are unaware of community affairs and the problems of metropolitan government. Others have little concern for the long-range interest of the jurisdiction as a whole. Many individuals pursue a single-issue agenda, whether that agenda is the welfare of a single neighborhood or some favored "cause."

As elected representatives grow less able to agree on or even to comprehend, public policy issues, the role of policy making has fallen on the shoulders of appointed career professionals. In fact, one panelist observed, "my job is to craft policy. My board understands that. Their job is to act as a focus group keeping me attuned to the community."

Our panelists also know that to treat their elected boards in this fashion represents a complete *role reversal* from that called for in each of the forms of government they have served. Without a legitimating framework for assuming this role, members of our panel are reluctant to be placed in the limelight. As one panelist admitts, "I have an unspoken pact with my council. I don't let on how little they understand what's going on and they can take the credit for what I and my staff do. In return, they don't bug me when I'm trying to deal with big issues." While the traditional Wilsonian model is extremely useful to disguise this role reversal, it does not solve the more important problem faced by career administrators: the acquisition of a legitimating framework to justify their active and broad participation in the processes of democratic governance.

As agents of a multiple set of moral obligations, our panel faces three almost insurmountable problems. First, at a personal level our administrators have no legitimating language to justify what they are called on to do on a daily basis. In fact, they deliberately hide what they do—strike private agreements with their governing boards and resort to the rhetorical use of language to disguise the full policy-initiating role they play.

At a broader public level, those who choose to take on ethical obligations outside the Wilsonian paradigm do so at the risk of being publicly charged with usurping the rights of elected officials in the democratic system. To make matters worse, some of the elected officials and clientele groups who in private urge an administrator to play an active role in the political system are the first to criticize that role in public. This is particularly so when the administrator's subsequent actions violate the critic's interest or go astray politically.

Third, at the level of constitutional governance the active political leadership role by career administrators in our governance process must be reconciled with the structure and substantive values of our regime of ordered liberty. By what right can—and/or should—career administrators play a role in democratic governance that has all the appearances of a role reversal?

Conclusion: Some Final Reflections and Recommendations on the Crisis of Role Reversal

What does the above analysis suggest for the direction of our future thinking about ethics and government service? When the ethical responsibilities of career administrators are viewed through the eyes of our panel of career administrators, there are two problems with the way we have tended to think about these responsibilities. First, we have tended to see efficiency and effectiveness in conflict with democratic control, much as Friedrich and Finer posed the problem in their famous debate more than fifty years ago (Friedrich 1940; Finer 1941). But our panel of practitioners does not view the world in this way. When they depart from the Wilsonian ship that began the American administrative voyage more than a century ago, they do so to make government work.

For our panel, to make government work means the ability to accommodate ambiguity, complexity, and conflict within the governance setting. It means taking up the slack to compensate for the reduced governance capacity of elected officials, intergovernmental constraints, reduced levels of resources, conflict among single-issue interest groups, heightened levels of citizen participation, and, most important of all, the role reversal that these conditions have produced. Viewed against this kind of backdrop, making government work means being efficient, effective, responsive, accountable, fair, just, and equitable in the treatment of citizens. Members of our panel of local career administrators assume a personal ethical obligation to all of these moral claims. In short, they do not see democratic government as some kind of trade-off between efficient government and accountable government. They see both as necessary for a community of ordered liberty and they see themselves as the primary agents of this trust.

We must focus our energies on providing career administrators with a moral framework that enables them to answer the question they face on a daily basis: By what right can/should I play such an active role in the activities of democratic governance? Without such a mediating framework, the languages of efficiency/effectiveness, pluralism, and the public interest can be used by career administrators in ways that soon lead to the worst excess inherent in each. Efficiency and effectiveness can become mindless instrumentalism, blindly serving any political master no matter how demagogic. Pluralism degenerates into an unconvincing excuse to mollify narrowly conceived self-interest. Finally, the "public interest" becomes a term easily appropriated by political actors who claim to represent "silent majorities" or who ride the waves of transitory and ephemeral elected majorities.

We end this essay with a call for reconstruction. In an era marked by growing pressures to measure the public sector by private-sector standards, it will become more important for career administrators to possess a moral framework that enables them to articulate a complex ordering of moral claims that are compatible with our constitutional system of government. Based on our research thus far, we believe career administrators possess the essential ingredients of this framework—efficiency, majority rule, and the public interest. However, we believe they need assistance from the academic community both to order these moral claims and to tie them to the values that undergird our peculiar form of constitutional governance. Without such assistance, local government will not attract or keep the quality of public leader required for the future.

Notes

1. The data obtained from the "panel" referred to in this article are part of a larger ongoing research project conducted by the authors. The project examines the way in which the administrative, legal, and political climate of local government administrators affects their sense of ethical obligation, decision making, and action. The study employs a small number of respondents whose views and experiences are examined in depth. The object is to capture the complex, subtle interaction of values that constitute the respondents' structure of ethical meaning. This approach is similar to that used by Bellah and others (1985) and, more specifically, Lane (1959).

The in-depth interviewing technique used for this study is patterned after the "focal group research" model (Merton, Fiske, and Kendall 1984; Lane 1959; Krueger 1988; D.L. Morgan 1988), which was selected for three reasons. First, it discourages the investigators from imposing their own cognitive structure on the respondents in the form of detailed questionnaires. Second, it permits the researchers to focus on ethical dilemmas actually faced by the participants rather than those "imported" by scholars in the form of "canned" cases. Third, it focuses the research on *dialogue*, which allows the authors to observe patterns of meaning that normally are inaccessible through other techniques.

The focal group consists of six executive-level administrators chosen for their reputation as highly effective local government officials. The group's discussions are focused by use of cases drawn from the participants' own experience as "stimulus materials." A simple case discussion format is used, and discussions are recorded on audio tape and with process notes. The notes and tape are cross-referenced during analysis of the discussion content. Emphasis is on a free-flowing give-and-take among the panel members over the case materials with minimum intervention by the researchers.

2. We have adopted Bellah's terminology to capture three major kinds of moral discourse that members of our panel employ to justify the exercise of their discretionary authority. The language of efficiency and effectiveness competes with the languages of pluralism and the public interest. Each language reflects a coherent set of moral claims that cannot be easily reconciled with the claims inherent in the other two languages of discourse.

3. James H. Svara's (1989a; 1989b) recent empirical work provides an interesting comparison to our findings on how professional administrators view the traditional dichotomy between policy making and administration. Svara's study of council–manager cities in North Carolina and Ohio suggests some revisions in the Wilsonian politics–administration dichotomy.

Svara argues that there are at least four levels of interaction between a professional administrator and elected council members: creation of a common *mission*, establishment of general *policy* guidelines, transformation of policy into *administrative* practice, and provision of *management* support for the policy and administrative functions. His empirical data suggest a model in which the council clearly dominates the formulation of a mission and the career executive exercises hegemony over management, while both share responsibilities for policy and administration.

Svara refers to this empirically derived model as "NeoTraditional." On the one hand, it clearly subordinates the career executive to a mission ultimately shaped by the council and at the same time gives the executive a determining role in management decisions. On the other hand, unlike the classical model, it obligates the career executive to exercise discretion in the realm of policy and administration within a framework of controls provided by mission goals and without the executive becoming an autonomous actor. From an ethical point of view the role obligations of the "Neo-Traditional" model "set high standards for managerial attainment, promote integrity and discretion of the manager and safeguard democratic principles" (Svara 1989a, 66).

Like Svara's findings, our own findings confirm a complex pattern of interactions between elected councils and career executives that is captured much more accurately by Svara's Neo-Traditional model, than by the classical dichotomy model, which tries neatly to separate politics from administration. However, we are not as confident as Svara that "given the continuing sensitivity of the management profession to the issue of respective roles, one may expect that city managers will continue to strengthen democracy in city government rather than to threaten it" (Svara 1989b, 89).

For a variety of reasons our panel of managers found themselves in an ethically weak position to carry out this strengthening role in their interactions with elected councils. This weakness is reflected in the subsequent resignation of two or perhaps three panel members in order to pursue other careers. First, contrary to the majority of councils in Svara's study, the majority on our panel often tried to escape the burden of mission setting and policy formation by having the career executive assume primary responsibility. Second, even when elected, council members were willing to share governance responsibility for policy and administrative matters; the majority of our career executives felt they were on weak ethical ground in resisting ill-conceived and/or unjust claims of elected council managers. In short, the ethical problems faced by our panel of local career executives can be only partially solved by Svara's "process-model." A fully adequate ethical model for guiding the exercise of administrative discretion must provide our career administrators with substantive standards as well as procedural/process standards for making better sense out of their world.

It is interesting to speculate on the extent to which the differences in findings between Svara's study and ours might be the result of differences between survey research and in-depth conversations with and among interviewees over an extended period of time.

References

Argyris, Chris, and Schon, D.A. 1974. *Theory in Practice*. San Francisco: Jossey-Bass.

Bellah, R., Madsen, R., Sullivan, W.M., Swidler, A., and Tripton, S.W. 1985. *Habits of the Heart: Individualism and Commitment in American Life*. New York: Harper and Row.

Dahl, R.A. 1956. *A Preface to Democratic Theory*. Chicago: University of Chicago.

Davis, Kenneth Culp. 1969. *Discretionary Justice: A Preliminary Inquiry*. Baton Rouge: Louisiana State University Press.

Finer, Herman. 1941. "Administrative Responsibility in Democratic Government." *Public Administration Review* 1 (Summer): 335.

Frederickson, H.G. 1971. "Toward a New Public Administration." In *Toward a New Public Administration*, edited by F. Marini. Scranton, PA: Chandler.

Friedrich, C.J. 1940. "Public Policy and the Nature of Administrative Responsibility." *Public Policy*. Cambridge, MA: Harvard University Press.

Krueger, R.A. 1988 *Focus Groups: A Practical Guide for Applied Research*. Newbury Park, CA: Sage.

Lane, R.E. 1959. *Political Life: Why People Get Involved in Politics*. Glencoe, IL: Free Press.

Lowi, T. 1979. *The End of Liberalism: The Second Republic of the United States*. 2d ed. New York: W.W. Norton.

Merton, R.K.; Fiske, M.; and Kendall, P. 1984. *The Focused Interview*. New York: Free Press.

Morgan, D.F. 1990. "Administrative Phronesis: Discretion and the Problem of Administrative Legitimacy in Our Constitutional System." In *Images and Identities in Public Administration*, edited by H. D. Kass and B. Catron. Newbury Park, CA: Sage.

Morgan, D.F. and Kass, Henry. 1991. "Legitimating Administrative Discretion through Constitutional Stewardship." In *Ethical Frontiers in Public Management: Seeking New Strategies for Resolving Ethical Dilemmas*, edited by James S. Bowman. San Francisco: Jossey-Bass.

Morgan, D.L. 1988. *Focus Groups as Qualitative Research*. Newbury Park, CA: Sage.

Morrow, W. L. 1987. "The Pluralist Legacy in American Public Administration." In *A Centennial History of the American Administrative State*, edited by R. Chandler. Glencoe, IL: Free Press, 1987.

Ostrom, V. 1974. *The Intellectual Crises in Public Administration*. University: University of Alabama Press.

Rittel, H.W.J., and Mill, W. 1973. "Dilemmas in a General Theory of Planning." *Policy Sciences* 4: 151–69.

Rohr, J.A. 1978. *Ethics for Bureaucrats: An Essay on Law and Values*. New York: Marcel Dekker.

———. 1986. *To Run A Constitution: The Legitimacy of the Administrative State*. Lawrence: University Press of Kansas.

Schon, D. 1983. *The Reflective Practitioner: How Professionals Think in Action*. New York: Basic Books.

Scott, William G., and Hart, David K. 1979. *Organizational America*. Boston: Houghton Mifflin.

Svara, James H. 1989a. "Dichotomy and Duality: Reconceptualizing the Relationship between Policy and Administration in Council–Manager Cities." In *Ideal and Practice in Council–Manager Government*, edited by H. George Frederickson, 53–69. Washington, DC: ICMA.

――― 1989b. "Policy and Administration: City Managers as Comprehensive Professional Leaders," In *Ideal and Practice in Council–Manager Government*, edited by H. George Frederickson, 70–92. Washington, DC: ICMA.

Truman, D.B. 1955. *The Governmental Process, Political Interests and Public Opinion*. New York: Alfred Knopf.

Zammuto, R.F. 1982. *Assessing Organizational Effectiveness*. Albany: State University of New York Press.

10

The Ethics Factor in Local Government: An Empirical Analysis

Donald C. Menzel

Scholarly interest in ethics in government has grown rapidly over the past decade and is quickly becoming a major field of research. The emergence of government ethics as an important research enterprise, however, will depend heavily on the extent to which scholars can validate, through systematic research involving rigorous data collection and analysis, the propositions so eloquently articulated in the literature. It seems fair to say that the existing stock of tested and validated knowledge of government ethics is sparse.

This chapter seeks to contribute to empirically based knowledge of government ethics by reporting the results of a study of the ethical work climates of two local governments. One objective of the study was to assess the extent to which an ethical work climate supports or is compatible with organizational work values such as efficiency and effectiveness. A second objective was to identify and assess the factors that contribute to an ethical work climate.

Ethical Climates in Public Organizations

The ethics literature has largely ignored the ethical climates of public organizations and the influence they may have on organizational goals and employee behavior. Rather, scholars have focused primarily on individual level behaviors, although often times in the context of complex public organizations (Willbern 1984; Thompson 1980; Stewart 1984; Morgan 1987; McSwain and White 1987).[1]

This is not to suggest that work climates in general have been ignored—indeed, quite to the contrary. Applied psychologists and organizational/management students have given the subject considerable attention, beginning as early as 1939 when psychologists conducted experiments to examine the relationship between work climates and aggressive behavior (Lewin, Lippitt, and White 1939). More recently, investigators have studied (a) how organizational climates influence the performance of managers and affect job satisfaction (Pritchard and Karasick 1973; Downey, Hellriegel, and Slocum 1975), (b) climate formation (Ashforth 1985), and (c) types of climates (Victor and Cullen 1987). The literature in this area is too voluminous to summarize here. For excellent reviews, the interested reader should consult Schneider (1983) and Schneider and Reichers (1983).

Organizational cultures also have been the subject of considerable interest in recent years. Motivated in part by corporate success stories in the United States and abroad—mainly Japan—popular books like Peters and Waterman's *In Search of Excellence* (1982), and scholars like Wilkins and Ouchi (1983) have drawn considerable attention to the significance of organizational culture. Although the two concepts—climate and culture—seem to have much in common, organizational students tend to embrace one but not the other. Why this seems to be the case and what the implications are cannot be discussed in the limited space provided here. (See Schneider [1990] for a thorough discussion of this point.)

Another emphasis in the ethics literature, other than individual-level behavior, has been on the philosophical or theoretical issues associated with ethical behavior in government. Writing primarily from a theoretical perspective, Cooper (1987) draws attention to the interplay between hierarchical organization with its emphasis on loyalty to superiors and the displacement of individual-level values such as moral autonomy and critical thinking. His work, however, stops short of documenting the linkages he believes to exist. Taking an even more ominous perspective, Scott and Hart (1979, 1989) and Denhardt (1981) have written at length about how organizational values suppress individual values, thereby producing organizational members who fail to develop as morally responsible human beings. Scott and Hart (1989, 30) put it bluntly in asserting that the organizational imperative defines what is good or bad for the individual, with good defined as doing what is necessary to ensure the success of the organization.

Still others have expressed an interest in providing public managers with prescriptions and guidelines for promoting ethical behavior. Gortner (1991, xiv) for example, argues that too little has been done to apply public administration ethics theory "to the lives of managers operating in the middle ranges of the public bureaucracy." His book, *Ethics for Public Managers*, is meant to fill this breach. Loverd (1990, 222) counsels public executives to "learn to listen" in order to "improve the viability and moral fabric of one's organization and maintain some measure of self-respect." In *Ethical Insight Ethical Action* (1988), an ethics reader published by the International City Management Association, an entire section is devoted to managing organizational ethics. More recently, the American Society for Public Administration (Richter, Burke, and Doig 1990) published a three hundred-page source book that, among other things, seeks to provide guidance on how to promote ethics in public organizations. One chapter is devoted exclusively to organizational strategies for combating corruption and encouraging ethics.

Other authors, although few in number, have been less prescriptive. Winn and Rice (1986) argue that individual ethics and organizational ethics are separate yet linked entities that should be studied separately and in relation to one another. Organizational ethics, they maintain, consist of organizational norms and values that induce ethical or unethical behavior on the part of members of the organization. More specifically, they argue that conflict between individual and organizational ethics can adversely affect organizational goals and that the two can and should be reinforcing.

Some authors invoke the terms *ethical environment, organizational ethics, the ethical organization,* and *ethics climate* to ascribe meaning to organizational behavior. Victor and Cullen (1988), for example, contend that organizations have distinct ethical work climates. Their study, which relied on confidential questionnaires completed by 872 employees in four private firms, found that ethical climates are multidimensional and can vary across organizations. Victor and Cullen also believe, although their findings did not confirm their belief, that ethical climates vary among subgroups or departments within an organization. Furthermore, they contend that ethical climates resemble other types of work climates and may affect organizational performance (1988, 122).

These studies are suggestive for an improved understanding of organizational ethics. At best, however, they represent a departure point for studying this important subject. This chapter attempts to build on these efforts by investigating how ethical climates of public organizations influence or condition organizational values and performance. Furthermore, an effort is made to identify those factors that lead to an ethical work climate.

An organization's ethical climate can be conceptualized in several ways. Victor and Cullen (1988, 101) define it as "the prevailing perceptions of typical organizational practices and procedures that have ethical content.... " This definition is broad but useful in that it permits one to separate out those aspects of the organizational climate that are without ethical content, for example, fact-finding methods or computational techniques. This definition, although it focuses specifically on *ethics* climates, is consistent with Schneider's (1990, 384) general definition of climate as "incumbents' perceptions of the events, practices, and procedures and the kinds of behaviors that get rewarded, supported, and expected in a setting."

Research Questions and Hypotheses

The research questions addressed in this chapter include:

1.   Do ethical climates of public organizations reinforce or detract from organizational values[2] such as efficiency, effectiveness, excellence, quality, and teamwork?

2.   Do more broad-based work climate values and practices such as trust, respect, friendliness, and bureaucratic rule orientation reinforce or detract from the ethical climate of a public organization? Relatedly, do ethical climates have more or less influence than organizational work climates and practices on organizational values?[3]

3.   What are the factors that foster or contribute to an ethical work climate? What factors reinforce or detract from ethics in the workplace?

Several working hypotheses guided the research. They are offered below along with their supporting rationale.

Hypothesis 1

As the ethical climate of an organization becomes stronger, organizational performance values such as efficiency, effectiveness, teamwork, excellence, and quality will be strongly supported.

Rationale

This hypothesis is contrary to the generally prevailing view that modern organizations with their emphasis on instrumentalism and rational choice tend to leave little room for ethical sensitivity or choice. As Denhardt (1988, 95) puts it: "For the administrator this means that in choosing an appropriate form of reasoning to achieve one set of values (efficiency and effectiveness), the implicit choice has been made to ignore other social values." Still, as she points out

> There is a need to develop and recognize that pursuing efficiency, effectiveness, and economy are not ends in themselves, but are valued because they are instrumental in serving social purposes by enhancing organizational goals, and are also valued in an ethical sense. (1988, 139)

Pastin (1986), although approaching the subject of organizational ethics from a business management perspective, argues that "good" ethics and "good" business go hand-in-hand. Organizations with a high level of performance do not ignore ethics questions or issues. Rather, they place them at the core of their organizational mission. In short, the argument advanced here is that high-performing organizations and strong ethical climates are compatible, indeed reinforcing value sets.

Hypothesis 2

Both a strong ethical climate and a supporting (positive) work climate will foster organizational values such as efficiency, effectiveness, quality, and excellence, but ethical climate will have the greater influence.

Rationale

This hypothesis is based on the pervasive (potential and real) influence of ethics in public organizations. Unlike private profit-making firms, governmental bodies owe their existence to basic laws and processes that command them to serve the public with faithfulness, fairness, integrity, and honesty. Moreover, all public service professional associations such as the American Society for Public Administration and the International City Management Association admonish their members not only to "do things right" but to "do the right thing" in carrying out their official duties and work-related responsibilities.

No hypothesis is offered with respect to the factors that might contribute to an ethical work climate. Instead, a series of variables such as the extent to which employees trust and respect each other, follow rules, engage in routinized work tasks, and assume responsibility are dealt with in an exploratory fashion.

Study Methodology

Study Sites

Two local governments participated in this study. One is a city with a population of 67,000 and a council–manager form of government. The other is a county with a population of 850,000 and a commission–administrator form of government. The city is located in the same county and in close proximity to the county headquarters. Both governments have a history of stability with appointed city/county managers who typically serve for many years. Given the sensitive nature of asking questions about ethics and the importance of obtaining candid replies, it was believed that local governments with the histories described above would be excellent subjects to study.

The primary data base consists of questionnaires completed by randomly selected samples of employees from each government. The city sample consisted of 500 employees among a total of 649 full-time employees. Two-hundred-sixty-five (N = 265) employees returned usable questionnaires for a response rate of 53 percent (nearly 41 percent of all employees). The county sample consisted of 750 employees among a total of 2,855 full-time employees. Four-hundred-sixty-five employees (N = 465) returned usable questionnaires for a response rate of 62 percent (16 percent of all employees).

Both samples were drawn from alphabetized payroll lists using a fixed interval selection method. All participants were informed that their participation was voluntary and all responses would be treated confidentially. Cover letters from the city manager, the chief personnel officer of the county, and the principal investigator explained the purpose of the study and assured anonymity. To provide additional anonymity, participants were not identified by sex, race, or work unit.

All major organizational subunits (police, fire, and so forth) in the city participated in the study. The county study population included all employees under the county administrator's jurisdiction, the supervisor of elections, the property appraiser's office, and the clerk of the circuit courts. Employees under the appointing authority of the sheriff did not participate in the study.

Surveys were mailed in-house to all county participants and half of the city participants in July/August 1990. Each respondent was provided a postage-paid envelope with the university's address clearly stamped on it.[4]

Questionnaire Development

The initial development of the questionnaire took place as a classroom exercise in a public administration graduate course on ethics. It was subsequently pretested on sixty-seven employees drawn from several local governments in the area. The responses were analyzed and assessed, and further modifications and improvements in the questionnaire were made. Following this effort, the principal investigator met with high-ranking administrators of the study governments to review the questionnaire for one final time. The result was a four-page questionnaire containing forty-five Likert-type items with four response categories: strongly agree, agree, disagree, strongly disagree. It also contained three scales that asked the respondent to characterize his/her own ethical standards, the ethical standards of co-workers, and the ethical standards of his/her work unit. Finally, the questionnaire included a series of questions about the respondent's background and organizational duties. Respondents could also make open-ended comments, and one-third did so. The questionnaires administered to city and county employees were identical in all aspects except for a few minor site-specific words.

Respondents as Observers

Each respondent was asked to provide information about the ethical climate of his/her organization. This approach assumes that the respondent can perform as a reasonably objective observer; it is similar to that followed by Victor and Cullen. As they put it, "the measure of ethical climate did not focus on whether the respondent believed he or she behaved ethically nor did it emphasize whether the respondent saw the ethical climate as good or bad" (Victor and Cullen 1988). The survey questionnaire elicited *descriptions* of, rather than feelings toward, the ethical climate.

Indicators and Scales

Table 10.1 contains the items used to construct an ethics climate scale (CLIMATE). These items reflect ethics issues (receiving gifts, misuse of position) commonly faced by local government employees. Although there is not complete agreement on appropriate behaviors, the ethics literature as well as many laws, local ordinances, and codes of conduct presumes that employees who take gifts, use their position for private gain, or leak information that benefits a third party engage in unethical behavior.

Table 10.1

Ethics Climate Items

1. It is not unusual for members of my department to accept small gifts for performing their duties.
2. Some members of my department use their position for private gain.
3. Members of my department have misused their position to influence the hiring of their relatives and friends in (city/county) government.
4. My supervisor encourages employees to act in an ethical manner.
5. Managers in my department have high ethical standards.
6. The people in my department demonstrate high standards of personal integrity.
7. There are serious ethical problems in my department.
8. Members of my department sometimes leak information that benefits persons who do business with the city.
9. My superiors set a good example of ethical behavior.

Other items on the CLIMATE scale attempt to capture behaviors by peers and superiors in fostering an ethical environment. Schmidt and Posner's (1986) study of federal level administrators reports that the behavior of superiors and peers is the most important influence that contributes to unethical behaviors or actions by managers. It should be noted that respondents were provided a generic definition of ethics as "values and principles that guide day-to-day behavior."

Table 10.2 contains scales and indicators of the organizational work climate. These include trust, respect, responsibility, friendliness, rule following, and procedural emphasis. In addition, certain job characteristics such as work pressure and stress, job efficacy, and work routinization could condition perceptions of an organization's ethical climate and influence organizational performance. For example, put as questions and implied hypotheses were the following: Does job stress make an organization/person more vulnerable to ethical transgressions? Does having a greater say in one's work duties reinforce ethics in the work place and promote organizational values (as the participatory management literature suggests)? Are persons with highly routinized work tasks likely to face fewer ethical dilemmas and therefore be less vulnerable to making "wrong" choices than persons whose work tasks are not routinized?

Table 10.3 contains five items that reflect widely held organizational values—efficiency, effectiveness, quality, excellence, and teamwork. These items are combined to form an organizational value scale (ORGVALUE) for subsequent analysis as a dependent variable.[5]

Findings

Multiple regression analysis was employed to test the following general model of the relationship between organizational performance values and ethics factors:[6]

Table 10.2

Organizational Work Climate Scales/Items*

Trust/Respect (TRUSTRES)
1. I respect my supervisor.
2. My supervisor trusts me.
3. Co-workers in my department respect each other.
4. I trust my supervisor.
5. My supervisor respects me.
6. Co-workers in my department trust each other.

Responsibility (RESPON)
1. One of the problems in my department is that people won't take responsibility.
2. Individuals in my department accept responsibility for the decisions they make.

Friendliness (FRIEND)
1. A friendly atmosphere prevails among people in my department.

Rule Orientation (RULE)
1. Ordinarily, we don't deviate from standard policies and procedures in my department.
2. Within my department, employees often bend the rules to get things done.
3. My supervisor often bends the rules to get things done.

Job Stress (STRESS)
1. In my department there is constant pressure to do more work.
2. The amount of work I am expected to do has remained about the same over the past year.
3. Around here, there is pressure to continually improve individual and group performance.
4. My work load is very heavy.

Routine
1. My work activities and responsibilities are about the same every day.
2. My daily routine is very predictable.

Job Say
1. I have to ask my supervisor before I do almost anything.
2. I have a large say in decisions that affect my job.

*Items in scales are equally weighted and scaled so that higher values correspond to increasing substantive interpretations. For example, a high score on the TRUSTRES scale indicates higher levels of trust and respect.

$$\text{ORGVALUE} = a + b_i \text{ ethics climate} + b_j \text{ work climate} + b_k \text{ job}$$

The discussion that follows will reference only the standardized (beta weights) coefficients since they indicate the relative influence of the independent variables. Multiple regression analysis was also drawn upon to examine the variables that contribute to an ethical climate. In other words, ethical climate is

Table 10.3

Organizational Values Items

1. Effectiveness is given a high priority in my department.
2. The people in my department constantly strive for excellence in carrying out their jobs.
3. Efficiency is given a high priority in my department.
4. Quality is given a high priority in my department.
5. I feel that I am a member of a well-functioning team.

---

treated as a dependent variable in order to sort out the relative influence that other components in the general work climate may have on it.

Organizational Values as the Dependent Variable

Table 10.4 shows the regression results for city and county samples when all variables, except routinized work behavior (ROUTINE), are included in the regression equation. ROUTINE is dropped because it does not have a statistically significant correlation with the organizational performance values scale.

The regression model for organizational values performs quite well in both study populations, having statistical significance levels at $p = 0.00$. Sixty-two percent and 63 percent of the total variance is explained in the city and county samples, respectively. Ethical climate has the largest influence in the city sample (beta = 0.28), while the scale that measures trust and respect (TRUSTRES) has a similar influence (beta = 0.30) in the county sample. Rule following and job efficacy have smaller weights in both study samples and are unimportant in the city sample when all variables are considered.

These statistics indicate that the ethical climate of an organization has an organizational impact, especially with respect to the combined values of efficiency, effectiveness, quality, excellence, and teamwork. Indeed, insofar as the city results are suggestive, ethical climate has the single most important influence on organizational performance values.

Ethics Climate as the Dependent Variable

The next task is to examine those variables that reinforce or detract from the development of ethical climates in public organizations. Stated differently, ethics climate can be viewed as a dependent variable. Table 10.5 reports the results of the regression analysis of the ethical climate scale with eight independent variables.

The regression model performs very well for both city and county samples, explaining 67 percent of the variance in the climate scale for both samples. All variables, except for friendliness in the county sample, are statistically significant.

Table 10.4

Regression Analysis for Organizational Values[a]

Variable	Standardized Regression Coefficients	
	City	County
INTERCEPT	n/a	n/a
CLIMATE	0.28**	0.16**
TRUSTRES	0.21**	0.30**
RESPON	0.26**	0.21**
FRIEND	0.17**	0.16**
RULE	0.01	0.09*
STRESS	0.17**	0.12**
JOBSAY	0.00	0.06

[a]ORGVALUE = efficiency, effectiveness, quality, excellence, and teamwork.

City: $F = 51.9$; $R^2 = 0.62$; $R = 0.79$
County: $F = 103.3$; $R^2 = 0.63$; $R = 0.80$

* Significant at $p < 0.01$ level, two-tailed test
** Significant at $p < 0.001$ level, two-tailed test

Rule following has the largest influence in the city sample, while trust and respect have the largest influence in the county sample. The importance of rule following in the city sample may be due to influence of a city manager who was with the city for many years and had a reputation of "going by the book." Although he was no longer the city manager when this survey was conducted, his influence might well have continued.

The importance of job stress as measured by the STRESS scale is an interesting finding. It shows up as significant in both governments (although the beta weights are small) and is in the opposite direction than hypothesized. This finding is not readily explainable. It may be that job stress acts as a positive tension up to some point or threshold after which it detracts from an ethical work environment. Unfortunately, the limitations of this study do not permit one to resolve this question. A second interesting finding is the small but statistically significant coefficients for routinized work patterns as measured by the scale ROUTINE. The signs are in the opposite direction expected; this suggests that respondents with more routinized jobs tend to work in an organizational environment with a weak ethical component. This finding may reflect the presence of professional versus nonprofessional work units in which the respondents belong. Employees who might be viewed as having professional duties are, by definition, likely to engage in nonroutinized work. Such employees may be more sensitive to the ethical components of their work setting and therefore perceive themselves as members of a more ethical work place.

Table 10.5

Regression Analysis for Ethics Climate[a]   +

Variable	Standardized Regression Coefficients	
	City	County
INTERCEPT	n/a	n/a
ROUTINE	−0.08*	−0.06*
TRUSTRES	0.26**	0.46**
RESPON	0.15**	0.13**
FRIEND	0.14**	0.04
RULE	0.38**	0.27**
STRESS	0.01**	0.07*
JOBSAY	0.13**	0.09*

[a]CLIMATE INDEX (see Table 10.1 for items)

City: $F = 65.4$; $R^2 = 0.67$; $R = 0.82$
County: $F = 121.6$; $R^2 = 0.67$; $R = 0.82$

*Significant at $p < 0.01$ level two-tailed test
**Significant at $p < 0.001$ level two-tailed test

Conclusion

This chapter documents the influence that the ethical climates of local government organizations have on organizational values such as efficiency, effectiveness, quality, excellence, and teamwork. These values are reinforced by a strong
rather than a weak ethical climate. The findings challenge much of the conventional wisdom that ethics and high performance are not compatible, at least as
they are defined in terms of the emphasis given to the time-honored administrative values of efficiency, effectiveness, and economy.

Another finding of this study that challenges conventional wisdom is that
bureaucratic environments, with their emphasis on hierarchy and rule following,
are incompatible with a strong commitment to organizational ethics. Indeed, at
least as defined in this study, the opposite seems to be true. Procedural emphases
in conjunction with other variables operative in the work place appear to reinforce ethics in public organizations. This study was limited to two local governments in a single state; the generalizations suggested here, therefore, are
necessarily constrained by this fact and must be viewed as tentative. Still, the
results are provocative in light of the extensive writing about the "evils" of hierarchy. Could it be that the defining, if not essential, characteristics of ethical public
organizations are order, authority, and rules? Or is it conceivable that hierarchy and
rule following merely reinforce the prevailing ethical climate regardless of how
strong or weak it may be? Only future studies can answer these questions.

This study did not produce evidence of different types of ethical climates across public organizations. Still, it would seem premature to rule out this possibility. More research is needed before an informed judgment or conclusion can be reached about the extent to which ethical climates vary among public organizations and how differences in ethical climates can make significant differences in organizational performance.

Like others who have adopted a more empirical approach to the study of government ethics (see Overman and Foss 1991), this chapter raises more questions than it answers. Answers may not be forthcoming, to paraphrase Overman and Foss, until other empirical inquiries into administrative ethics are completed.

Notes

1. An exception is Denhardt (1988), who argues that equal attention should be given to individual-level ethics and the organizational context in which ethics decisions are made.

2. Organizational values are sometimes treated as organizational goals or, more specifically, as administrative process goals.

3. Work climate researchers generally contend there is no singularly defined generic work climate. Rather, work climate is defined by its specific referents. Ethics work climates, then, can be thought of as a specific type of work climate. The distinction drawn in this chapter between the general work climate and ethics climates must be viewed in terms of the specific referents of the two types of climates.

4. An examination of several statistics suggest that those who completed the questionnaire do not differ from the study populations as a whole. City respondents, for example, indicated they had been employed by the city 7.6 years. Statistics from city records show that the average city employee had been with the city between seven and nine years. A breakdown by age categories also showed that 20 percent of the survey respondents were between the ages of eighteen and twenty-nine compared to 24 percent of all employees; 31 percent of the respondents were between the ages of thirty and thirty-nine and the same number was true for all employees; 28 percent of the respondents were between the ages of forty and forty-nine compared to 24 percent for all employees; 15 percent of the respondents were between the ages of fifty and fifty-nine compared to 14 percent for all employees; and identical percentages (6 percent) for the study sample and all employees characterized those sixty years of age or more.

In comparing the county respondents with all county employees, county records show that the typical employee had been with the county between 6.9 and 9.6 years while the typical survey respondent had been employed by the county 8.3 years. A breakdown by age categories shows that 15 percent of the survey respondents were between eighteen and twenty-nine compared to 19 percent of all employees who were younger than thirty-one; 28 percent of the respondents were between thirty and thirty-nine compared to 32 percent of all employees who were between thirty-one and forty; 28 percent of the respondents were between forty and forty-nine compared to 24 percent who were between forty-one and fifty; 20 percent of the respondents were between fifty and fifty-nine compared to 19 percent of all employees who were between the ages of fifty-one and sixty; and 10 percent of the respondents were sixty or older while 8 percent of all employees were sixty-one or more years of age.

5. All scales were subjected to reliability tests employing *Cronbach's Alpha*—an internal consistency test. Most scales have alpha coefficients exceeding 0.80, which indicates high reliability. ROUTINE and JOBSAY are the only scales to drop below alpha = 0.60;

CLIMATE, ORGVALUE, and TRUSTRES have alphas of 0.86/0.86, 0.85/0.86, 0.85/0.86 for city and county samples, respectively.

6. Difference of means tests (T-tests) were performed on all scales to determine if the city and county samples differed in any statistically significant ways. The T-tests showed that the study samples did not differ. City and county ethical climates appear to be quite similar.

References

Ashforth, Blake E. 1985. "Climate Formation: Issues and Extensions." *Academy of Management Review* 10: 837–47.

Cooper, Terry L. 1987. "Hierarchy, Virtue, and the Practice of Public Administration: A Perspective for Normative Ethics." *Public Administration Review* 47 (July/August): 320–28.

Denhardt, Kathryn G. 1988. *The Ethics of Public Service: Resolving Moral Dilemmas in Public Organizations.* Westport, CT: Greenwood Press.

Denhardt, Robert B. 1981. *In the Shadow of Organization.* Lawrence: University Press of Kansas.

Downey, H. Kirk; Hellriegel, Don; and Slocum, John W. 1975. "Congruence between Individual Needs, Organizational Climate, Job Satisfaction and Performance." *Academy of Management Journal* 18: 149–55.

Gortner, Harold F. 1991. *Ethics for Public Managers.* New York: Praeger.

Lewin, Karl; Lippitt, Ronald; and White, Ralph K. 1939. "Patterns of Aggressive Behavior in Experimentally Created Social Climates." *Journal of Social Psychology* 10: 257–78.

Loverd, Richard A. 1990. "Dealing with Dissent: Learning to Listen for an Ethical Organization." In *Combating Corruption, Encouraging Ethics*, edited by William L. Richter, Frances Burke, and Jameson W. Doig. Washington, DC: American Society for Public Administration.

McSwain, Cynthia J., and White, Orion F., Jr. 1987. "The Case for Lying, Cheating, and Stealing—Personal Development as Ethical Guidance for Managers." *Administration & Society* 18 (February): 411–32.

Morgan, Douglas R. 1987. "Varieties of Administrative Abuse: Some Reflections on Ethics and Discretion." *Administration & Society* 19 (November): 267–84.

Overman, E. Sam, and Foss, Linda. 1991. "Professional Ethics: An Empirical Test of the 'Separatist Thesis.' " *Journal of Public Administration Research and Theory* 1 (April): 131–46.

Pastin, Mark. 1986. *The Hard Problems of Management.* San Francisco: Jossey-Bass.

Peters, Thomas J., and Waterman, R.H. 1982. *In Search of Excellence.* New York: Harper & Row.

Pritchard, Robert D., and Karasick, Bernard W. 1973. "The Effects of Organizational Climate on Managerial Job Performance and Job Satisfaction." *Organizational Behavior and Human Performance* 9:126–46.

Richter, William L., Burke, Frances, and Doig, Jameson W., eds. 1990. *Combating Corruption, Encouraging Ethics.* Washington, DC: American Society for Public Administration.

Schmidt, Warren H., and Barry Z. Posner, 1986. "Values and Expectations of Federal Service Executives." *Public Administration Review* 46 (September/October): 447–54.

Schneider, B. 1983. "Work Climates: An Interactionist Perspective." In *Environmental Psychology: Directions and Perspectives*, edited by N.W. Feimer and E.S. Geller. New York: Praeger.

Schneider, B. and Reichers, A.E. 1983. "On the Etiology of Climates." *Personnel Psychology* 36: 19–39.

Schneider, Benjamin, ed. 1990. *Organizational Climate and Culture*. San Francisco: Jossey-Bass.

Scott, William G., and Hart, David K. 1979. *Organizational America*. Boston: Houghton Mifflin.

———. 1989. *Organizational Values in America*. New Brunswick, NJ: Transaction Publishers.

Stewart, Debra W. 1984. "An Ethical Framework for Human Resource Decision Making." *Public Administration Review*: 44 (January/February): 14–22.

Thompson, Dennis F. 1980. "Moral Responsibility of Public Officials: The Problem of Many Hands." *American Political Science Review* 74 (December): 905–16.

Victor, Bart, and Cullen, John B. 1987. "A Theory and Measure of Ethical Climate in Organizations." In *Research in Corporate Social Performance and Policy*, edited by William C. Frederick. Greenwich, CT: JAI Press.

———. 1988. "The Organizational Bases of Ethical Work Climates." *Administrative Science Quarterly* 33: 101–25.

Wilkins, Alan L., and Ouchi, William G. 1983. "Efficient Cultures: Exploring the Relationship between Culture and Organizational Performance." *Administrative Science Quarterly* 28 (September): 468–81.

Willbern, York. 1984. "Types and Levels of Public Morality." *Public Administration Review* 44 (March/April): 102–108.

Winn, Mylon, and Rice, Mitchell F. 1986. "Individual and Organizational Ethics: A Case for Compatibility." *New Directions in Public Administration Research* 1 (April): 14–29.

11

The Impact of Demographic, Professional, and Organizational Variables and Domain on the Moral Reasoning of Public Administrators

Debra W. Stewart and Norman A. Sprinthall

Most studies of managerial ethics focus on the attitudes and values of the respondents, and the lion's share of the empirical work has looked at American business managers rather than at public administrators. This chapter reports on a study of moral reasoning rather than simply on ethical attitudes or values, and explores empirically that reasoning in samples of public administrators and public administration graduate students. Variables thought to explain variation in aspects of ethics include age, gender, seniority (Hodgkinson 1971); education (Purcell 1977); function and level of responsibility (Hunt, Wood, and Chonko 1989; Harris 1989; Posner and Schmidt 1984), and organizational context (Conner and Becker 1975; Hunt et al. 1989; Trevino 1986). In this study we explore the relationship between each of these variables and levels of moral reasoning among public administrators. Our research allows us to look at these relationships in three ethical domains and to consider the aggregate relationships as well. This study represents an effort to move beyond case study and admonition toward understanding the way moral reasoning and ethical behavior are influenced in organizations.

Assumptions and Background

This essay assumes that the public administrator is a moral agent. While we recognize that the development of individual agency is not a simple process (McDonald and Victor 1988), we assume that it is an essential feature of life in public-sector organizations (Stewart 1985; Denhardt 1988). But to agree with Denhardt (1988) that the ethical administrator has a responsibility to utilize moral assessments is to leave unanswered the question of how to conduct that moral assessment. In an earlier essay we argued for the need to conduct more research on the systems of ethical reasoning that public administrators may employ in resolving ethical dilemmas. We also presented a new instrument to assess stages of moral reasoning exhibited by public administrators (Stewart and Sprinthall 1991). It was based on the Kohlberg (1984) theory that moral development occurs in a specific sequence of stages, and that ethical or moral judgment is neither fixed nor relativistic but rather forms a sequence of ethical models. We argued previously that the higher order models are more democratic and just in their comprehensiveness and thus are compatible with the ideals of public service (Stewart and Sprinthall 1991). The instrument we developed assesses levels of moral reasoning among individuals in a public administration context.

Data and Methods

Detailed information on the development of the instrument, the Stewart Sprinthall Management Survey (SSMS), is reported elsewhere (Stewart and Sprinthall 1991). The survey is based on Lawrence Kohlberg's finding that moral development occurs in a specific series of stages across cultures. By studying empirically the system of thinking that people employ to deal with moral questions, Kohlberg identified an invariant sequence of stages of moral growth that ranges from a straightforward concern about self to a stage focused on the application of universal moral principles such as those that relate to justice and equality (Kohlberg 1984). James Rest developed the Defining Issues Test (DIT) as an objective adaptation of Kohlberg's interview (Rest 1986). Like the Kohlberg instrument, the DIT presents general moral dilemmas and classifies individuals according to the arguments they invoke to solve these dilemmas. The SSMS parallels the DIT but is designed to assess moral reasoning evoked in a public-sector management context. The dilemmas provided in the SSMS deal with the actual ethical quandaries individuals encounter in public administration. In that context the SSMS reflects reasoning across five stages of moral development. The stages are as follows:

Stage 1: *Concern for Obedience and Punishment*. To avoid punishment one must be obedient—fear of punishment is a major motivator.
Stage 2: *Concern for Cooperation and Reciprocity in a Single Instance*. Cooperative interactions are entered because each party has something to gain. "Let's make a deal." It is the exchange that makes it fair. Bargains are struck to achieve self-interest. Materialism predominates.
Stage 3: *Concern for Enduring Personal Relationships*. Maintaining of good relationships over time is valued; approval of others is important. Be kind and

considerate and you will get along with others. Engage in reciprocal role taking; social conformity is the highest value.

Stage 4: *Concern for Law and Duty.* Authority maintains morality; everyone in society is obligated and protected by the law; respect for the authority of law is part of one's obligation to society.

Stage 5: *(P): Principled Reasoning.* This mode of reasoning envisions the mind of a hypothetical rational person—what agreement would a hypothetical group of rational people accept? Impartiality is central. Democratic principles of justice and fairness are the core values.

In the SSMS the individual dilemmas deal with three domains of administrative decision making: promotion, with the attendant issues of affirmative action and patronage; procurement, with the ever-present concerns of conflict of interest; and data base management, with the related issues of data file integrity. In each domain the SSMS provides opportunity for the respondent to reflect upon the mode of reasoning employed. The total SSMS scores represent averages across all three administrative domains. For an individual respondent the stage scores reflect the tendency for that individual to select reasons that correspond to different levels of moral development.

Analysis

The instrument was administered to three separate samples in North Carolina: graduate students in public administration (N = 75), local government managers attending a series of executive training programs (N = 136), and city and county managers and assistant managers (N = 190). Across all three samples the pattern of distribution is similar, with the most commonly selected reasons falling in stage 4 and the principled stage. There was a clear pulling toward "law and duty" reasoning with almost 40 percent of the respondents in each sample, reflecting principled reasoning. This figure corresponds to the level of moral reasoning found in the U.S. population as a whole for individuals who have completed college. However, it is significantly higher than that reported for the southern region (Sapp 1985).

As shown in Table 11.1, the percentages indicate the number of persons whose reasoning could be classified according to stage type. Thus, 40 percent of the graduate student sample, or thirty subjects, employed principled reasons in resolution of the administrative dilemmas. Thirty-five of these subjects used stage 4, or the legal code, as their means of resolving the issues. The number of subjects according to stage in the other two groups is similar. Since the survey measure is a recognition test, the percentages reflect the subjects' ability to identify stage type reasons from a list of choices. It has been shown in other research on moral reasoning that such an approach actually overestimates by one stage the level of reasons that the subject can produce *de novo* or can actually

Table 11.1

Total SSMS Stage Score Comparison across All Groups

Stage Scores	Students (%) (N=75)	Local Gov't Mgr. (%) (N=136)	City/County Mgr. (%) (N=190)
1+2	5	6	7
3	5	7	10
4	46	45	42
5	40	39	38

Note: The percentages vary due to rounding and a few unclassified subjects.

employ in real dilemma situations (Rest 1986; Kohlberg 1984). Thus, a person who identifies a preference for principled solutions may actually employ stage 4, or the legal code, in a real situation. Similarly, a preference for stage 4 would likely shift closer to stage 3, social conformity, in an actual administrative dilemma. The base rate for our sample is similar to college educated adults in general and is higher than adults in general from the South and Southeast. The actual level of reasoning, however, is probably one stage lower than the level obtained by a recognition test. We will now turn to an analysis of possible differences within our sample according to demography, organizational responsibilities, and context.

Demographic Factors

In this analysis we look at the impact of a set of demographic factors that have been thought to influence the kinds of ethical choices individuals are likely to make and the factors they are likely to consider important in this decision-making process. As Tables 11.2 through 11.5 suggest, there are no significant differences that can be attributed to gender, race or education level across any of the three samples.

Carol Gilligan (1982) has speculated specifically on the importance of gender differences and level of ethical reasoning. She has argued that women tend to reason about moral conflict based on a notion of morality as care, while men reason through such conflicts based on morality as justice. Our results, however, show quite clearly that males and females are virtually the same in the numbers who identify principled or justice-based reasoning. These results are also in line with recent meta-analyses indicating that gender is irrelevant as a factor in moral reasoning (Walker 1988). With all four demographic factors, only age turned out to be significant, and that for only one of the three groups, the graduate student sample. This finding may be an artifact of graduate school admission and a small *n* in that category. Usually, age after college does not bear a significant relationship to ethical reasoning (Rest 1986).

Table 11.2

Comparison of Principled Reasoning by Gender for Each Group

Gender (N=75)	Students (%) (N=75)	Local Gov't. Mgr. (%) (N=136)	City/County Mgr. (%) (N=190)
Male	39 (N=36)	39 (N=95)	38 (N=174)
Female	42 (N=38)	39 (N=41)	39 (N=16)

Table 11.3

Comparison of Principled Reasoning by Race for Each Group

Race	Students (%) (N=0)	Local Gov't. Mgr. (%) (N=136)	City/County Mgr. (%) (N=190)
Black	—	35 (N=15)	40 (N=4)
White	—	40 (N=120)	38 (N=186)

*Race information was not available for the graduate student group.

Table 11.4

Comparison of Principled Reasoning by Education for Each Group

	Students (%) (N=75)	Local Gov't. Mgr. (%) (N=136)	City/County Mgr. (%) (N=190)
1. Less than BA	—	40	39
2. BA or more	40	39	36
3. MA or more	—	40	40

Table 11.5

Comparison of Principled Reasoning by Age for Each Group

Gender (N=75)	Students (%) (N=75)	Local Gov't. Mgr. (%) (N=136)	City/County Mgr. (%) (N=190)
25–30	35	37	38
31–40	37	39	38
41–50	44	40	37
51+	57	39	41

*Difference significant at 0.0002
Eta 0.49

Table 11.6

Comparison of Stage Score by Level of Responsibility for Local Government Manager Sample and County/City Manager Sample Combined on Total SSMS

	Level of Position				
Stage Score	Manager (%) (N=156)	Ass't Mgr. (%) (N=46)	Dept. Head (%) (N=52)	Div. Head (%) (N=31)	Supervisor (%) (N=34)
1+2	7	6	7	6	6
3	9	11	7	7	6
4	43	41	46	46	44
5	38	39	40	36	40

Note: Columns do not total 100 percent due to rounding error and meaningless response option.

Table 11.7

Comparison of Mean Principled Reasoning Scores by Line vs. Staff for Local Government Managers, City/County Managers, and All Managers

	Line			Staff		
	Local Gov't. Mgr. (N=53)	City/County Mgr. (N=150)	All Mgrs. (N=203)	Local Gov't. Mgr. (N=72)	City/County Mgr. (N=40)	All Mgrs. (N=112)
SSMS Level P Reasoning	38%	38%	38%	40%	38%	39%

Functional and Organizational Responsibilities

A second set of factors that were found to affect the ethical thinking in organizations may be grouped under the rubric of functional and organizational responsibility. While these variables may be operationalized in a variety of ways, this study looked at level of responsibility, line versus staff, and functional task as factors that might explain variation. Tables 11.6 and 11.7 display the findings for level of responsibility and line vs. staff.

Table 11.6 indicates that across levels of responsibility within organizations, a combination of the local government manager and the city/county manager samples, there is no expression of principled reasoning that can be attributed to level of responsibility in position. The modest differences that do appear seem unrelated to level of position.

Table 11.7 suggests that there is no relationship between principled reasoning and line versus staff position in either of the sample groups of local government managers or city/county managers.

In a third exercise we simply reviewed the job titles of all respondents who indicated a propensity to select principled reasons (P = 50 or more). This inspection revealed no pattern that might be attributed to functional responsibility; that is, in making their decisions city managers, their assistants, planners, budget directors, and personnel managers appeared equally likely or unlikely to consider stage 5 reasons.

Organizational Context

Finally, we considered whether the context within which the decision maker was located would affect the likelihood of identifying principled reasons in resolving ethical dilemmas. The context factors that we considered relevant to local-level managers were the type of jurisdiction where they are located, the size of their jurisdiction, and whether or not their organization has a code of ethics. First we combined the two samples and considered all managers together.

As Table 11.8 shows, the simple context of city vs. county vs. region clearly has no impact on the likelihood of selecting principled reasons in decision making. The mean response is roughly equivalent across cities, counties, and regions.

Table 11.9 displays stage score response across small, medium, and large cities and counties. There are no significant differences that can be attributed to size of jurisdiction, whether city or county. The final context factor was the existence of a code of ethics in the jurisdiction. The city/county manager survey provided data on that question.

Table 11.10 reports no significant difference in the mean response scores that can be attributed to whether or not a jurisdiction has a code of ethics.

Difference in Ethical Domains

The analysis thus far reveals no differences that can be attributed to commonly cited demographic, organizational, or contextual factors as the reasons selected by public managers for resolution of ethical quandaries. The data do reveal differences across ethical domains. Since statistically significant positive relationships hold between each of three stories and the total SSMS scores, the total SSMS score measures overall capacity to function at a particular stage or level. However the strength of one's capacity to function at the principled reasoning level appears to vary across domains. A few recent empirical studies provide background on this point.

In the measurement of moral judgment there are often differences in levels of reasoning according to the actual dilemma content. Developmental psychologists usually refer to such differences as examples of cognitive *décalage*—systematic

Table 11.8

Comparison of Mean Principled Reasoning across Cities, Counties, and Regions

SSMS	City (N=204)	County (N=117)	Region (N=4)
Mean Principled Reasoning	39%	38%	42%

Table 11.9

Comparison of Stage Scores across Size of Jurisdiction for Cities and Counties

	County			City		
Stage Score	Less than 25,000 % (N=11)	25,000– 100,000 % (N=59)	Greater than 100,000 % (N=51)	Less than 10,000 % (N=100)	10,000– 25,000 % (N–35)	Greater than 25,000– 25,000 % (N=69)
1+2	6	8	7	6	5	7
3	13	8	8	7	7	11
4	42	42	43	45	45	41
5	37	38	38	40	39	38

Table 11.10

Mean Stage Scores on SSMS Comparing Jurisdictions with and without Codes of Ethics

Stage Scores On SSMS	Yes Code (%) (N=58)	No Code (%) (N=30)
1 + 2	6	8
3	11	9
4	42	43
5	37	39

gaps in reasoning levels by problem areas (Kohlberg 1980). An important determining factor appears to be how close to real experience is the dilemma content as well as the extent to which there are known and articulated positions. Thus, when adult subjects were confronted with real-life issues as opposed to third-party hypothetical problems, the reasoning level declined (Walker, deVries, and Trevethan 1987). Similarly, in a study with adolescents the reasoning level declined when the content of the dilemmas shifted from abstract questions such as, Should a person in a foreign country steal a drug to save his spouse? to everyday issues such as obedience to one's parents versus loyalty to one's own peer group (Gilligan et al. 1971). In the latter case, the level of reasoning declined by almost one stage for both male and female subjects. Rest (1986) has noted that the ability to identify principled reasons involves a complex process of comprehension, awareness of consequences, selection of courses of action that are consistent with such principles, and enough personal strength to withstand criticism. Such factors develop as a result of experience in dealing with controversial issues and in taking action. This means experience dealing with issues that have not been rehearsed or hashed out and that are personally involving—that is, close to real life—and that levels employed will be lower than with experiences assessed through standard or more familiar dilemmas.

There is another source of possible domain discrepancy. Jennifer Hochschild (1981) found that different beliefs about distributive justice prevail in different domains of life. Her in-depth interviews with a sample of rich and poor respondents in the Standard Metropolitan Statistical Area of New Haven showed that people may use egalitarian norms when they address issues in the socializing or political domain, but they shift to differentiating norms in the economic domain (Hochschild 1981, 48, 49, 82). Thus they come to different conclusions in different domains because they are applying different principles of justice (Hochschild 1981). This type of discrepancy could only be assessed in our case through the creation of an additional set of principled reasons based on different justice concepts. Thus far, the enormous number of studies in the moral development distributive justice format does provide us with a ready source of comparison in that general moral domain. That data base (Kuhmerker 1991) continues to grow both within this country and cross-culturally. This means that the differences we find in levels of moral development on the specific issues faced by professionals in the field of public administration can be compared to general levels in the adult population and with appropriate cultural translations to public administrators in other countries as well.[1]

In the study reported in this paper we can say that there appears to be a shift in the preference for a principled mode of reasoning across the three stories posed in the SSMS instrument, from over 50 percent stage scores for principled reasoning across all three samples for the first story, to less than 30 percent selection of principled responses across each of the three samples for the third story. Table 11.11 displays these data. We believe this suggests that there are different ethical decision domains and that some domains are more likely to elicit principled reasoning than others.

Table 11.11

Comparison within Stories and across Groups on Stage Score

Stage Scores	Students (N=74)			Local Gov't Mgr. (%) (N=136)			City/County Mgr. (%) (N=190)		
	Story 1	Story 2	Story 3	Story 1	Story 2	Story 3	Story 1	Story 2	Story 3
1 + 2	2	7	7	2	6	9	2	6	10
3	8	7	3	5	12	2	8	17	2
4	36	45	58	39	39	62	35	33	59
5	52	42	28	52	43	22	51	42	20

The three stories are as follows:

Story 1: Promotion

Bob was hired to revitalize a somewhat lackluster division in a state agency. Soon after becoming division director, he held a meeting with all division personnel and announced that all future promotions would be based on demonstrated merit and affirmative action. The patronage practice of the former director would be discontinued. Bob issued a written statement to confirm this new policy.

About a month later Bob's boss told him that he expected Joe Jones, an individual on Bob's staff, to be promoted. Joe was a marginally effective white male and there were several other employees in the division much more deserving of promotion. Bob pointed out to his boss all of the reasons for not wanting to promote Joe Jones at that time. But the boss responded that he really would like to see Joe promoted and that Bob's ability to create more promotional opportunities for his staff in the future (new positions, successful job reclassification, etc.) depended on his cooperation in this situation.

Story 2: Friends in Government

In our agency, as in many others, private vendors are hired to provide goods and services. I deal directly with these representatives and have become good friends with one representative. Our wives have become friends and our families enjoy one another. I occasionally join him for lunch and he picks up the check as a company expense. This has always been acceptable in our organization.

However, a dilemma arose recently when my friend invited my family and me to join his family and other friends at his beach cottage for a week. He was going to pay for the food and drink, and since the others were private clients, his firm was going to write it off. We knew it would be a great trip and we really wanted to go. I also knew that it could be seen by the press as a payoff for a large contract that my agency had just awarded to my friend's company.

Story 3: Data Re-creation

Jack heads the Management Information System section for his agency. Through no fault of Jack's some benefit payment data were accidentally deleted from the agency computer file. There was no way to retrieve these data within the system. The local governments charged with inputting these data originally complained bitterly about the burden of this task, so the agency's top management wanted to keep the recent data loss quiet. Top management told Jack to devise a scheme to recreate the data based on the assumption that certain relationships existed between the data elements. But Jack argued that this would result in some people receiving more benefits than they should and others receiving fewer. Top management in the agency felt that to meet payment deadlines of local government, there was no choice. Jack was told to re-create the file as best he could.

Respondents are asked to read the stories and decide what plan of action they would follow. Then they are asked to review a list of possible considerations and indicate which they would consider most important in the situation.

Clearly, the domain does make a difference across all three samples. While our conclusions on this point are preliminary, we suggest that the difference can be explained in terms of familiarity with the domain and depth of individual experience in resolving ethical quandaries in the area. The promotion story raises issues that have been under intensive discussion in public administration over the past twenty years. The competition between "merit" and "equity" claims is a standard topic in all public-sector arenas from the formal classroom or training session to the office coffee klatsch. More important, it has been a topic on the agenda of society at large for more than two decades. Accordingly, we find mean principled scores above 50 percent for all three groups.

The "Friends in Government" dilemma is by contrast a less intensively discussed social issue for the general public. There has been significant public media attention focused on conflict-of-interest issues regarding governmental procurement and other practices; however, the intensity of the public debate pales by comparison with the affirmative action–merit controversy. Still, within public agencies serious attention is given to the issue of conflict of interest through agency training programs, written policies, and simple admonitions from agency officials. It is reasonable to expect that respondents in this study have strong familiarity with the issue and have had opportunities to discuss and to reflect on a dilemma similar to the one raised in "Friends in Government." Their scores on principled reasoning of 47 percent, 43 percent, and 42 percent, respectively, across the three groups support this assumption.

The third story, "Data Re-creation," is the least familiar of the three. The problem posed, that of simulating a large and lost data set, is a relatively new problem in the annals of public administration. The problem is occasioned by a technology known, but probably not well understood, by most respondents.

Clearly this is not a topic discussed by the broader society. Rarely would such a dilemma be encountered by public managers. The specialized character of this problem makes the attendant ethics an unlikely topic for discussion in agency training seminars. In short, in identifying issues in this story, respondents are left without the benefit of discussions, either within the agency or in society, that would provide the background for reflection and decision. Hence we find across all three groups that the mean score on principled reasoning was at the highest (28 percent) in the student group, followed by 22 percent and 20 percent for the other groups. It may be unsettling to note that the average percentage of principled reasoning on this dilemma is only slightly higher than the average reasoning of junior high school students on hypothetical dilemmas (Rest 1986).

At the construct validity level, we can say that all the groups, regardless of position, comprehended the sets of reasons in a similar manner across all three situations. The rank order by principled level was always the same, with Story 1 receiving the highest percent of principled responses and Story 3 the lowest percent across nine comparisons. This means that the subjects were reading the story choices in a consistent manner according to level of understanding and familiarity. At a theory construct level it is noteworthy that the second modal stage was always in juxtaposition to the first modal stage. Thus in Story 1, stage 5 was the predominant stage selected, over 50 percent of the time. For the same story, stage 4 was always the second most common choice. Similarly in Story 3, stage 4 was the predominant mode while stage 5 was second.

These findings also indicate that the subjects remained consistent in their ability to select theoretically coherent levels as opposed to random choices. Behavioral science research in moral/ethical development has shown that a base-line criterion is the ability of an instrument to assess levels of reasoning in an invariant sequence (Kohlberg 1980). The subjects should select reasons that represent their general mode at one particular level and the next level will always be at plus or minus one. The only exception to the overall invariant sequence in our study is with the lowest stages, for example the combined stage 1 and stage 2 responses, for specific stories. On an overall basis however, for all subjects on all three stories, the sequence is invariant (Table 11.1) with the peak at stage 4. These results do support the theoretical validity of stage and sequence concepts with empirical outcomes from our samples. The reliability of the instrument can be supported by the fact that the measure has been used with four different samples (two separate administrations for graduate students and two for the groups of public administrators). In each case the rank order of story choice for the combined stories has always been the same, which indicates that the concurrent reliability is strong. We have not yet estimated the stability of the instrument over time. Other research with the general objective measure of moral/ethical judgment, upon which our instrument was based, has shown test/retest correlations in the +0.70 range (Rest 1986).

Conclusions

It should be noted that surveys such as ours measure the ability to identify levels of ethical reasons and do not assess actual moral behavior in real-world situations. Other research (Blasi 1980), however, has shown a consistent behavioral relationship between thought and action. It is certainly clear that if persons cannot process issues at a principled level or cannot recognize democratic principles, such persons are much less likely to act in accord with ethical principles. The ability to recognize such issues is a necessary first step in the process of ethical behavior (Rest 1986). In this sense, a first conclusion from our study indicates that the greatest variability in level of reasoning is derived from the content of the problem situation. If the content is familiar and there has been considerable discussion and analysis of the issues, there is a greater likelihood of higher stage reasoning. The opposite is also true. In unfamiliar situations where little has been discussed or processed, individuals are highly likely to employ less democratic and more self-serving reasons.

A second conclusion is that the usual factors of demography and organizational context have almost no influence on the level of moral reasoning. Notwithstanding the need for public executives to manifest a broader ethical vision that recognizes interconnectedness and that operates on a longer time horizon (Luke 1991), public executives in this study are no more able to identify principled reasoning than mid-level or first-line managers. Perhaps more ironically, the existence of ethical codes provides no influence on the ability to identify ethical reasons. These findings indicate that ethical reasoning and public administration are dynamic and interactive. The levels are independent of status and organization context. Those variables obviously play an important role in many areas of administration but not when focused on issues of ethics.

A third conclusion is that there may be a need to reexamine both graduate and professional in-service education. Development of extensive codes of ethics appears to be a sterile enterprise. It may be more profitable to consider dialogue on issues of ethical controversy both during graduate school and throughout professional practice. Certainly it is no easy task to learn to identify the ethical premises in difficult situations, and clearly it cannot be learned through the lecture method. Open discussion and challenge, on the other hand, can facilitate the growth process even in such a complex area as ethical reasoning (Thoma 1984).

A fourth conclusion points to future research. Since all respondents in the three studies were drawn from North Carolina, and since we know there may be regional differences associated with levels of moral reasoning, more research needs to be done across regions to identify possible differences. In addition, it is important to understand more about the relationship between stage score responses and actual behavior in public administrator roles. Finally, more research is needed to understand the most effective methods of ethics training. With the use of SSMS as our starting point, this will form our continuing research agenda.

Note

1. We are currently piloting the SSMS with a small group of public administrators in several districts in Warsaw, Poland. The project ultimately entails comparison of local-level public administrators in the United States and Poland.

References

Blasi, A. 1980. "Bridging Moral Cognition and Moral Action." *Psychological Bulletin* 88: 1–45.
Conner, P.E., and Becker, B.W. 1975. "Values and the Organization: Suggestions for Research." *Academy of Management Journal* 18: 550–61.
Denhardt, K.G. 1988. *The Ethics of the Public Services: Resolving Moral Dilemmas in Public Organizations*. New York: Greenwood.
Gilligan C. 1982. *In a Different Voice*. Cambridge MA: Harvard University Press.
Gilligan, C.; Kohlberg, L.; Lerner, M.; and Belenky, M. 1971. "Moral Reasoning about Sexual Dilemmas." *U.S. Commission on Obscenity and Pornography*. Washington, DC: U. S. Government Printing Office.
Harris, J. 1989. "Ethical Values and Decision Processes of Business Students and Business Practitioners: A Review and Extension." Unpublished manuscript, cited in J. Harris, 1990, "Ethical Values of Individuals at Different Levels in the Organizational Hierarchy of a Single Firm." *Journal of Business Ethics* 9: 741–50.
Hochschild, Jennifer L. 1981. *What's Fair? American Beliefs about Distributive Justice*. Cambridge, MA: Harvard University Press.
Hodgkinson, C. 1971. "Organizational Influence on Value Systems." *Educational Administration Quarterly* 7: 46–55.
Hunt, S.D.; Wood, V.R.; and Chonko, L.B. 1989. "Corporate Ethical Values and Organizational Commitment in Marketing." *Journal of Marketing* 53: 79–90.
Kohlberg, L. 1980. *The Meaning and Measurement of Moral Development*. Worcester, MA: Clark University Press.
———. 1984. *Essays on Moral Development*. Vol. 2. New York: Harper and Row.
Kuhmerker, L. 1991. *The Kohlberg Legacy*. Birmingham, AL: REP Books.
Luke, J. S. 1991. "New Leadership Requirements for Public Managers: From Managerial to Policy Ethics." In *Ethical Frontiers in Public Management*, edited by J. S. Bowman, 158–82. San Francisco: Jossey-Bass.
McDonald, R.A., and Victor, B. 1988. "Towards the Integration of Individual and Moral Agencies." *Business and Professional Ethics Journal* 7: 103–18.
Posner, B.Z., and Schmidt, W.H. 1984. "Values of the American Manager: An Update." *California Management Review* 16: 202–16.
Purcell, T.V. 1977. "Do Courses in Business Ethics Pay Off ?" *California Management Review* 19: 50–58.
Rest, J. 1986. *Moral Development: Advances in Research and Theory*, 2d edition. New York: Praeger.
Sapp, G.L. 1985. *Moral Development: Modes, Processes and Techniques*. Birmingham, AL: REP Books.
Stewart, D. 1985. "Ethics and the Profession of Public Administration: The Moral Responsibility of Individuals in Public Sector Organizations." *Public Administration Quarterly* 8: 4.
Stewart, D., and Sprinthall, N. 1991. "Strengthening Ethical Judgement in Public Administration." In *Ethical Frontiers in Public Management*, edited by J. S. Bowman, 243–60. San Francisco: Jossey-Bass.

Thoma, S. 1984. "Do Moral Education Programs Facilitate Moral Judgement?" *Moral Education Forum* 9 (4): 20–25.

Trevino, L. K. 1986. "Ethical Decision Making in Organizations: A Person–Situation Interactionist Model." *Academy of Management Review* 11: 601–17.

Walker L. 1988. "The Development of Moral Reasoning." *Annals of Child Development* 5: 33–78.

Walker, L.J.; deVries, B.; and Trevethan, S.D. 1987. "Moral Stages and Moral Orientations in Real-Life and Hypothetical Dilemmas." *Child Development* 58: 842–59.

12

Ethical Attitudes of Members of Congress and American Military Officers toward War

Howard Tamashiro, Donald E. Secrest, and
Gregory G. Brunk

The U.S. Congress has major foreign policy powers under the Constitution. Its prerogatives include the ability to declare war, fund the military, ratify treaties, and oversee governmental operations. Yet we know little about how members of Congress view the most fundamental decision-making problems that are involved in foreign policy. In the current effort we build upon our research concerning the attitudes of American military officers. We will examine congressional attitudes to determine if Congress members' decision-making framework is similar to that of the American military.

Further, we seek to discover whether members of Congress hold attitudes that are consistent with any traditional school of international affairs. We would like to know whether they follow a *moral* approach that involves concern and respect for other nations, or whether they tend to be particularistic and nationalistic.

While there have been numerous studies of foreign policy attitudes (e.g., Rosenau 1961; Holsti and Rosenau 1979 and 1986; Wittkopf and Maggiotto 1983a, 1983b, and 1986; Ferguson 1986), until recently social scientists have done little empirically to study *moral and ethical* constraints on decision making (see Brunk et al. 1990; Tamashiro et al. 1989; Secrest et al. 1991a, 1991b). The literature does suggest, however, that moral constraints might be viewed as *decision-making rules*, which offer guidance regarding what "should" be done, what is "fair," and what maximizes "good" outcomes.

In *A Theory of Justice*, Rawls (1971) argued that if individuals could divorce themselves from their biased positions in life, a set of "fair" rules could be found. Even this fundamental assumption has been challenged, and it is uncertain that "fair" has the same meaning for all people (Reynolds and Shelly 1985). A key problem facing scholars is that we know little about how individuals incorporate decision-making rules into their belief systems. These belief systems might be so complicated as to defy analysis, or they might be relatively easy to comprehend; we cannot be certain here. However, the potential tractability of moral reasoning in matters of public policy is suggested by the use of traditional, just-war thinking by President George Bush to justify the war against Iraq in 1991 (Rosenthal 1991).

Many theologians (for example, Aquinas 1266) and philosophers (see Donagan 1977) have contended that the most common approaches to running government flow *deductively* from a few simple rules and assumptions about human nature. This perspective leads one to the ideal of "professionalism" in governmental service. It is also the foundation of many political ideologies which emphasize that a political cause must be justified through empirical evidence and deductive logic.

Recently the normative belief system approach has attracted increased attention among social scientists. Even economists are starting to argue that ethical decision making rules affect real world decisions, that such rules are not just rhetoric, and that our knowledge of human behavior will not be complete until we better understand how such decision-making rules influence the policy process. Some recent examples of this approach include works by Levy (1981), Stark (1985), Tamashiro et al. (1989), and Brunk et al. (1990). The empirical examination of normative belief systems also has been given impetus by game theory scholars. They have demonstrated that certain "normative" or ideological rules are utility maximizing (e.g., Brams 1977; Axelrod 1984; Roemer 1985). Such normative rules seem to develop because they have survival benefits (e.g., Axelrod 1984), time-saving advantages (e.g., Asher and Weisberg 1978), or other utility-maximizing aspects (e.g., Weingast 1979; Panning 1982; Brunk et al. 1990).[1]

A number of scholars have argued that the complex ethical distinctions found in the academic literature go undiscerned by nonspecialists (e.g., Donagan 1977; Hare 1981; Kohlberg 1981). If this is true, then instead of a complicated morass of hard-to-interpret philosophical doctrines, a few simple dimensions of evaluation should be apparent in an empirical analysis of everyday ethical reasoning.

Such relative simplicity is, in fact, observable among American military officers using standardized surveys on moral attitudes toward war (Tamashiro et al. 1989; Brunk et al. 1990). For the current research effort, we surveyed members of Congress on their moral attitudes toward war and compared these results with the attitudes exhibited earlier by military officers. All survey items were designed to tap the major moral precepts and perspectives toward war reflected in the traditional philosophical, theological, and political literature.

Major Moral and Amoral Perspectives in International Relations

Over a dozen major moral and amoral perspectives on war can be identified in the traditional and the international relations literature. Some of these, such as fatalism, appear to be rare in the West and are confined mainly to traditional cultures (Tamashiro et al. 1989). Ten major positions appear to capture most Western approaches. These are:

Golden Rule. In its traditional formulation, this position argues "Do unto others as you would have them do unto you." In foreign affairs, the United States should take no unwanted actions against other nations.

Perfectionism. According to the perfectionist approach, some moral principles are absolute and apply in all situations. At the other end of the scale is nonperfectionism, which contends that any action potentially may be justified as long as it is the least destructive option available.

Moral Crusade. Some goals are so important and some enemies are so evil that *any* action can be justified to achieve America's goals or defeat America's enemies.

Pacifism. It is wrong to take another's life.

Nuclear Pacifism. Since nuclear war cannot serve any practical end it must be condemned.

Just War. Only "just" wars are legitimate. There are seven commonly cited criteria for a just war (Ramsey 1961, 1968; O'Brien 1981; National Conference of Catholic Bishops 1983). These are: A war must be declared by the proper legal authority; the damage caused to *both* sides must be proportional to the good achieved by the war; the injury that caused the war must be real and recent; a nation must have a reasonable chance of winning a war; war must be a last resort after all other options have failed; a nation must have right intentions in waging war; and a war must be waged morally.

Supreme Emergency. Under extreme circumstances, such as the possibility of total defeat by an enemy who threatens one's way of life, one can ignore the usual rules of war (Walzer 1977).

Retaliatory Ethic. One has the right to suspend moral behavior when the enemy acts immorally.

Legalism. One's primary duty is to obey legal authorities.

Reason of State. Governments should be guided only by the goals of victory and national survival.

These perspectives are broadly representative of the amoral and moral approaches to international relations. They are not an exhaustive classification scheme, for some viewpoints are broad orientations while others are very specific. As examples, perfectionists can adopt either a moral crusading or a pacifist viewpoint, while nuclear pacifism can be derived either from pacifism or by application of the just-war doctrine.

The Survey Instruments

Our data come from surveys sent to retired military officers and members of Congress (see Tamashiro et al. 1989; Brunk et al. 1990). After extensive pretesting, the survey was mailed in 1986 to one thousand retired members of a national military association. The response rate was 62 percent. In 1988 we sent the same survey to all retired U.S. senators and representatives. Their mailing addresses are listed in the *Directory of the United States Association of Former Members of Congress*.

In both mailings, potential respondents were sent a personal letter asking if they would participate in our study. To minimize the potential for interviewer bias, the cover letter specified that respondents should use their own judgment in interpreting normative terms in our questionnaire, such as "moral," "better," or "wrong." All the questions used in the primary analysis are five-point Likert items, whose responses range from "strongly disagree" to "strongly agree." The survey items are reproduced in the Appendix, and we will refer to them in our discussion.

A potential problem in this type of research is how to ensure that the responses analyzed are from the desired population and not from congressional secretaries or staff. To ensure this, we specified that it would be all right for staff members to answer the questionnaire, and an item was included asking whether the respondent was a former member of Congress or staff. Thus it was possible to separate the two groups. The staff responses were discarded for purposes of this analysis, which is based upon the opinions of 169 former senators and representatives.

Because we felt that the responses would be controversial, we avoided personal descriptor questions, which would have allowed identification of individual members of Congress. Instead, we asked only general questions about ethics, morality, and religion and the role they play in government.[2] The only political descriptor included was a measure of ideology. Past research has shown that political ideology is one of the few important variables relating to support for moral belief systems (e.g., Brunk et al. 1990; Secrest et al. 1991b). Of the senators and representatives included in the study, 25 percent indicated that they were "liberal," 48 percent indicated that they were "moderate," and 27 percent indicated that they were "conservative." Of the military, only 3 percent answered that they were "liberal," 41 percent answered that they were "moderate," and 56 percent answered that they were "conservative."

Support for Moral Perspectives in International Relations

Our research examines the attitudes of members of Congress to see if they are similar to those discovered for military officers (Tamashiro et al. 1989; Brunk et al. 1990). If the patterns are similar, then we can infer that a *fundamental orderli-*

Table 12.1

Average Support for Various Approaches (%)

Framework	Congress	Military
Golden Rule	71.2	63.3
Just War	51.0	36.2
Legalism	45.6	61.1
Supreme Emergency	38.6	43.9
Retaliatory Ethic	35.4	43.5
Reason of State	31.0	40.9
Perfectionism	27.1	18.5
Nuclear Pacifism	16.2	4.9
Pacifism	10.9	5.5
Moral Crusade	10.2	10.6

Note: The percentages refer to average support across precepts of a moral school. Support is defined as answering "strongly agree" or "agree," while opposition is defined as answering "strongly disagree" or "disagree."

The averages for the military also appear in Brunk et al. (1990, 92).

ness underlies the moral judgments of these two elite groups. In exploring this issue we first turn to the average level of support given to the ten moral and amoral positions by members of Congress and the American military. Table 12.1 presents the evidence.[3] Support is defined as responding "agree" or "strongly agree" to a positively worded statement or "disagree" or "strongly disagree" to a negatively worded statement. While there are clear similarities between members of Congress and military officers in the support given to some approaches, there are also major differences.

Both groups give broad support to the principle that one nation should do nothing to another nation that it would not approve the other nation's doing to it. This is the foreign policy version of the golden rule. Both military officers and members of Congress overwhelmingly reject moral crusading, pacifism, nuclear pacifism, and perfectionist reasoning. The doctrinal positions of just war, legalism, supreme emergency, the retaliatory ethic, and reason of state receive intermediate support from both groups.

There are notable differences as well between the two groups. The just-war approach receives almost 15 percent more support from members of Congress than it receives from the military. On the other hand, the military is 15 percent more supportive of legalism than are members of Congress. Finally, while both groups overwhelmingly reject nuclear pacifism as impractical in international affairs, the military almost unanimously rejects this approach, while 16.2 percent of Congress members are supportive of it.

There is no consensus in the literature about the percentage of those surveyed who must accept a proposition for it to be considered a norm, although 80 or 90 percent seems reasonable (e.g., Bernick and Wiggins 1983). None of these frameworks is accepted at the 90 percent level by members of Congress, and only pacifism and nuclear pacifism are rejected at this level by the military. Only three frameworks make the 80 percent cutoff for Congress. Moral crusading, pacifism, and nuclear pacifism all are rejected by them as norms.

These are not strong findings, nor do they indicate any systematic approach to decision making. The data seem to reflect congressional disarray. To strengthen this assertion, let us examine the tabular evidence in more detail. Among congressional members there is substantial support for the golden rule; there is also significant support for the retaliatory ethic, which is also known as the negative golden rule. The Machiavellian, or reason of state, approach receives substantial support. So too does the supreme emergency idea, which was called upon by Lincoln to justify his otherwise illegal orders issued during the Civil War. The latter approaches clearly conflict with the ideals of just-war theory, which are supported by more than half the members of Congress. Just-war theory argues that nations can only take specific, restrained actions in the international system.

The theoretical problem is obvious. How can respondents simultaneously show aggregate support for such a diverse and conflicting array of decision-making approaches? One obvious possibility is that attitudes are confused on these issues and no deeper pattern can be found. James Fallows (1979, 42), a speechwriter for President Jimmy Carter, noted this possibility when he wrote:

> I came to think that Carter believes fifty things, but no one thing. He holds explicit, thorough positions on every issue under the sun, but he has no large view of the relations between them, no line indicating which goals will take precedence over which when the goals conflict. Spelling out these choices makes the difference between a position and a philosophy, but it is an act foreign to Carter's mind.

If, as many have argued, traditional "normative" approaches are confused and unworkable, then cost–benefit calculations should serve as public policy guidelines. However, even if we accept this argument, there is no agreement among members of Congress on the correct non-normative framework that should be used. Such "rational" approaches also are contained in our questionnaire in the guise of various amoral and immoral frameworks, such as reason of state, which is supported by only 31 percent of Congress members.

An alternative possibility is that the moral view of members of Congress is best conceived as a multidimensional space. Such an outlook might clarify congressional inconsistencies. This conjecture finds guarded support from Charles Kegley. "It appears that foreign policy beliefs consist of several dimensions or components but we do not know yet what they are, how many there are, or what the relationships among them are" (Kegley 1986, 456).

Mounting research also suggests the empirical utility of a multidimensional approach to the understanding of attitudinal discrepancies. For example, fluctuations in U.S. foreign policy have been explained in terms of two dimensions—

cooperative internationalism and military internationalism (see Bardes and Oldendick 1978; Wittkopf and Maggiotto 1983a; 1986; Holsti and Rosenau 1986). A similar multidimensional argument has been proposed by Maddox and Lilie (1984), who contend that the American political universe is dominated by two-dimensional reasoning, arising from four ideological groupings: liberals, conservatives, populists, and libertarians.

In the next section, consistent with this multidimensional line of inquiry, we shall examine whether such an approach can clarify congressional moral dispari-ties. In particular, we shall determine whether there are systematic features that underlie congressional moral attitudes and whether these are similar to those of the American military community.

A Factor Analysis of Moral Beliefs

Factor analysis allows us to identify and examine patterns in our survey data. The amount of explained variance in our factor analysis is a measure of the explanatory power that can be attributed to systematic components, the "factors" that underlie moral attitudes. This methodology allows one to make inferences that are impossible with simple frequency counts. By revealing the underlying relationships among survey items, empirically derived factors allow us to infer basic belief patterns derived from the traditional moral and amoral schools of international politics. In this way, a factor analysis can uncover the fundamental building blocks that are used by elites in reaching moral judgments about spe-cific situations. It allows a clearer understanding of moral decisions that may not be apparent in traditional, normative analysis.

The Number of Decision-Making Factors

A coherent, underlying factor structure would suggest a core set of decision-making values. We first conducted a principal components analysis of the survey items, and discovered that nine factors have eigenvalues greater than 1.00 for the congressional survey. They collectively explain 58.4 percent of the variance in responses, but it seems likely that most of these factors are random noise, which cannot be given any clear substantive interpretation. As an aid to determining which factors are random noise, we examined a scree plot. The rationale behind a scree test comes from geography. Statisticians have argued that factors com-posed of random noise will appear littered like scree at the edge of a glacier. There is a dominant factor with an eigenvalue of over 8.3 and two other substan-tively significant factors with eigenvalues of about 3.0.

This three-factor solution explains 42 percent of the variance in congressional responses. Further, the factors are related only weakly to each other, indicating the presence of three separate dimensions underlying respondent moral attitudes. The correlations between the factors from an oblique analysis range from –0.23 to 0.15.

Factor Interpretation

The factor structure that we find for Congress is virtually identical to that found for the American military (Tamashiro et al. 1989). The primary factor accounts for 24.4 percent of the variance. We refer to it as "risk sensitivity," and it is a combination of the values of a large number of traditional moral schools. The second and third factors represent "constraints on war entry and conduct" and "legitimacy of force." They account for 9.0 and 8.5 percent of the variance, respectively. These latter factors are closely related to the just-war doctrine, but are not identical to it. All three factors require additional explanation. Table 12.2 presents the factor coefficients we discovered for the Congress and those for the American military (Tamashiro et al. 1989). *The similarity is remarkable.* Despite great differences between members of Congress and military officers in training, purpose, and legal authority, and significant aggregate differences in opinion on major foreign policy issues, three virtually identical factors emerged for both groups.

In no instance does a question that clearly defines any of the three factors load differently for members of Congress and the military. There are different principal loadings for the factors in only four instances (items 9, 15, 19, and 24), and these differences are minor. As can be seen by an examination of Table 12.2, the coefficients of the military and congressional groups tend to be the same. There are no primary loading sign reversals. The average absolute difference in magnitude of items on their primary dimension is 0.11 for the sixteen items loading most heavily on factor one, 0.15 for the nine items loading most heavily on factor two, and 0.11 for the nine items loading most heavily on factor three.

The differences that exist between these two groups are not differences in basic factor structure but in the explanatory power of the three dimensions. Congressional respondents have a substantially higher level of explained variance. While the factors explain 30.7 percent of the variance in responses for military officers, they explain 41.9 percent of the variance for members of Congress. In other words, the decision-making attitudes of congressional members are substantially more structured regarding international relations problems. This is particularly evident on the first factor, which explains almost one-fourth of all the variance in responses for representatives and senators. In the following discussion we will offer a more detailed examination of the three dimensions.

Risk Sensitivity

The first dimension combines the principles of many different traditional approaches to war, but all these approaches are unified in a concern for risk in the international environment. All questions from the retaliatory ethic, supreme emergency school, and legalism, and two items from the reason of state approach, load strongly on this dimension. The negative loadings on perfectionism

Table 12.2

Factor Coefficients

Issue	Factor 1: Risk Sensitivity		Factor 2: Constraints on War Entry and Conduct		Factor 3: Legitimacy	
	Congress	Military	Congress	Military	Congress	Military
Item 26	**0.72**	**0.55**	−0.11	−0.01	−0.07	−0.24
Item 23	**0.69**	**0.72**	−0.17	−0.06	−0.04	0.06
Item 25	**−0.69**	**−0.71**	0.02	0.06	0.09	−0.07
Item 27	**0.68**	**0.70**	−0.26	−0.12	0.04	0.06
Item 32	**0.66**	**0.62**	−0.20	0.06	−0.11	0.00
Item 33	**0.65**	**0.54**	−0.17	−0.10	−0.33	−0.20
Item 28	**0.62**	0.38	−0.29	−0.30	−0.05	−0.12
Item 7	**0.59**	**0.51**	−0.34	−0.25	0.05	0.07
Item 31	**0.57**	**0.47**	0.19	0.05	−0.19	−0.35
Item 5	**0.56**	**0.55**	−0.06	−0.12	−0.26	−0.22
Item 29	**0.55**	**0.65**	−0.33	−0.09	−0.13	−0.03
Item 24	**0.43**	0.28	−0.35	**−0.47**	−0.20	−0.09
Item 30	**0.43**	0.37	−0.13	−0.25	**−0.43**	−0.28
Item 15	**0.43**	0.22	−0.13	0.02	−0.39	**−0.43**
Item 9	0.30	0.00	−0.21	−0.15	0.22	0.30
Item 4	−0.27	−0.31	−0.05	0.16	0.25	0.03
Item 2	−0.07	−0.08	**0.75**	**0.53**	0.15	−0.15
Item 34	0.32	0.26	**−0.74**	**−0.45**	0.19	0.27
Item 3	−0.17	−0.04	**0.74**	**0.49**	0.06	−0.01
Item 8	0.28	0.24	**−0.73**	**−0.52**	0.02	0.08
Item 20	−0.15	−0.13	**0.58**	**0.61**	0.15	0.18
Item 17	0.04	0.05	**0.56**	**0.62**	**0.42**	0.14
Item 18	0.25	0.02	**0.49**	**0.54**	0.39	0.24
Item 21	−0.14	−0.12	**0.40**	**0.43**	0.20	0.30
Item 19	−0.10	−0.05	0.18	0.01	0.05	0.31
Item 10	−0.06	0.10	0.12	0.13	**0.72**	**0.43**
Item 12	−0.19	−0.04	0.07	0.12	**0.64**	**0.48**
Item 6	−0.09	−0.24	0.00	0.10	**0.61**	**0.47**
Item 14	−0.39	−0.13	0.15	0.05	**0.57**	**0.54**
Item 11	0.00	0.08	**−0.46**	0.01	**0.54**	**0.40**
Item 13	−0.36	−0.29	0.14	0.10	**0.53**	**0.54**
Item 1	−0.18	−0.01	0.10	0.06	**0.46**	**0.46**
Item 16	0.08	0.01	0.15	0.36	**0.43**	0.27
Item 22	0.33	0.25	0.22	0.21	0.36	0.30
Variance Explained	24.4	16.7	9.0	7.8	8.5	6.2
Eigenvalue	8.3	5.7	3.1	2.6	2.9	2.1

Note: The factor coefficients for the military also appear in Tamashiro et al. (1989, 145), and Brunk et al. (1990, 94).
The factor loadings in bold type signify values above 0.4 in absolute value.

indicate that a nonperfectionist viewpoint is supported by members of Congress. If one examines the items in detail, a clear pattern emerges.[4] All the questions that load heavily on this first dimension represent sensitivity to risk which, in this context, means exposing one's own in-group to serious harm. On this dimension, risk-averse individuals have positive values and risk-accepting individuals have negative values.

At least four types of uncertainty in the international system are represented by questions loading heavily on this dimension. These represent the possibility of military defeat (items 5 and 29); uncertainty regarding the intentions of other countries (items 31 and 33); the nature of the enemy (items 23, 25, and 29); and the possibility of the collapse of mutual restraint during war (items 26, 27, and 28) of the sort discussed by Axelrod (1984). The risk-averse in Congress look toward national interest, rather than formalistic rules, as a guide in decision making. The most interesting aspect of our interpretation is that the key criterion behind the ethical evaluation of foreign policy actions is a common economic variable—risk. *How one stands on risk aversion is of crucial importance in determining what moral or amoral philosophical school is adopted and what foreign policy actions are advocated.*

Constraints on War Entry and Conduct

It is believed that the just-war approach is a major influence in American foreign policy since it is the basis of most international law on warfare and has been supported by most American churches (Lewis 1975; Secrest et al. 1991b). The second dimension relates to just-war logic. We see that five just-war items load most heavily here, along with two golden rule items. The golden rule loadings are particularly significant. Catholic theologians have been at the forefront in the development of the just-war theory. They claim that just-war doctrine can be logically deduced from a simple belief in the golden rule and a few other basic principles (Aquinas 1266; Donagan 1977; Secrest et al. 1991a).

The just-war principles that load most heavily for members of Congress on this dimension are the ideas of proportionality in warfare (item 20), use of war as a last resort (item 17), the self-defensive quality of a "just war" (item 18), and noncombatant immunity (item 21). The essence of this dimension is that those who form American public policy should have a nonbelligerent outlook that takes into account the lives of individuals in other nations.

Legitimacy of Force

The third factor is a measure of the general legitimacy of force and force planning. All pacifism items and two nuclear pacifism and just-war items load most heavily on this dimension. Another way to interpret this dimension is to say that factor two deals with constraints on the use of force, while factor three provides warrants for the use of force.

Three types of force legitimacy issues are tapped by this factor: whether the use of force is allowable in principle (all pacifism items), whether nuclear force is allowable (all nuclear pacifism items), and the circumstances that legitimize war or war planning. The pacifist position is located at one extreme end of this dimension.

Comparison between Members of Congress and the Military

While the factor scores tell us that the pattern of moral reasoning is similar for the two groups, they cannot tell us how the groups stand relative to each other since factor analysis is a standardized technique. In Table 12.3 we present the average values for the two groups on the five items that load most heavily on each of the three dimensions. A number of differences should be noted. Members of Congress tend to be more risk-accepting than the members of the military, more constrained in their use of war as a policy tool, and more likely to see force as less legitimate in foreign policy.

On two items associated with the first dimension, members of the military depart significantly from Congress members. The first difference concerns the degree to which harsh action is justified in response to a surprise attack (item 26). Although both groups show strong support for retaliation, the military's support is notably stronger. The second item concerns whether "the only thing that matters in war is victory." The military is more supportive of this position, but otherwise the differences between the two groups are not sizable. While military officers tend to be slightly more risk-averse than are Congress members, they are not significantly more risk-averse except on the two issues that concern them the most.

There are three significant differences between Congress and the military concerning items loading on the second dimension. The military is less inclined to treat other governments as we wish to be treated (item 3). This is reflected in the lower level of support the military gives to the golden rule (see Table 12.1). Second, although both groups oppose the use of force to convert others to our beliefs (item 8), military opposition is weaker than congressional opposition. Finally, military officers are less inclined to show restraint when waging war, although both the military and congressional respondents generally support the proposition that one should show restraint in destruction of an enemy's society.

To summarize our findings, we have seen that both the military and members of Congress use the *same type of decision-making framework* in the evaluation of international relations problems. While there are significant differences in responses between the military and Congress, there is not much difference in their opinions on the first two dimensions. Disagreement primarily concerns the third dimension regarding the general legitimacy of force in international affairs. Not surprisingly, military officers see force as more legitimate than does the average member of Congress. There are significant differences on all five items loading

Table 12.3

Differences in Responses between Military Officers and Members of Congress

Item	Congress	Military	T Value
Risk Sensitivity Dimension			
26. Harsh and unrestrained military actions are justified against an enemy who launches an unprovoked attack on our nation.	3.58	3.99	−3.92*
23. Sometimes our enemies are so evil that it may be necessary to ignore moral concerns in order to win a war.	3.12	3.31	−1.73
25. If an enemy's goal is the destruction of our nation, morality should still influence our actions in times of war.	3.20	3.33	−1.10
27. If a foreign enemy stops observing moral principles, we should also stop observing moral principles.	2.29	2.34	−0.56
32. The only thing that matters in war is victory.	2.92	3.36	−3.66*
Constraints on War Entry and Conduct			
2. If we want other countries to keep their treaty promises, we should keep our treaty promises.	4.35	4.25	1.88
34. We should go to war whenever it is to our advantage.	1.60	1.71	−1.73
3. Our government should treat other countries the same way that we want to be treated.	4.17	4.00	2.18*
8. It is all right to use military force to convert others to our beliefs.	1.71	1.93	−3.04*
20. A moral war must seek only to defeat the enemy's military and not to destroy his society totally.	3.86	3.63	2.56*
Legitimacy of Force Dimension			
10. If one must choose either nonviolent resistance or participation in a war, nonviolent resistance is the only moral choice.	2.13	1.52	7.86*
12. It is always wrong to kill another person, even in a war.	2.02	1.72	3.51*
6. Our country's decision to go to war should be based only on universal moral principles and not on the particular context facing our nation.	2.33	1.83	7.03*
14. It is better to accept defeat than to participate in a nuclear war.	1.98	1.42	8.27*
11. Morality requires that a nation should not resist if attacked by a foreign country.	1.41	1.15	5.07*

Note: Responses are coded on a five-point Likert scale: strongly disagree (1); disagree (2); uncertain (3); agree (4); strongly agree (5). A total of 620 military officers and 169 retired representatives and senators responded to the survey.

* Indicates a significant difference in means at the 0.05 level for two-tailed tests.

heavily on factor three. In particular, and as Table 12.1 shows, military officers reject the premises of pacifism and nuclear pacifism to a greater degree than do members of Congress.

The Role of Ideology

Since Congress and the military differ primarily on the third and weakest dimension of evaluating foreign policy decisions, the sources of major differences between individuals may have little to do with their occupations or roles. Unfortunately, there is little systematic research that addresses this issue and what exists is largely atheoretical.[5]

Within the past decade, ideology has emerged as a major predictor of foreign policy attitudes. It is associated with increased interest in congressional oversight by members of the House Committee on International Relations (Kaiser 1977) and elite attitudes and congressional roll-call voting patterns on foreign policy issues (Russett 1970; Moyer 1973; Bernstein and Anthony 1974; Schneider 1983; Smith 1981; McCormick and Black 1983; Rasmussen and McCormick 1985; Holsti and Rosenau 1986). Ideology also is associated with foreign policy issues in foreign legislatures (e.g., Rasmussen and McCormick 1985). As a generalization, liberals tend to be more supportive of a cooperative form of internationalism and more opposed to militant internationalism (Wittkopf and Maggiotto 1983b, 1986). Conservatives act in the opposite manner.

At best, previous researchers have developed only weak predictive models for the three decision-making factors of risk sensitivity, constraints on war, and force legitimacy (Brunk et al. 1990). Such models only explain between 5 and 18 percent of the variance in regression equations that include up to nine variables, for example, combat experience, rank, and level of education. The most significant predictor has been ideology.

Figure 12.1 shows the average location of military liberals, conservatives and moderates in the factor space. Liberals are more risk-accepting than conservatives, and moderates fall between them. This implies that military liberals are more supportive of ethical constraints in war than are conservatives. This liberal–conservative split requires discussion since other research indicates that ideology in the general public is not related to moral attitudes (Peffley and Hurwitz 1985). At least three schools of thought regarding differences in risk sensitivity between military liberals and conservatives can be found in the literature.

First, some military attitudes may be related to a "cavalier warrior ethic" that places a high value on glory, gallantry, and chivalry. Such an outlook, sometimes associated with the American South, might glorify certain risky, ethical restraints in war (McMurry 1987). However, our evidence indicates that a southern background is not associated with risk sensitivity. Hence, this conjecture finds little support.

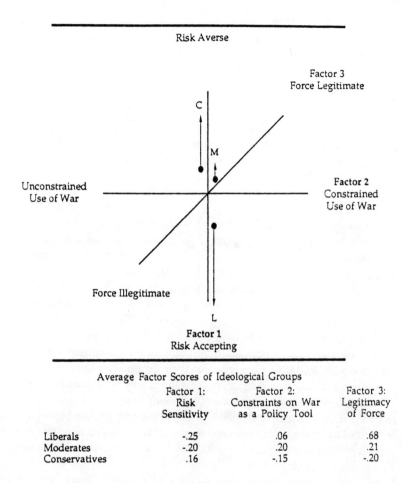

Figure 12.1. **Location of Ideological Groups of Military Officers in the Factor Space**

Average Factor Scores of Ideological Groups

	Factor 1: Risk Sensitivity	Factor 2: Constraints on War as a Policy Tool	Factor 3: Legitimacy of Force
Liberals	-.25	.06	.68
Moderates	-.20	.20	.21
Conservatives	.16	-.15	-.20

Second, conservatives may rely primarily on strict, rule-based ethics in war, where the "right" rather than risk is the major concern (Walker 1983). This may lead conservatives to be more accepting of risk. In contrast, military liberals may place more emphasis on situational factors when they reach ethical decisions in war. Hence, they might become more risk-sensitive than their conservative, rule-following colleagues. Some evidence for this conjecture exists (Brunk et al. 1990), but Figure 12.1 does not support it.

Third, the liberal–conservative split on risk sensitivity may be a statistical artifact. The vast majority of military respondents were conservative, and only 3 percent identified themselves as liberal. Hence, the distribution of ideological positions held by our military respondents was highly skewed. Accordingly, the

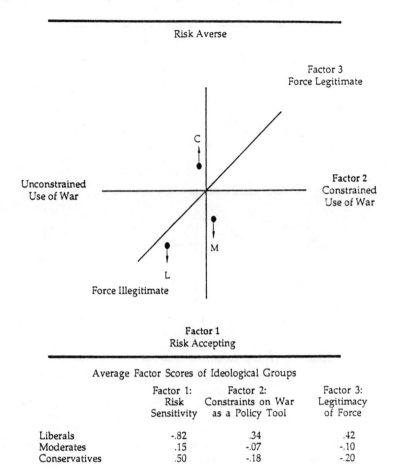

Figure 12.2. **Location of Ideological Groups of Members of Congress in the Factor Space**

	Factor 1: Risk Sensitivity	Factor 2: Constraints on War as a Policy Tool	Factor 3: Legitimacy of Force
Liberals	-.82	.34	.42
Moderates	.15	-.07	-.10
Conservatives	.50	-.18	-.20

Average Factor Scores of Ideological Groups

risk sensitivity found among these military liberals may be a result of chance statistical fluctuations arising from the relatively small number of liberals in our sample rather than of their "liberalness." If this is so, one would expect the disappearance of this association when a larger number of liberals is examined. The analysis of congressional respondents tends to support this view.

In Figure 12.2 we have plotted the average location of congressional liberals, conservatives, and moderates in the factor space. Unlike the military officers in our sample, the proportion of liberal congressional respondents was greater than twenty percent. A clear difference emerges among members of Congress that matches our intuitive understanding of American politics. Conservatives in Congress tend to be very sensitive to risks in the international system, while liberals are relatively risk-insensitive. Moderates are in the middle. All three groups are located at significantly different positions within the factor space. It is interesting that if the military liberals in Figure 12.1 are treated as outlier cases, and are removed from the analysis, the factor structures of both Figures 12.1 and 12.2 become nearly identical.

In summary, for both the American military and Congress, ideology seems to account for some modest variation in attitudes. While ideology is a weak predictor of constraints on war entry and conduct and on the legitimacy of force, its primary explanatory power is found on risk sensitivity. Conservatives are very sensitive to risks when they are faced with moral decisions in war. Congressional liberals are much less sensitive to risk. The connection between ideology and risk sensitivity among military officers is seen to be quite similar when the attitudes of moderates and conservatives are examined and the military liberals are dropped from the sample.

Discussion

We find major similarities, but some differences as well, between the decision-making frameworks of military officers and members of Congress. The primary similarity is that the same three-factor framework is useful to explain the attitudes of both groups. A notable difference is that professional politicians have more structured attitudes than do those in the military. This added structure is reflected by the 42 percent variance explained for congressional attitudes in contrast to the smaller 31 percent variance for the military.

Nevertheless, for both the military and Congress, there is enough attitudinal latitude explained to speak of a *shared decision-making framework* toward morality and foreign policy that has *broad applicability*. We can now discuss generalized aspects of risk aversion, force legitimacy, and constraints on war entry and conduct, rather than just talk about the intricacies of a dozen traditional schools of moral thought toward war. These three factors can be combined with a few other precepts in various ways to form the basis of most of the major views toward war that have been developed over the centuries by theologians, philosophers, and international relations scholars.

What we see among many members of Congress and American military officers is the philosophical position that advocates a moral reason-of-state approach to foreign policy. As the nation-state became institutionalized, people attributed ethical qualities to it, and national safety frequently was cast in universal moral terms (Meinecke 1957; Niebuhr 1930, 6–20; Morgenthau and Thompson 1985, 260–78). This moral reason-of-state view is reflected by the risk aversion dimension when one's principal concern is to protect the nation and one's own. Since risk aversion is the strongest predictor of attitudes in our studies, it is quite likely that the moral reason-of-state view is widely held among both the military and members of Congress.

Finally, our analysis suggests a possible explanation for the commonly encountered contention that foreign policy attitudes are unstable and subject to quick change (see Kegley 1986, 457–60). While some of this change might be due to non-opinions, much instability in attitudes may be misidentified. *Beliefs about fundamental values and precepts should not be subject to quick change. What can change very quickly is an individual's perception of the amount of risk involved in a situation.* This can trigger a sudden shift in one's attitude toward a given public policy issue. Such an argument suggests that ideology is not as fundamental in determining shifts in moral attitudes as is risk aversion. *If this hunch is correct, then it raises the suspicion that many "ideological" disputes over ethics and policy are really disputes over risk.* H. L. Menken, it seems, spotted something significant when he suggested that politics is less about principle and more about prudence and privilege.

Appendix: Major Survey Items

Golden Rule

1. If we do not want other nations to spy on us, we should not spy on them.
2. If we want other countries to keep their treaty promises, we should keep our treaty promises.
3. Our government should treat other countries in the same way that we want to be treated.

Moral Perfectionism/Moral Nonperfectionism

4. Moral principles are absolute and do not depend on the situation.
5. Our military planners should not rule out any type of future military actions because of moral principles.
6. Our country's decision to go to war should be based only on universal moral principles and not on a particular problem facing our nation.

Moral Crusade

7. When we are at war, we have a moral duty to punish and totally destroy the enemy.
8. It is all right to use military force to convert others to our beliefs.
9. There are moral values so important that we should not deal with those who disagree with these values.

Pacifism

10. If one must choose either nonviolent resistance or participation in a war, nonviolent resistance is the only moral choice.
11. Morality requires that a nation should not resist if attacked by a foreign country.
12. It is always wrong to kill another person, even in a war.

Nuclear Pacifism

13. Destruction of enemy cities with nuclear weapons is immoral even if our cities are attacked with nuclear weapons first.
14. It is better to accept defeat than to participate in a nuclear war.
15. It is morally acceptable to threaten to use nuclear weapons against enemy cities as a way to prevent nuclear attacks against our cities.

Just War

16. A war must be legally authorized before it can be considered to be moral.
17. It is not moral to fight a war until all peaceful alternatives have been tried.
18. A war must be an act of self-defense in order for it to be moral.
19. The amount of war damage and number of casualties on both sides is important in deciding whether a war is moral.
20. A moral war must seek to defeat only the enemy's military forces and not to totally destroy his society.
21. In order for a war to be moral, efforts must be made to avoid killing civilians.
22. It is not moral to fight a war that one has no chance to win.

Supreme Emergency

23. Sometimes our enemies are so evil that it may be necessary to ignore moral concerns in order to win a war.
24. It is all right to attack an enemy first, before he becomes strong enough to defeat us.
25. Even if an enemy's goal is the total destruction of our nation, morality should still influence our actions in times of war.

Retaliatory Ethic

26. Harsh and unrestrained military actions are justified against an enemy who launches an unprovoked attack on our nation.
27. If a foreign enemy stops observing moral principles we should also stop observing moral principles.
28. Revenge against an enemy's civilians is morally acceptable if that nation has attacked our civilians.

Legalism

29. If the only way to avoid defeat in a battle is to commit a "war crime," then we should do so.

30. It is all right to launch a surprise attack against another country if it is legally ordered by our government.
31. If there is a conflict between one's moral beliefs and our country's law, one should obey the law.

Reason of State

32. The only thing that matters in war is victory.
33. National interest, rather than morality, should determine our foreign policy.
34. We should go to war whenever it is to our advantage.

Notes

1. From any narrowly defined perspective, such as a politician's attempts to maximize voter support, most frameworks of rule-following behavior seem at first to be irrational. Some schools of foreign policy argue exactly this position, but many traditional schools dispute the conclusion, and some social choice theorists have begun to argue likewise. One of the first works to explore the utility-maximizing aspects of rules was Buchanan and Tullock's *The Calculus of Consent* (1962).

2. In the current analysis, we have not used the items that measure religious factors.

3. The evidence regarding military attitudes that appears in Tables 12.1 and 12.2 is taken from Tamashiro et al. (1989) and Brunk et al. (1990).

4. For a more detailed question-by-question analysis of the patterns for military respondents, see Tamashiro et al. (1989).

5. For a review of this literature, see Cockerham and Cohen (1979, 1980, 1981).

References

Aquinas, T. 1266. *Summa Theologica.*
Asher, H.B., and Weisberg, H.F. 1978. "Voting Change in Congress: Some Perspectives on an Evolutionary Process." *American Political Science Review*, 22: 391–425.
Axelrod, R. 1984. *The Evolution of Cooperation.* New York: Basic Books.
Bardes, B., and Oldendick, R.W. 1978. "Beyond Internationalism: The Case for Multiple Dimensions in the Structure of Foreign Policy Attitudes." *Social Science Quarterly* 59: 496–508.
Bernick, E.L., and Wiggins, C.W. 1983. "Legislative Norms in Eleven States." *Legislative Studies Quarterly* 8: 191–200.
Bernstein, R.A., and Anthony, W.W. 1974. "The ABM Issue in the Senate, 1968–1970: The Importance of Ideology." *American Political Science Review* 68: 1198–1206.
Brams, S.J. 1977. "Deception in 2X2 Games." *Journal of Peace Science* 2: 171–203.
Brunk, G.G.; Secrest, D.; and Tamashiro, H. 1990. "Military Views of Morality and War: An Empirical Study of Retired American Officers," *International Studies Quarterly* 34: 83–109.
Buchanan, J.M., and Tullock, G. 1962. *The Calculus of Consent.* Ann Arbor: University of Michigan Press.
Cockerham, W.C., and Cohen, L.E. 1979. "Attitudes of U.S. Army Paratroopers toward Participation in the Quelling of Civil Disorders." *Journal of Political and Military Sociology* 7: 257–69.

————. 1980. "Obedience to Orders: Issues of Morality and Legality in Combat among U.S. Army Paratroopers." *Social Forces* 58: 1272–88.

————. 1981. "Volunteering for Foreign Combat Missions: An Attitudinal Study of U.S. Army Paratroopers," *Pacific Sociological Review* 24: 329–54.

Donagan, A. 1977. *The Theory of Morality.* Chicago: University of Chicago Press.

Fallows, J. 1979. "The Passionless Presidency." *Atlantic Monthly* 243 (5): 33–48.

Ferguson, T. 1986. "The Right Consensus? Holsti and Rosenau's New Foreign Policy Belief Systems." *International Studies Quarterly* 30: 411–23.

Hare, R.M. 1981. *Applications of Moral Philosophy.* New York: Oxford University Press.

Holsti, O.R., and Rosenau, J.N. 1979. "Vietnam, Consensus, and the Belief Systems of American Leaders." *World Politics* 30: 1–56.

————. 1986. "Consensus Lost, Consensus Regained: Foreign Policy Beliefs of American Leaders, 1976–1980." *International Studies Quarterly* 30: 375–409.

Kaiser, F. 1977. "Oversight on Foreign Policy: The U.S. House Committee on International Relations," *Legislative Studies Quarterly* 3: 255–79.

Kegley, C.W. 1986. "Assumptions and Dilemmas in the Study of Americans' Foreign Policy Beliefs: A Caveat." *International Studies Quarterly* 30: 447–71.

Kohlberg, L. 1981. *Essays on Moral Development.* San Francisco: Harper and Row.

Levy, D. 1981. "Toward a Neo-Aristotelian Theory of Politics: A Positive Theory of Fairness." *Public Choice* 42: 39–54.

Lewis, R.A. 1975. "A Contemporary Religious Enigma: Churches and War." *Journal of Political and Military Sociology* 3: 57–70.

McCormick, J.M., and Black, M. 1983. "Ideology and Senate Voting on the Panama Canal Treaties," *Legislative Studies Quarterly* 8: 45–63.

McMurry, R. 1987. *Two Great Rebel Armies.* Chapel Hill: University of North Carolina Press.

Maddox, W.S., and Lilie, S.A. 1984. *Beyond Liberal and Conservative: Reassessing the Political Spectrum.* Washington, DC: Cato Institute.

Maggiotto, M.A., and Wittkopf, E.R. 1981. "American Public Attitudes toward Foreign Policy." *International Studies Quarterly* 25: 601–31.

Meinecke, F. 1957. *Machiavellism: The Doctrine of Raison d'Etat and Its Place in Modern History.* New Haven, CT: Yale University Press.

Morgenthau, Hans J., and Thompson, K.W. 1985. *Politics among Nations: The Struggle for Power and Peace.* New York: Alfred Knopf.

Moyer, W. 1973. "House Voting on Defense: An Ideological Explanation." In *Military Force and American Society,* edited by Bruce M. Russett and Alfred Stepan. New York: Harper and Row.

National Conference of Catholic Bishops ad hoc Committee on Peace and Disarmament. 1983. *The Challenge of Peace: God's Promise and Our Response.* Washington, DC: National Conference of Catholic Bishops.

Niebuhr, R. 1930. *Moral Man and Immoral Society.* New York: Charles Scribner's Sons.

O'Brien, W.V. 1981. *The Conduct of Just and Limited War.* New York: Praeger.

Panning, W.H. 1982. "Public Choice and Congressional Norms." *Western Political Quarterly* 35: 193–203.

Peffley, M., and Hurwitz, J. 1985. "A Hierarchical Model of Attitude Constraint." *American Political Science Review* 79: 871–90.

Ramsey, P. 1961. *War and the Christian Conscience: How Shall Modern War Be Conducted Justly?* Durham, NC: Duke University Press.

————. 1968. *The Just War: Force and Political Responsibility.* New York: Charles Scribner's Sons.

Rasmussen, J.S., and McCormick, J.M. 1985. "The Influence of Ideology on British Labour MPs in Voting on EEC Issues." *Legislative Studies Quarterly* 10: 203–21.

Rawls, J. 1971. *A Theory of Justice.* Cambridge, MA: Harvard University Press.

Reynolds, D.R., and Shelly, F. 1985. "Procedural Justice and Local Democracy." *Political Geography Quarterly* 4: 267–88.

Rielly, J.E. 1983. *American Public Opinion and U.S. Foreign Policy.* Chicago: Chicago Council on Foreign Relations.

Roemer, J.E. 1985. "Rationalizing Revolutionary Ideology." *Econometrica* 53: 85–108.

Rosenau, J.N. 1961. *Public Opinion and Foreign Policy.* New York: Random House.

Rosenthal, A. 1991. "Bush Vows to Tackle Middle East Issues." *New York Times,* January 29, A13.

Russett, B.M. 1970. *What Price Vigilance? The Burdens of National Defense.* New Haven, CT: Yale University Press.

Russett, B.M., and Hanson, E.C. 1975. *Interest and Ideology: The Foreign Policy Beliefs of American Businessmen.* San Francisco: W.H. Freeman.

Schneider, J.E. 1970. *Ideological Coalitions in Congress.* Westport, CT: Greenwood Press.

Schneider, W. 1983. "Conservatism, Not Interventionism: Trends in Foreign Policy Opinion, 1974–1982." In *Eagle Defiant: United States Foreign Policy in the 1980s,* edited by K.A. Oye, R.J. Lieber, and D. Rothchild. Boston: Little, Brown.

Secrest, D.; Brunk, G.G.; and Tamashiro, H. 1991a. "Empirical Investigation of Normative Discourse on War: The Case of the Donagan–Aquinas Thesis." forthcoming in *Journal of Peace Research* 28: 293–306.

———. 1991b. "Moral Justifications for Resort to War with Nicaragua: The Attitudes of Three American Elite Groups," forthcoming in *Western Political Quarterly* 44: 541–59.

Smith, S.S. 1981. "The Consistency and Ideological Structure of U.S. Senate Voting Alignments, 1957–1976." *American Journal of Political Science* 25: 780–95.

Stark, O. 1985. "On Private Charity and Altruism." *Public Choice* 46: 325–29.

Tamashiro, H.; Secrest, D.; and Brunk, G.G. 1989. "The Underlying Structure of Ethical Beliefs toward War." *Journal of Peace Research* 26: 139–52.

Walker, S.G. 1983. "The Motivational Foundations of Belief Systems." *International Studies Quarterly* 27: 179–201.

Walzer, M. 1977. *Just and Unjust Wars: A Moral Argument with Historical Illustrations.* New York: Basic Books.

Weingast, B.R. 1979. "A Rational Choice Perspective on Congressional Norms." *American Journal of Political Science* 23: 245–62.

Wittkopf, E.R., and Maggiotto, M.A. 1983a."Two Faces of Internationalism: Public Attitudes toward American Foreign Policy in the 1970s—And Beyond?" *Social Science Quarterly* 64: 288–304.

———. 1983b. "Elites and Masses: A Comparative Analysis of Attitudes toward America's World Role," *Journal of Politics* 45: 303–34.

———. 1986. "On the Foreign Policy Beliefs of the American People: A Critique and Some Evidence." *International Studies Quarterly* 30: 425–45.

Part Four

Conclusions

13

Ethics and Public Administration: Some Assertions

H. George Frederickson

Introduction

This conclusion attempts a synthesis of the preceding chapters and a broad-gauged treatment of the subject of ethics and public administration in the context of research. The categories used for this synthesis are purposely broad, generally conforming to theoretical constructs in the field of ethics. Research in governmental ethics, however, tends to be in narrower categories and on more limited questions. It is, then, necessary to fit research findings into what appear to be the most appropriate theoretical categories. Even though ethics theorists and researchers may quarrel with the groupings used here, we are less concerned with the perfection of the categories and more concerned with generally advancing what we know about government ethics. There is first a consideration of the classic question of whether persons in public administration are good or bad and if research is illuminating on this subject. This is followed by a treatment of the question of whether political or governmental decisions are right or wrong. Third is a consideration of research on the traditional question of administrative accountability and the issue of the appropriate breadth of administrative discretion. Fourth is a consideration of research perspectives on the bigger questions of the rightness or wrongness of public policy. Finally, the chapter deals with issues of methodology and education in ethics in public administration.

Some Assertions

The Nature of Persons: Good or Bad

There are interesting parallels between assertions in political philosophy about human nature and the evolution of the conception of the administrative person. Hobbesian man is struggling in a harsh and brutal world, a world in which base passions rule. His Leviathan, the product of his "science of politics," would cause the people to covenant together to subject themselves to a single body of sovereign authority, in order to maintain order and preserve peace. In this way natural lawless and warlike passions could be controlled. Civil government is formed, following Locke, because people fail in the Law of Nature to exercise pure freedom responsibly and therefore must make a compact with a sovereign for the purposes of peace and order. In modern political thinking, the works of Lowi seem most nearly to resemble the Hobbesian-Lockian view.

The Kantian person, on the other hand, can only find morality in a state of freedom. This morality will be naturally and metaphysically derived, thus enabling the free person and, presumably, groups of free men to reason together in the pursuit of order and peace. The contemporary work of Rawls and Dworkin seems similar to that of Kant.

Administrative man in the Theory X framework, following McGregor, practices management by control and through the hierarchy. His Theory Y framework favors the techniques of human relations and associated forms of collective or collegial management (Harmon and Mayer 1986). That Theory X is to organization theory as Hobbesian person is to political philosophy and that Theory Y is similar to the Kantian view of human nature is hardly a new observation. It is likely that the range of good and bad persons found in politics is roughly comparable to the goodness and badness of persons in administration. What may, however, be more important is whether political and administrative persons are different and whether this difference accounts for significant variations in the definition of ethics and ethical behavior in political, as against administrative, settings.

It is demonstrable that political and administrative persons are different from each other. That the political person, absent controls and enforced standards, will often pursue personal gain at public expense is clear (Holbrook and Maier, this volume). That professionals in different fields define ethics differently is also clear (Overman and Foss, this volume). For example, values such as empathy, fairness, innovativeness, and a concern for the general or public interest tend to be stronger among persons preparing for or in public service careers than in persons preparing for or in business careers (Nalbandian and Edwards 1983). Persons who chose public service careers tend to be more inclined toward job security and are more risk-averse than persons in business careers (Bellanta and Link 1981). Attitudes toward corruption and ethical conduct appear to be situationally determined, which is to say that definitions of corruption and what constitutes ethical behavior vary depending on whether the setting is business, medical, legal, political, or public administrative. Persons in public service have a greater interest in power and influence, which seems to indicate that Machiavelli was right. Persons in business and commerce have stronger acquisitive interests, which seems to indicate that Bentham was right. It seems reasonable to find that persons choose their field of work, when such choices are available, on the basis of personality characteristics and value preferences. And, the attitudes of professionals toward ethical behavior are "higher" than attitudes toward ethical behavior in the general population (Overman and Foss, this volume). All of this suggests that rather than asking whether man is good or bad, it is more useful to disaggregate the question and ask several questions: Is political person good or bad? Is business person good or bad? Is administrative person good or bad? Is medical or legal man good or bad? While we do not know if persons are good or bad in the entire, we do know that persons are different depending on their tasks and that the standards of goodness or badness are situational, depending on the setting and the task.

This contextual approach to dealing with the issue of whether men are good or bad is similar to two fundamental concepts in organization theory. The first is that organizations, professions, legislatures, businesses, and so on are "culture-bearing milieux" (Louis 1983). The symbols, myths, metaphors, language systems, and legends of governmental agencies, houses of representatives, and businesses are the artifacts of their organizational culture. Second, organizations are systems of shared meanings as much as they are collectives of persons working toward shared objectives. The organizational culture defines what is good and bad and it attributes meaning or importance to goodness and badness (Smirich 1983). Research on the contrasting response of Danish and German civil servants to the Holocaust bears this out. The culture and shared meanings of Danish civil servants was not accepting of the deportation and killing of the Jews whereas it was accepted by most German civil servants (Frederickson and Hart 1985). The structures of Canadian and United States governments have led to different understandings of, and approaches to, public-sector conflict-of-interest laws (Stark, this volume). And, it is history and culture that explain much of the variation in traditional corruption in American cities (Holbrook and Meier, this volume).

In the governmental context, persons are parsed into two general groupings—political and administrative. The political is meant to include both elected and politically appointed officials while the administrative is the merit-based civil servant and certain executives appointed on the basis of professional rather than political criteria, such as city managers. In the federal government the Civil Service Reform Act of 1978 provided for a sharp increase in political (in this case presidential) appointees to provide for greater "policy responsiveness" on the part of the bureaucracy. During the Reagan presidency these positions were filled with persons generally loyal to the policy preferences of the president. They rarely had government experience and most were from business. By any measure there was very significant policy responsiveness to the president's preferences, even when that policy responsiveness was counter to both the Constitution and the law. The Reagan administration was also the most corrupt administration in recent memory.

Did this happen primarily because bad men were brought into the administration? Did it happen because these new appointees found themselves in a governmental setting that they did not entirely understand and so they engaged in practices that would have been either accepted or tolerated in business or professional settings? Or, did it happen because many of these appointees had little respect for government, because government was, after all, the problem? The likely answer is some combination of each of these. But of the three explanations, the most influential was probably that there are different standards for ethics in government than there are in business.

Abscam and the lesser scams would seem to indicate that some members of Congress and of state legislatures were willing to take bribes, and there can be no defense for bribe taking based on the uniqueness of the legislative setting. The savings and loan scandal and especially the Keating Five matter indicate that the close connection between political campaign contributions and the intervention of legislators in regulatory and administrative processes is laden with questions of ethics. Clearly, accepting bribes is understood to be unethical and illegal while intervening on behalf of a contributor may be unethical but it is legal.

The Ill Winds defense contracting scandal involved both politically appointed and merit-based public officials. But both the laws and standards of ethics in defense procurement are clear for civil servants and appointees, and both were violated. The point is that definitions of what constitutes corruption are clearer in the administrative setting than in the legislative setting.

The "better types" argument is widely used to explain how government can be improved. Better types can mean, in political terms, electing someone else to office. Indeed, the research of Holbrook and Meier shows that levels of local government corruption are reduced by high levels of electoral competition and high voter turnout (1993). But better types more generally means types like us. When the term "better types" is used by business executives it means that there should be persons either elected or appointed to office who are from the business world or who share the values of business. Better types is used in the anti-bureaucratic sense, usually by politicians or business leaders, to suggest that bureaucrats are lazy or unresponsive and that political or business persons would be preferable. In the reform era, better types meant eliminating the spoils system, replacing it with a merit-based civil service, and weakening political parties at the local level by structural changes that result in the election of business leaders and community-oriented types. In many ways, the better types argument corroborates the view that the issue of whether a person is good or bad is not nearly as important as whether the person is political, bureaucratic, business, legal, medical, or otherwise.

The "levels of moral reasoning" perspective is an interesting cousin of the better types argument. Following Kohlberg, there are lesser-to-greater levels of moral reasoning depending on a variety of personality, demographic, contextual, and other factors. There are, then, different levels of moral/ethical development that can be demonstrated (Kohlberg 1980; Rest 1986). Lesser or greater levels of moral reasoning are dependent on knowledge of the problem or situation, the time given to analysis and understanding, and the nature of the problem (Stewart and Sprinthall, this volume). Demography and organizational context among administrators does not influence levels of moral reasoning. All of this is to the point that careful and analytic approaches to problems improve the chances for moral/ethical solutions, at least in public administration settings (Stewart and Sprinthall). It is implicit in much of this research that it is possible to improve the moral reasoning of public administrators by education, reasoning, and analytic processes (Lewis 1991). So, within a given context persons can be made better. That is certainly the message in much of the humanistic and group decision-making perspective on public administration ethics (Denhardt 1988).

What, then, can be concluded about the nature-of-man issue and the question of ethics in government administration? First, that definitions of corruption vary by profession, setting, and culture, and that standards of ethical behavior vary also. Second, that the general bell curve of men from good to bad probably holds for each setting and profession. Third, that it is in government that one finds the most stringent standards and ethics expectations, especially in the administrative parts of government. Fourth, that persons from other settings, when placed in government, are more likely than are governmental persons to breach standards of ethics. Fifth, that within government there are significant differences between the standards and ethics expectations of elected or political persons and appointed or civil service persons. Sixth, that is possible to improve the moral reasoning of persons in any organized context.

Making Ethical Decisions: Doing Right or Wrong

We shift from the question of whether man is inherently good or bad to the question of the rightness or wrongness of decisions. This suspends the question of contextual variation in definitions of goodness and badness and the nature of man in different contexts and simply asks whether a particular decision, a set of decisions, or a pattern of decisions is right or wrong, and why. The approach used here rests on two broad philosophical traditions; the first is deontological, consisting of decisions based on fundamental principles, the other is teleological, consisting of decisions based on calculations of their likely consequences or results (Lewis 1991; Bok 1978; French 1983; Strauss and Cropsey 1987). In the deontological tradition, most particularly associated with Aquinas and Kant, decisions are based on duties or principles that are either right or wrong in themselves, the results being irrelevant to moral judgment.

> Deontological reasoning comes in many shades, depending upon whether the rules of behavior are seen as permanent and universal; knowable or unknowable; derived from revelation, human law, or community norms; and so on. All permutations dictate that there are certain underlying rules according to which behavior is judged, and no matter how desirable the consequences, there are certain things managers (and government) may not do. (Lewis 1991, 88)

The teleological tradition, most particularly associated with Mill and Bentham, is often referred to in the modern context as utilitarianism. In this tradition, decisions are judged by their consequences depending on the results to be maximized—security, happiness, pleasure, dignity. Results can be judged on the basis of the individual, the family, the neighborhood, the group or organization, the political jurisdiction, the nation-state.

Explicit standards of right and wrong are a defining feature of American government. The U.S. Constitution and laws, the state constitutions and laws, and the charters and laws of the lesser jurisdictions of the states when taken together are, by any measure, an impressive collection of definitions of right and wrong. In addition, there are countless administrative regulations adopted pursuant to laws and carrying the force of law. Add to this mix an entire branch of government established in part to interpret and protect the constitutions and the laws. Although it is trite, ours is a nation of laws and not of men. Certainly we have an impressive deontological array of constitutions, laws, and regulations that codify our values and define the principles of right and wrong as we see them. Much of the study of ethics in American government is embedded in the constitutional–legal perspective (Rohr 1989; Rosenbloom 1986; Cooper 1992).

Despite the law, there is some considerable tolerance among the citizens for less egregious forms of corruption such as conflicts of interest, the blatant exercise of political influence, and small monetary exchanges (Malec, this volume). On the other hand, bribery, extortion, or the exchange of large sums of money are ethically unacceptable. Regardless of the law, there is relatively widespread tolerance of petty corruption in American government (Malec). This would seem to indicate that absolute principles of ethics, in the deontological tradition, are usually bent depending on the seriousness of the ethical breach.

If there is among the citizens a considerable tolerance for petty corruption, is there also a problem of "regime legitimacy"? Is government held in low regard and therefore unable to sustain strong public support because of petty corruption? Probably not. But there is strong evidence that people are much more inclined to obey the law if they believe the law to be just and fair and if they are of the opinion that there is procedural justice in the administration of the law (Tyler 1990). Regime legitimacy is a function of fairness and equity and some level of official benevolence in the administration of the law. To the extent that petty or grand corruption detract from fairness, equity, and benevolence, they reduce regime legitimacy. The larger deontological issue here is the identification of fairness, equity, and official benevolence as high-order ethical principles.

The current disquiet over the electoral advantage of incumbents is a further illustration that issues of fairness and equity seem to be importantly connected to regime legitimacy. Efforts to limit the number of terms served by incumbents presumably would level the electoral playing field. That seems more important to voters than the experience or expertise of legislators.

Procedural controls established during the reform movement to reduce corruption were generally successful. Judged in any comparative way, American government is among the most clean or ethical. But these procedures are the "red tape" that causes government to be slow, non–risk taking, bureaucratic, and nonresponsive. Perhaps the best evidence, however, that these anticorruption procedures work is the research indicating that when such procedures are taken away to make government more businesslike, there is an increase in corruption (Henriques 1986).

At the time of the reform movement it was thought that elected officials worked in the realm of values in making laws and setting budgets. Administration was neutral, a value-free implementation of law and legislative intent. With the destruction of the policy–administration dichotomy it became clear that values and political power are operative from the agenda-setting stage of the public policy process to the street-level implementation of policy (Waldo 1948). The values and patterns of moral reasoning of public administrators and civil servants became, then, almost as important as the values of elected officials (Cooper 1992). Professional associations for public administrators rapidly developed codes of ethics and ethics courses and training programs. Many jurisdictions adopted codes and standards. These documents and programs are primarily deontological—the statement of agreed-upon or settled values. And the assumptions have been Kantian—that there are absolute principles of right and wrong, independent of results or consequences, and that public administrators will adhere to these values. Research on ethics for public administrators indicates that the Kantian assumption is essentially correct, that civil servants are significantly inclined to support values such as civic virtue, honesty, procedural fairness, equity, and human dignity (Menzel, this volume; Lewis 1991). There is also good evidence that citizens expect their government to be fair and equitable even though those concepts are difficult to define (Hochschild 1981).

On its face this seems an odd finding because public administrators live and work in a world that is unrelentingly teleological, a world in which policy and programs results rule. In this world the public administrator practices, to borrow from Simon, "bounded ethics." In bounded ethics the administrator functions within the limits of enabling legislation, with limited budgets, usually advocating or at least supporting the purposes of the agency. Fundamental questioning of the purposes and practices of the agency, on the basis of issues of morality, is seldom found and rarely encouraged (Meltsner 1979; Amy 1984). Whistleblowing is very risky to the whistleblower and seldom results in fundamental organizational change (Perry, this volume; Glazer and Glazer 1989; Johnson and Kraft 1989; Jos, Thompkins, and Hays 1989). Following bounded ethics, the public administrator is, within the limits of organizational purpose and funding, almost always honest, virtuous, procedurally fair, and efficient. Indeed, many top public administrators have been and are examples of morality in government (Cooper and Wright 1992). To accept this conclusion, however, one must accept the boundaries within which the public administrator works.

There is another explanation for the apparent relative sense of right and wrong or morality of civil servants. Their work is embedded in rules, guidelines, inspectors, forms, and reports, and the other impedimenta of ethics enforcement. There can be little doubt that these requirements are "ethics enhancing" although it is likely that they slow work, inhibit creativity, and reduce responsiveness. With all of these procedural guides, inspectors, and oversight, why was there a HUD scandal, an Ill Winds scandal, an S&L scandal? The answer is that these are primarily political rather than bureaucratic scandals. As Paul Light puts it when he describes how the impending HUD scandal was regularly reported to Congress by the Inspectors General: "As for the influence-peddling scheme at the top of the agency, the IGs simply were not equipped to pursue such high-level wrongdoing. Their task was primarily to look down for scandal, not *up*." (see chapter five, this volume).

The antigovernment-probusiness ethos of the last fifteen years has taken its toll on governmental ethics. Concepts of privatization and third-party government are especially in favor. Government, to use the currently trendy word, is being "reinvented" to put together public–private partnerships, to "empower" citizens with choices, and so on. In sum, it is fashionable to degovernmentalize on the promise of saving money and improving services. As previously governmental functions are shifted to the private sector or shared, it is a safe bet that corruption will increase. It is no small irony that government moves in the direction of privatization at the same time that there is a rising concern for governmental ethics.

There is a similar paradox in the universities. In public administration and public policy studies the teleological perspective holds the high ground. The wholesale adoption of policy analysis based on the measurement of results in terms of efficiency is a factor. So too is the popularity of the market model and theories of games, public choice, and cost–benefit analysis. What is right or wrong, what is moral or ethical is to be judged in terms of utility of consequences. That such an approach is without a larger sense of absolute right or wrong is generally understood (Amy 1984; Tong 1986). Yet in the presence of this utilitarian hegemony the universities are rediscovering ethics. It is especially interesting that many of the leaders of the new ethics groups on campuses are neo-Kantians (Thompson, D. 1987; Jennings 1991).

What, then, can be concluded about ethical decision making in government and the doing of right and wrong? First, that the ethics of decisions are often based in the constitution(s), the law, and the regulations. Second, that rules, regulations, reports, oversight, inspectors, and the like do enhance the potential for ethical decisions. Third, that professional standards and codes of ethics also enhance ethical decision making. Fourth, that public administrators practice a form of bounded ethics that generally accepts the purposes and policies of the agency and practices ethics within those bounds. Fifth, that the most notable ethical breaches in recent years have been political rather than administrative. Sixth, that citizens are concerned with issues of fairness, equity, and justice and are likely to view government as less legitimate when these issues are not met and when there are scandals. Seventh, that as government moves in the direction of privatization the potential for ethical breaches increases. Eighth, that the study of public policy and the practice of policy analysis in American universities is teleological and utilitarian while most of the theory coming from those associated with the new centers for the study of ethics is deontological.

Democracy and Ethics: The Issue of Accountability

Central to the practice of government administration is the issue of accountability. Before the policy–administration dichotomy was rendered mythical it was possible to beg the question of accountability, falling back on the rhetoric if not the substance of neutrality. No more. Beginning fifty years ago with Herman Finer and continuing to this day is a stream of scholarship that seeks forms of democratic control over the bureaucracy. In our time Lowi argues for a juridical democracy in which the laws are precise and bureaucratic latitude in carrying out those laws is nil. Gruber seeks bureaucratic control through both legislative and presidential actions. Burke looks for balance between democratic control through legislators and elected executives and informed digression on the part of bureaucrats, but on the assumption that there is a bureaucratic control problem.

Carl Friedrich countered Finer with the argument that the effective conduct of government administration requires bureaucratic expertise and the discretion to apply that expertise. A host of public administration scholars have, over the years, supported this position (Bailey 1964; Willbern 1984; Long 1949; Lilla 1981). In recent years the "taking personal responsibility" for decisions and actions school, especially associated with Dennis Thompson, is put forward as the way to cope with the problems of dirty hands and many hands. A bureaucrat cannot take personal responsibility unless discretion is available, except in the case of refusing to act or to exit. John Rohr argues persuasively that there is a constitutional-legal basis for an extensive bureaucratic discretion. Charles Goodsell claims that without bureaucratic discretion government will be ineffective.

The entire issue turns on the question of whether, or to what extent, bureaucracy acts without controls or accountability. Much of the discussion of bureaucratic controls and accountability simply assumes their absence. In fact, the question of controls and accountability is usually caught up in the political battle between the policy preferences of legislators (Congress, state legislatures, city councils) and elected executives (president, governors, strong mayors). It is standard political rhetoric for presidents or governors to call for greater bureaucratic controls when the administration is carrying out the law and spending authorized appropriations on programs the president or the governor does not like. Legislators do the same. Does this mean that the bureaucracy is out of control or is unaccountable? No. Still, a surprising number of scholars accept the rhetoric as true and proceed to the question of controls and accountability.

Such research as there is on the subject indicates the following: bureaucrats tend to be responsive, within the law and their appropriations, to executive direction (Seidman and Gilmour 1986; Moe 1987; Weingast and Moran 1983; Wood and Waterman 1991); in cases of the absence of accountability or the violation of the law or standards of ethics, such as the FBI under Hoover, both congressional and presidential oversight and controls failed (Hart and Hart 1992); administrative agencies and their leaders are both experts and advocates for their tasks or missions and will seek support among legislators and elected executives (Kelman 1987); interest groups and clients will support the programs and budgets of agencies supporting their interests (James D. Thompson 1967).

Simply put, there are very few examples of bureaucratic agencies operating outside the ordinary range of legislative and executive accountability. (The activities of Oliver North in the Reagan administration come to mind, but his was hardly a regularly established administrative agency with enabling legislation, a bureaucracy, or a congressionally approved budget.)

Perception is more important than reality. It is widely believed, particularly among elected officials, that there are serious problems of bureaucratic control and accountability. Consequently, there has been a wide range of legislation establishing prohibitions against conflicts of interest and elaborate reporting procedures designed to prevent such conflicts—"designated ethics officers" in federal agencies, "Inspectors General" in federal departments, agency codes of ethics, ethics hotlines, ethics boards and commissions at the state and local level, and so on. Do they work? Yes, the Inspector General system does serve as an effective check against possible corruption (Light, this volume). Yes, codes of ethics "do less than everything and more than nothing" (Lewis 1991). Whistleblowing is a deterrent to possible agency misbehavior (Perry, this volume). Most important, these controls have very likely increased democratic controls and decreased administrative discretion (Lewis 1991). We may be close to Lowi's juridical democracy.

The problem, of course, is that the effective administration of governmental affairs is diminished. In addition, unlike earlier managerial ethics controls designed to *prevent* unethical behavior, these procedures are primarily designed to catch those who are unethical. As procedural-managerial controls have been relaxed in many jurisdictions, they have been replaced with "gotcha" ethics controls. That such controls inhibit innovation and creativity is certain.

Consider the opposite argument. Morgan and Kass discovered that local-level public administrators are experiencing a "role reversal" in which elected officials either will not or cannot decide issues and make policy. Is it unethical, under such circumstances, for bureaucrats to do nothing, especially if doing nothing would be fundamentally harmful to the public? Should the civil servant "take responsibility" when elected officials will not or cannot? Is the "policy gridlock" such that there can be no common ground on highly charged emotional issues such as abortion or on especially complicated social issues such as health care policy? Under such circumstances do we have questions of role reversal? Can we turn the policy–administration dichotomy on its head? In the dichotomy, elected officials set policy and appointed officials carry it out—they manage. We appear to be more nearly able to agree on how to do certain things—to manage—than we are able to agree on what should be done. Morgan and Kass call for a revised moral framework that enables administrators to articulate a complex ordering of moral claims that are compatible with our constitutional system of government. This is relatively close to Rohr's description of a constitutional basis for the legitimacy of the administrative role in American government.

There is no evidence, however, that Congress, state legislatures, and city and county councils are inclined to more specificity in the law, to precise policy direction, or to adequate funding to carry out policy or to cease intervening in administrative affairs. The problems for administrators are still there, and now they have less discretion to deal with the problems. As policy gridlock at the national level worsens, will there be a resurrection of the bureaucracy? Or is the administration of the national government so diminished in latitude and so hamstrung with congressional micro-management that we have the worst of both worlds—a Congress that cannot make policy and a bureaucracy that cannot manage?

What can be concluded about ethics and democracy and the issue of accountability? First, there has been the widespread perception that public bureaucracies are beyond control or unaccountable, although there is little evidence to support such perceptions. Second, most evidence indicates that bureaucrats are accountable and controlled. But there is also evidence that certain bureaucracies are powerful participants in the policy-making process and have influential political protectors. Third, there has been a sharp increase in ethics controls on bureaucrats and a decline in latitude or administrative discretion. Fourth, adding to procedural-managerial approaches to preventing unethical behavior there are now many procedures designed to catch the unethical. Fifth, policy gridlock may result in the possibility of administrative role reversal with an accompanying ethical dilemma for government administrators.

Policy Ethics and Politics

The careful reader will have noticed the absence of consideration of the *big questions* in ethics; indeed some might regard the earlier sections of this chapter to be concerned mostly with petty ethics—government corruption. Because the main emphasis of the chapter is government administration, there is virtually no treatment of legislative or electoral ethics, but these too are often regarded as petty ethics. There is a significant literature on political ethics, especially associated with the funding of elections and electoral competition. This has resulted in control systems such as contribution limits and ethics hearings. Because of this focus on the ethics of elected officials and the application of controls, the practice of "ethics politics" has emerged. Ethics procedures can be used to disadvantage political groups (Holbrook and Meier, this volume) or individuals and to advantage others (Dobel, this volume). Bureaucracies do, however, connect to and sometimes influence larger matters of ethics, policy ethics, so they will be briefly considered here.

In a democratic polity it would be correct to assume that the main venue for the consideration of policy ethics is legislative. In fact, however, many policy ethics issues have become the province of the judicial branch. The question of war is an exception, having been left to the executive and legislative branches of government. War is perhaps the issue most laden with questions of morality. In comparing the attitudes of members of congress and military officers toward war it was found that both groups agree on national self-protection and the moral authority of the state as appropriate justifications for war and the involuntary taking of life (Tamashiro, Secrest and Brunk, this volume). But, members of Congress are more willing than members of the military to accept the risks of war, while military persons are more inclined than members of Congress to view war as a policy tool. Certainly the contrasting perspectives of General Colin Powell and Secretary of Defense Richard Cheney on when and how to enter the Gulf War confirm these differing perspectives on the risks of war.

Many of the other big policy ethics issues, while belonging to the legislature(s), are decided by the courts. The vexing issues of equity in per-student spending for public education is in the courts in more than one-third of the states. Abortion is likely to be up for review by the Supreme Court. Property rights versus environmental protection issues are decided by the courts. Most states have had to sharply increase their prison capacity in response to the courts. The point is clear—both elected executives and legislatures no longer wrestle with all of the great issues. They, along with the bureaucracy, often react to the courts. It is for this reason that proposed appointments to the U.S. Supreme Court receive as much attention and scrutiny as senatorial or presidential candidates. It should also not surprise us that scholars who study the big issues of ethics now tend to be professors of law. In public administration and political science the tendency of scholars is to focus on smaller ethical issues. Fortunately philosophers still work on big ethical issues (Rawls 1971; MacIntire 1981; Pincoffs 1986).

The big policy ethics issues that remain the province of the legislative and executive branches often have to do with distributive justice (Frederickson 1990). The examples would include the morality of a health-care "system" that fails to provide access to significant numbers of citizens; the problem of homelessness and low-quality housing; a transportation system that emphasizes highway construction and maintenance but does comparatively little to improve inner-city public transportation; the problem of intergenerational inequity, as in the case of the relatively favorable circumstances of the elderly versus those of the children of the poor, or the transferring of most of the costs of toxic and other waste disposal from this generation to the next; and the relative emphasis on funding research on one disease such as AIDS, as opposed to another disease such as breast cancer. Of all the moral/ethical issues faced by government, it is clear that to the people, the most significant ones have to do with fairness and justice.

Under conditions of majority rule it is likely that the terms of taxes and benefits will favor the majority, or at least a coalition of influential minorities. There is maldistribution and sometimes massive maldistribution. Where does the bureaucracy fit in this? Insofar as we have evidence on this matter, it appears that at the service level there is both an ethic and the practice of forms of social equity, and these ameliorate some of the effects of majority rule (Lineberry 1977).

What, then, can be concluded about policy ethics? First, many issues of policy ethics are handled by the courts. Second, legislatures, elected executives, and bureaucracies often react to judge-made policy. Third, as a consequence, both elected and appointed government officials often deal with issues of middle-level and petty ethics. Fourth, the major ethical issues faced by elected officials and public administrators have to do with distributive justice.

Methodology and Knowledge in Public Administration Ethics

Like most research in the social sciences, the primary and dominant approach to the study of ethics and public administration is positivist, rational, and empirical. In positivism, knowledge is based on the observation of natural phenomena and their properties. These properties and the relations among them can be observed and derived by the physical senses. There are discernible and describable patterns of order and chaos in both the physical and social worlds. Empiricism is the view that knowledge of the world can or should be acquired by sense experience. To the rationalist, reason alone can provide knowledge of the existence and nature of things. Rationality is also used to describe the view that reality is a unified, coherent, and explicable system. Taken together, positivism, rationality, and empiricism form the epistemology or theory of knowledge that guides contemporary research in most of the study of public administration (Frederickson, forthcoming).

Knowledge derived in this way is objective and scientific, distinct from belief, values, or preferences. This is the critically important distinction of facts from values found in logical positivism. In this approach to research there is also the assumption that there are discernible patterns of relationship between phenomena which would indicate that action A will produce result B. This is individual or organizational rationality, which is assumed to be goal oriented.

This approach to research has five primary methodologies. The first and most often used is the self-reporting questionnaire or survey research. In this volume, the research of Menzel, Overman and Foss, and Steward and Sprinthall uses this method. This methodology is especially useful for determining attitudes, values, preferences.

The second most used methodology in the positivist research approach is the interview. Interview methods range from the administration of highly structured instruments that resemble questionnaires to open-ended discussions. In this volume the research of Paul Light and Morgan and Kass is in this tradition. The advantage of interviews is the ability in a face-to-face setting to clarify questions and answers and to probe the reasons behind a particular answer. Both questionnaires and interviews can be one-time or panels in which persons are questioned more than once over a period of time.

The third most common approach to research in public administration ethics is the use of secondary data. The chapters by Holbrook and Meier and by Perry use this technique. Governments gather and store extensive data, some of which lends itself to analysis.

The next research approach is the case study of a particular ethical event or issue. The chapter by Dobel in this volume is illustrative. In the case study approach it is assumed that the case is reported objectively following the canons of social science.

Finally, experiments are sometimes used in research in public administration ethics (Wittmer 1992). These experiments ordinarily involve students taking roles and attempting to solve ethical dilemmas. The researcher observes the actions of the subjects in the experiment.

It is common for researchers to use more than one methodology when studying an ethical issue. It is assumed that the same finding resulting from the use of more than one method provides substantial scientific verification for that finding.

The positivist-empirical-rational approach to research in public administration ethics is especially useful in determining the values and attitudes of administrators and the effects of particular ethical guides and standards on beliefs and attitudes. Much of this research does not, however, inform the question of ethical behavior. With the exception of case studies, this research largely begs the question of whether public administrators behave ethically. This research could be described as pre-behavior, indicating what administrators believe and how they view ethical issues. And beliefs and attitudes may be helpful predictors of actual ethical behavior. Case studies help put ethical issues in context and they often effectively describe the behavior of public officials. The problem is that they ordinarily do not account effectively for why public officials behave as they do.

In recent years there has been a significant attack on the positivist perspective. The post-positivist critique of the presumed objectivity of the positivist-empirical-rational school is that social structures such as laws, rules, organizations, and governments "do not exist independent of human consciousness" (Harmon and Mayer 1986, 287). In this view, "there is no objective truth 'out there' waiting to be discovered. Rather all 'reality' is socially constructed" (Kelly and Maynard-Moody, forthcoming, 1993). In the positivist tradition the social world is external to individual cognition, a real world of hard, tangible empirical entities. The approach to studying this world is taken from the natural sciences, using the process of testing hypotheses following the techniques of scientific rigor. The post-positivists reject this view, arguing that genuine objectivity is virtually impossible and that subjective methodological approaches achieve a deeper understanding of social experience. Rather than research being value-free and objective, the post-positivist would argue that research should be value centered, the values of the researcher being made explicit. To the post-positivist analysis *is* interpretation, not an objective interpretation of the facts. The separation of facts and values as in logical positivism is impossible because facts reflect values and values change the interpretation of facts. They cannot be separated.

The primary methods of the post-positivists are history, stories, and ethnography, or naturalistic inquiry. In this collection, the research of Dobel and of Morgan and Kass comes closest to the post-positivist perspective. The most famous recent work in this methodological family is Bellah et al., *Habits of the Heart* (1985). Bellah and his colleagues used most of the techniques in the positivist methodological kit bag as well as extensive interpretation and elaboration in the form of a research team working with research subjects to describe and put in social context the opinions and actions of the subjects.

The best recent example of interpretative history as both case study and elaboration is found in Neustadt and May's *Thinking in Time: The Uses of History for Decision-Makers* (1986). For students of the larger questions of policy ethics this is an especially useful treatment of cases such as the decisions to enter the Korean and Vietnam wars, the Cuban Missile Crisis, the Bay of Pigs case, and many more. In addition, Neustadt and May review the ethical challenges facing leaders such as John Kennedy, Lyndon Johnson, Martin Luther King, Malcolm X, and Harold Macmillan.

Stories are often powerful guides for action in bureaucratic settings. John Van Maanen, Marisa Kelly and Steven Maynard-Moody, and Roger C. Schank all describe how stories combine facts, values, myths, legends, history, and rules-of-thumb to influence behavior. Stories are especially useful as windows on the ethical culture of public organizations. For example, the research of Perry on whistleblowing reported here is confirmed by Kelly and Maynard-Moody based on stories bureaucrats tell: "The singular message in these stories for would-be whistleblowers is 'don't.' Not only do supervisors demand compliance and punish dissent, but co-workers ostracize colleagues who pass information on to the press or elective officials" (1992, 31).

The advantages of post-positivist research on public administration ethics is the extent to which it can focus on actual ethical behavior. It is often rich in context, providing a setting for action. And it is usually rather interesting reading. The problem is that post-positivist research is much less common in the study of administrative ethics. Much of this research is done by university faculty and advanced graduate students. In American universities the positivist model is much more widely accepted and used by these scholars.

Both positivist and post-positivist research on ethics in public administration are helpful. Research findings on a particular subject achieved using one method can be validated or questioned by research using another method. Positivist methods are especially useful in determining the beliefs, attitudes, and feelings of public administrators toward ethical questions. Post-positivist methods are more useful in describing actual ethical behavior. The epistemological perspectives of these two approaches differ significantly, but when applied to public administration ethics the results of research using either family of methods should be complementary.

Some Conclusions

The government reform movement had a lasting effect on American government. Will the current ethics reform movement have the same "staying power" and permanent results? The answer is probably yes, especially if there is a continuing increase in incidence of government corruption. However, in the earlier case corruption was reduced by increasing administrative capacity and decreasing politics. In the present case we are moving in the opposite direction, reducing administrative capacity and increasing political control, with the probability that there will be more rather than less corruption. There are, of course, more controls on political corruption than in the past. Whether they will work remains to be seen.

The end of each section of this chapter sets out a list of assertions. These assertions are preliminary attempts to synthesize and summarize what is known about ethics in government administration. They are meant to stimulate research and analysis and should be thought of as subject to testing and verification.

In addition, I suggest that the future ethics research agenda should include the following six tasks:

1. It is evident that standards of right and wrong vary significantly from context to context. Yet much of the literature on ethics, especially the deontological literature, sets out universal standards of behavior. For certain matters of right and wrong this is sensible, such as standards of human dignity, the sanctity of life, adherence to the constitution(s) and the law(s). But for many ethical issues, standards and expectations are situationally determined. Future research should focus on the settings, professions, and cultures in which ethical issues occur and measure behavior against the cultural expectations and professional standards appropriate to the research context.

2. Once this is done, researchers should compare ethical standards and behavior between settings, professions, and cultures. In this way the richness and variety of the common ethical themes and variations on those themes can be described.
3. Researchers should assess the effect or result on the behavior of government officials, both political and administrative, of traditional procedural and managerial controls with modern approaches such as ethics officers, codes of ethics, Inspectors General, and whistleblowers.
4. Education and training are two of the most important modern techniques by which governments, professions, and universities attempt to enhance ethical behavior. Researchers should measure the actual results of education and training on behavior.
5. Researchers should assess the influence of privatization on government corruption and on ethics.
6. Researchers should measure the effects of reduced administrative discretion on both administrative effectiveness and ethics.

Much of the research on ethics in government is based on surveys of opinion. While opinions are important, there needs to be a body of research on government ethics based on field observation. Case studies and post-positivist forms of data gathering are essential to building a reliable body of knowledge. With an improved body of knowledge it will be possible to build a descriptive theory in government ethics to complement and challenge deductive theories.

References

Amy, Douglas J. 1984. "Why Policy Analysis and Ethics Are Incompatible." *Journal of Policy Analysis and Management*, 3: 573–91.
Bailey, Stephen K. 1964. "Ethics and the Public Service." *Public Administration Review*, no. 24: 234–43.
Bellah, R.N.; Madsen, R.; Sullivan, W.M.; Swidler, A.; and Tipton, S.M. 1985. *Habits of the Heart: Individualism and Community in American Life.* Berkeley: University of California Press.
Bellanta, B., and A.N. Link. 1981. "Are Public Sector Workers More Risk Averse Than Private Sector Workers?" *Industrial and Labor Relations Review*, no. 34: 408–12.
Bok, Sissela. 1978. *Lying: Moral Choice in Public and Private Life.* New York: Vintage.
Burke, John P. 1986. *Bureaucratic Responsibility.* Baltimore: Johns Hopkins University Press.
Cooper, Phillip. 1992. *Hard Judicial Choices.* New York: Oxford.
Cooper, Terry L. 1990. *The Responsible Administrator: An Approach to Ethics for the Administrative Role.* San Francisco: Jossey-Bass.
Cooper, Terry L., and Wright, N. Dale, eds. 1992. *Exemplary Public Administrators: Character and Leadership in Government.* San Francisco: Jossey-Bass.
Denhardt, Kathryn G. 1988. *The Ethics of Public Service: Resolving Moral Dilemmas in Public Organizations.* New York: Greenwood.
Finer, Herman. 1941. "Administrative Responsibility in Democratic Government." *Public Administration Review.* 14: 335–50.

Frederickson, H. George. 1990. "Public Administration and Social Equity." *Public Administration Review*, 50: 228–37.

———. Forthcoming 1993. "Research and Knowledge in Administrative Ethics." In Terry L. Cooper, ed., *Handbook of Administrative Ethics*. New York: Marcel Dekker.

Frederickson, H. George, and Hart, David K. 1985. "The Public Service and the Patriotism of Benevolence." *Public Administration Review*, 45: 547–53.

French, P.A. 1983. *Ethics in Government*. Englewood Cliffs, NJ: Prentice Hall.

Friedrich, Carl J. 1940. "The Nature of Administrative Responsibility." *Public Policy*, 1: 3–24.

Glazer, Myron P., and Glazer, Penina M. 1989. *The Whistleblowers: Exposing Corruption in Government and Industry*. New York: Basic Books.

Goodsell, Charles T. 1983. *The Case for Bureaucracy: A Public Administration Polemic*. Chatham, NJ: Chatham House.

Gruber, Judith E. 1988. *Controlling Bureaucracies: Dilemmas in Democratic Governance*. Berkeley: University of California Press.

Harmon, Michael M., and Mayer, Richard T. 1986. *Organization Theory for Public Administration*. Boston: Little, Brown.

Hart, David K., and Hart, David W. 1992. "George C. Marshall and J. Edgar Hoover: Noblesse Oblige and Self-Serving Power." In Terry L. Cooper and N. Dale Wright, eds., *Exemplary Public Administrators: Character and Leadership in Government*. San Francisco: Jossey-Bass.

Henriques, Diana B. 1986. *The Machinery of Greed: Public Authority Abuse and What to Do about It*. Lexington, MA: D.C. Heath.

Hochschield, Jennifer L. 1981. *What's Fair? American Beliefs about Distributive Justice*. Cambridge, MA: Harvard University Press.

Jennings, Bruce. 1991. "Taking Ethics Seriously in Administrative Life: Constitutionalism, Ethical Reasoning and Moral Judgement." In James S. Bowman, ed., *Ethical Frontiers in Public Management*. San Francisco: Jossey-Bass.

Johnson, Roberta A., and Kraft, Michael E. 1989. *Bureaucratic Whistleblowing and Policy Change*. Government Printing Office: United States Department of Agriculture.

Jos, Phillip H.; Thompkins, Mark E.; and Hays, Stephen W. 1989. "In Praise of Difficult People: A Portrait of the Committed Whistleblower." *Public Administration Review*, 49: 552–61.

Kelly, Marisa, and Maynard-Moody, Steven. Forthcoming 1993. "Policy Analysis in the Post-Positivist Era: Engaging Stakeholders in Evaluating the Economic Development District Program." *Public Administration Review*.

Kelman, Steven. 1987. *Making Public Policy: A Hopeful View of American Government*. New York: Basic Books.

Kohlberg, L. 1980. *The Meaning and Measurement of Moral Development*. Worcester, MA: Clark University Press.

Lewis, Carol W. 1991. *The Ethics Challenge in Public Service*. San Francisco: Jossey-Bass.

Lilla, Mark. 1981. "Ethos, 'Ethics,' and Public Service." *Public Interest*, 63: 317.

Lineberry, Robert L. 1977. *Equality and Urban Policy: The Distribution of Municipal Public Services*. Beverly Hills, CA: Sage Publications.

Long, Norton E. 1949. "Power and Administration." *Public Administration Review*, no. 9: 257–64.

Louis, Merl Reis. 1983. "Organizations as Culture-Bearing Milieux." In L.R. Pondy et al., eds., *Organizational Symbolism*. Greenwich, CT: JAI Press, 39–54.

Lowi, Theodore. 1969. *The End of Liberalism: Ideology, Policy and the Crisis of Public Authority*. New York: W.W. Norton.

McGregor, Douglas. 1960. *The Human Side of Enterprise*. New York: McGraw-Hill.

MacIntire, Alasdair. 1981. *After Virtue*. Notre Dame, IN: University of Notre Dame Press.
Meltsner, Arnold. 1979. *Policy Analysis in the Bureaucracy*. Berkeley: University of California Press.
Moe, Ronald C. 1987. "Exploring the Limits of Privatization." *Public Administration Review*, 47: 453–60.
Moe, Terry M. 1982. "Regulatory Performance and Presidential Administration." *American Journal of Political Science*, 26: 197–224.
———. 1987. "An Assessment of the Positive Theory of 'Congressional Dominance.' " *Legislative Studies Quarterly*, 12: 475–520.
Nalbandian, John, and Edwards, J.T. 1983. "The Values of Public Administration: A Comparison with Lawyers, Social Workers and Business Administrators." *A Review of Public Personnel Administration*, 4: 114–129.
Neustadt, R.E., and May, E.R. 1986. *Thinking in Time: The Uses of History for Decision-Makers*. New York: The Free Press.
Norman, J. Baldwin 1991. "Public Versus Private Employees: Debunking Stereotypes." *Review of Public Personnel Administration*, 11: 1–27.
Pincoffs, Edmund L. 1986. *Quandaries and Virtues: Against Reductivism in Ethics*. Lawrence: University Press of Kansas.
Rawls, John. 1971. *A Theory of Justice*. Cambridge, MA: Belknap Press of Harvard University Press.
Rest, J. 1986. *Moral Development: Advances in Research and Theory*. New York: Praeger.
Rohr, John A. 1989. *Ethics for Bureaucrats: An Essay on Law and Virtue*. 2d ed. New York: Marcel Dekker.
Rosenbloom, David H. 1986. *Public Administration: Understanding Management, Politics, and Law in the Public Sector*. New York: Random House.
Seidman, Harold, and Gilmour, Robert. 1986. *Politics, Position and Power: From the Positive to the Regulatory State*. 4th ed. New York: Oxford University Press.
Smirich, Linda. 1983. "Organizations as Shared Meanings." In L.R. Pondy et al., eds., *Organizational Symbolism*. Greenwich, CT: JAI Press, 55–65.
Strauss, L., and Cropsey, J., eds. 1987. *History of Political Philosophy*. Chicago: University of Chicago Press.
Thompson, Dennis. 1987. *Political Ethics and Public Office*. Cambridge, MA: Harvard University Press.
Thompson, James D. 1967. *Organizations in Action*. New York: McGraw-Hill.
Tong, Rosemary. 1986. *Ethics in Policy Analysis*. Englewood Cliffs, NJ: Prentice Hall.
Tyler, Tom R. 1990. *Why People Obey the Law*. New Haven, CT: Yale University Press.
Van Maanen, J. 1978. "Observations on the Making of a Policeman." In P.K. Manning and J. Van Maanen, eds., *Policing: A View from the Street*. Santa Monica, CA: Goodyear.
Waldo, Dwight. 1948. *The Administrative State*. New York: Ronald Press.
Weingast, Barry R., and Mark J. Moran. 1983. "Bureaucracy: Discretionary Congressional Control? Regulatory Policy Making by the Federal Trade Commission." *Journal of Political Economy*, 91: 756–800.
Willbern, York. 1984. "Types and Levels of Public Morality." *Public Administration Review*, 44: 102–108.
Wittmer, Dennis. 1992. "Ethics and Public Management: Some Experimental Results." *Journal of Public Administration Research and Theory*, no. 2: 443–62.
Wood, B. Dan, and Waterman, Richard W. 1991. "The Dynamics of Political Control over the Bureaucracy." *American Political Science Review*, 85: 801–28.

Index